D0160505

THE ANNALS
OF EUROPEAN
CIVILIZATION
1501–1900

ALFRED MAYER

THE
ANNALS
OF
EUROPEAN
CIVILIZATION
1501–1900

BARNES
&NOBLE
BOOKS
NEW YORK

This edition published by Barnes & Noble, Inc.

1993 Barnes & Noble Books

ISBN 1-56619-155-6

Printed and bound in the United States of America

M 9 8 7 6 5 4 3 2 1

TO MY WIFE

Great nations write their autobiographies
in three manuscripts;—the book of their
deeds, the book of their words, and the
book of their art. Not one of these books
can be understood unless we read the two
others. . . .

RUSKIN, *St. Mark's Rest.*

FOREWORD

By Dr. G. P. GOOCH

THE PURPOSE and methods of this work are so fully and so clearly explained in the Preface that my only task is to commend it to students of all ages. By students I mean not only the generation which is thinking of examinations or the budding historian who is learning his trade, but the wider public which carries into middle and later life an intelligent interest in things of the mind. Many years of patient labour and research have gone to the making of this handbook, so much more detailed and comprehensive than anything which has hitherto appeared. Here we find mention in almost dazzling profusion of the choicest fruits of the human spirit during the four centuries which have chiefly fashioned the Europe that we know. If anything could teach us the essential unity of civilization, the insufficiency of cultural no less than political nationalism, the relative superficiality of racial and linguistic boundaries, it is this impressive panorama of creative effort, in which every country, big and small, has played its honourable part. If there is much in political history to make us weep, there is still more in the opulent record of the arts and sciences to make us rejoice.

Specialists will turn with critical eyes to their own chosen field, and there is nothing to prevent them from making such additions or omissions as they please. No compiler expects to satisfy every one, and even experts have been known to disagree. Dr. Mayer has done his best to provide a fair and accurate summary of his vast material by seeking and taking expert advice. Where is the reader, however manifold his interests and however profound his erudition, who will not learn many things from these crowded pages ? Which of us, for instance, could tell where the most celebrated pictures in the world are to be seen ? The system of double entry is particularly valuable, for it is as essential to know the place which a poem or a play, a treatise or an invention, occupies in its special province as it is to keep in mind the social and intellectual landscape of the age which saw its birth. This useful book is intended by the author to remind us that we are indeed the fortunate heirs of all the ages. The doors of the treasure-house stand wide open, and, guide in hand, we have only to walk in.

CONTENTS

INTRODUCTION

THE READER of a book, and especially a book of dates and events, usually passes over the preface without reading it, promising himself to make good the omission at his leisure on some future occasion. I beg him, therefore, all the more earnestly to read this Introduction before he plunges into the system of the book. For its purpose is not only to show him his way about, but also to explain a number of things which may seem strange to him, and to justify a number of things which he may be prompted to criticize.

This book has a two-fold purpose.

Its first and more obvious aim is to serve as a useful book of reference. With this in view, I have taken pains to combine chronological accuracy with a sound selection of material.

Few works of chronology hitherto have given a history of European civilization in its totality, and when they have it has always been in a context of political and economic events. The task which my predecessors have set themselves was to exhibit the temporal connections between the political life of nations and the development of cultures. They have neither wished nor attempted to give a biography of the European spirit independently of the life of nations. They have been concerned for the most part to record the existence of the principal works of human creativeness and their authors in a specific period of time. I have tried, on the other hand, to record these works, in their original titles, and in their cultural continuity, in such a way that they may be considered independently of political history, and so that the book can at the same time be used as a bibliographical guide.

This book, therefore, presumes in its readers a general knowledge of political and economic events between the years 1500 and 1900, and refers them, if need be, to the numerous and excellent tables of political history which already exist in many European languages.

If, then, it is to provide biographical and bibliographical information, the book must satisfy certain particular requirements.

In the Annals it presents in chronological order, year by year, the principal events of European cultural history.

I have here assumed that the reader has sufficient acquaintance with the principal European languages to be able to recognize a work in its original title. Works of literature in the widest sense, works of music, and numerous works of painting are therefore quoted in their original titles, and even, when it appeared significant, in their original spelling.

Only for the Slavonic languages and Hungarian have I departed from this practice, because I could not suppose a knowledge of these languages in my English reader, any more than I have myself.

When there is no other indication, the dates refer to the year of the first public appearance of a work. The year when an idea was born, or when a work of literature or music was created, cannot always be established. The year of first publication, however, is in general manifest, and is the significant date for the influence which the work has had on the history of civilization. If the year of the first printing or of the first performance is uncertain, the work has been entered under the year of its first authentic appearance. The possibility of an earlier performance or an earlier printing has then been recorded.

In the selection of material my principle has been to treat fully those things which have been significant for European life, either in their own time or for all time, and to restrict the treatment of those things whose significance was essentially regional.

I have to admit that in this I have not always avoided the danger of introducing my personal preferences. This danger has, however, been somewhat reduced by ending the book with the year 1900. In this way I wished to exclude much that is in question in the present-day battle of opinions, and at the same time to avoid the danger of overlooking significant works by living artists and thinkers, and so unintentionally doing an injustice to their authors. I hope that the book, thus restricted, will have gained in objectivity what it has lost in actuality.

However, it is not possible to eliminate personal judgment altogether, nor is it even desirable, so long as the selection is the result of reflection and not of bias. As I was concerned to bring out those things which in my opinion lent character to the period, the personality of the compiler, in spite of his best efforts to remain in the background, could not but be discernible at times.

ABBREVIATIONS

bgn.	. . . .	begun
compl.	. . .	completed
ed. prin.	. . .	editio princeps
end.	. . . .	ended
est.	. . . . .	established
fnd.	. . . .	founded
Fr.	. . . .	French
inv.	. . . .	invention of, invented
iss.	. . . .	issued
op., opnd.	. . .	opened
posth.	. . . .	posthumous
pr.	. . . .	printed
prod.	. . . .	produced, production
pt(s).	. . . .	part(s)

INDEX OF NAMES

INDEX OF NAMES

[3]

[7]

[8]

[18]

RHAETICUS, Georg Joachim (1514-76), 1540, 1596
RIBADENEYRA, Pedro de (1527-1611), 1595
RIBERA, José Antonio de (1588-1652), 1632, 1633, 1635, 1637, 1638, 1650, 1651
RICARDO, David (1772-1823), 1817
RICHARDSON, Samuel (1689-1761), 1740, 1748, 1753
RICHTER, Jean Paul Friedrich. See Jean Paul
Richter, Ludwig (1803-84), 1837
RIDINGER, Georg (1568-?), 1614
RIEMANN, Georg Friedrich Bernhard (1826-66), 1854, 1859
RIEMENSCHNEIDER, Tilman (1468-1531), 1513, 1516
RIESE, Adam (1489-1559), 1550
RIGAUD, Hyacinthe (1659-1743), 1701
RIMBAUD, Arthur (1854-91), 1873, 1886
RIMSKY-KORSAKOV, Nicolai Andreyevich (1844-1908), 1865, 1888, 1889, 1898
RINUCCINI, Ottavio (1566-1621), 1594
RITTER, Carl (1779-1859), 1817
RIVAS, Angel de Saavedra, Duque de (1791-1865), 1835
ROBERTSON, William (1721-93), 1759, 1769, 1777
RODENBACH, Georges (1855-98), 1892
RODIN, Auguste (1840-1917), 1864, 1877, 1879, 1884, 1886, 1898
RODÓ, José Enrique (1872-1917), 1900
ROEBUCK, John (1718-1794), 1746
ROEMER, Olaf (1644-1710), 1675, 1735
ROENTGEN, Wilhelm (1845-1923), 1895
ROGERS, John (T. Matthew) (d. 1555), 1537
ROJAS, Fernando de (about 1475-about 1537), 1502
ROJAS ZORRILLA, Francisco de (1607-1660), 1650
ROKITANSKY, Carl, Freiherr von (1804-78), 1842
ROLLAND, Romain (1868-1944), 1900
ROMNEY, George (1734-1802), 1781, 1789
RONSARD, Pierre de (1524-85), 1550, 1552, 1560, 1565, 1572
ROSENHANE, Gustaf (1619-84), 1680
ROSS, John (1777-1856), 1831
ROSS, Ronald (1857-1932), 1897
ROSSETTI, Christina Georgina (1830-1894), 1862, 1893, 1896
ROSSETTI, Dante Gabriel (1828-82), 1850, 1861, 1863, 1870, 1881
ROSSINI, Gioacchino (1792-1868), 1813, 1816, 1817, 1818, 1829, 1841
ROSTAND, Edmond (1868-1918), 1897, 1900

ROTROU, Jean (1609-50), 1645, 1646, 1647
ROUGET DE LISLE, Claude-Joseph (1760-1836), 1792
ROUSSEAU, Jean-Baptiste (1671-1741), 1712
ROUSSEAU, Jean-Jacques (1712-78), 1752, 1753, 1761, 1762, 1782
RUBENS, Peter Paul (1577-1640), 1604, 1606, 1609, 1614, 1615, 1616, 1620, 1623, 1625, 1627, 1630, 1632, 1635, 1638, 1639
RUBINSTEIN, Anton (1829-94), 1852
RUCELLAI, Giovanni (1475-1525), 1525
RUDBECK, Olaf (1630-1702), 1652, 1653
RUECKERT, Friedrich (1788-1866), 1823
RUISDAEL, Jacob van (1628-82), 1654
RUÍZ DE ALARCÓN, Juan (about 1581-1639), 1628
RUNEBERG, Johan Ludvig (1804-77), 1832, 1848
RUNGE, Philipp Otto (1777-1810), 1805
RUSIÑOL, Santiago (1861-1931), 1898
RUSKIN, John (1819-1900), 1843, 1849, 1851, 1862, 1865, 1871, 1872
RUTHERFORD, Ernest, Lord (1871-1937), 1896, 1900
RYLÉYEV, Kondrati Fjedorovich (1795-1826), 1825

SAAVEDRA, Angel de. See Rivas
SAAVEDRA FAJARDO, Diego (1584-1648), 1640
SACHS, Hans (1494-1576), 1517, 1523, 1546, 1549, 1551, 1553, 1557, 1558
SACKVILLE, Richard (?-1566), 1559
SACKVILLE, Thomas (1536-1608), 1561
SAINT-EVREMOND, Charles de Marguetel de Saint-Denis, Seigneur de (1610-1703), 1668
SAINT-PIERRE, Charles-Irénée Castel de (1658-1743), 1713
SAINT-PIERRE, Jacques-Henri-Bernardin de (1737-1814), 1787, 1791
SAINT-SAËNS, Camille (1835-1921), 1871, 1874, 1877
SAINT-SIMON, Claude-Henri, Comte de (1760-1825), 1807, 1819, 1823, 1825
SAINT-SIMON, Louis de Rouvroy, Duc de (1675-1755), 1829
SAINTE-BEUVE, Charles-Augustin (1804-1869), 1840, 1857, 1863
SAINTE-MARTHE, Scévole de (1536-1623), 1584
SALES, Saint François de (1567-1622), 1609, 1614
SALIERI, Antonio (1750-1825), 1784, 1787

INDEX OF PLACES

INDEX OF PLACES

THE ANNALS
1501-1900

THE ANNALS

1501

BRITISH ISLES

England	Architecture	Peterborough Cathedral East End compl. (bgn. 1441)
Scotland	Literature	DOUGLAS, Gawin. *Palace of Honour* (*The palis of honoure*)

THE LOW COUNTRIES

Flanders	Painting	DAVID, Gerard. *The Mystic Marriage of St. Catherine* (Nat. Gal. Lond.)

CENTRAL EUROPE

Germany	Literature	*Opera Hrosvite* (Ed. Prin. Medieval Plays of Hroswitha of Gandersheim, ed. Conrad Celtes)

LATIN EUROPE

Italy	Painting	BOTTICELLI, Sandro. *Virgin adoring the Child* (Nat. Gal. Lond.)
		LIPPI, Filippino. *St. Catherine* (Bologna)
Spain	Universities	Santiago de Compostela fnd.

1502

THE LOW COUNTRIES

Flanders	Music	DES PRÈS, Josquin. *Missae Liber primus*
	Painting	DAVID, Gerard. *Baptism of Christ* (Bruges)

CENTRAL EUROPE

Germany	Architecture	Marienkirche, Danzig compl. (bgn. 1343)
	Literature	BEBEL, Heinrich. *Liber Facetiarum*
		CELTES, Conrad. *Liber Amorum*
	Universities	Wittenberg fnd.

LATIN EUROPE

Italy	Architecture	BRAMANTE, Donato Lazzaro. Tempietto of S. Pietro in Montorio, Rome, blt.
	Literature	SANNAZARO, Jacopo. *Arcadia.*
	Painting	RAPHAEL. *Coronation of the Virgin* (Vatican)
	Philology	Ed. Prin. Herodotus, Sophocles, Thucydides (Aldus, Venice)
Spain	Literature	ROJAS, Fernando de. *Tragicomedia de Calisto y Melibea*
	Travels	Fourth Expedition of Columbus

[45]

SLAVONIC EUROPE

Czechoslovakia Architecture Vladislav Hall, Prague, compl. (bgn. 1484)

1503

BRITISH ISLES

England Literature ARNOLD, Richard. *Chronicle* (cont. *The Nut-Brown Maid ;* Van Berghem, Antwerp)

Scotland Literature BARCLAY, Alexander. *The Castell of Laboure* (Vérard, Paris)
DUNBAR, William. *The Thrissill and the Rois*

THE LOW COUNTRIES

Holland Theology ERASMUS. *Enchiridion Militis Christiani*

CENTRAL EUROPE

Germany Painting CRANACH, Lucas, the Elder. *Crucifixion* (Munich)
DÜRER, Albrecht. *The Virgin with the Bird* (engravings)
GRUENEWALD, Matthias. *Crucifixion* (*circa*; Basle)

LATIN EUROPE

Italy Geography VESPUCCI, Amerigo. *Mundus Novus*
    Painting LEONARDO DA VINCI, *La Gioconda* ("Mona Lisa," compl. 1519 ; Louvre)
LIPPI, Filippino. *Virgin and Saints* (Genoa)
    Philology CORNAZANO, Antonio. *De Proverbiorum Origine*
Ed. Prin. Euripides (Aldus, Venice)
Ed. Prin. Xenophon's *Hellenica* (Aldus, Venice)

1504

CENTRAL EUROPE

Germany Painting CRANACH, Lucas, the Elder. *Rest on the Flight into Egypt* (Kais. Fried. Mus., Berlin)
DÜRER, Albrecht. *Adoration of the Magi* (Uffizi)
DÜRER, Albrecht. "*Great*" *Passion* (wood engravings)
DÜRER, Albrecht. "*Green*" *Passion* (drawings; Albertina, Vienna)
    Theology REUCHLIN, Johannes. *De Arte Praedicandi.*

LATIN EUROPE

Italy   Architecture   Palazzo Contarini, Venice bgn.
            Painting   GIORGIONE; Giorgio Barbarelli. *Madonna of Castelfranco* (Venice)
                           MANTEGNA, Andrea. *The Triumph of Scipio* (Nat. Gal. Lond.)
                           RAPHAEL. *Marriage of the Virgin* (Milan)
                           SIGNORELLI, Luca. Orvieto Cathedral, Frescoes compl. (bgn. 1499)
            Philology   Ed. Prin. Demosthenes (Aldus, Venice)
            Sculpture   MICHELANGELO. *David* (National Mus., Florence)

1505

BRITISH ISLES

England   Universities   Christ's College, Cambridge, fnd.
Scotland Universities   Royal College of Surgeons, Edinburgh, fnd.

CENTRAL EUROPE

Germany   Inventions   HENLEIN. The watch (Nuremberg)
              Painting   CRANACH, Lucas, the Elder. *Virgin and Three Saints* (woodcut)

LATIN EUROPE

Italy   Architecture   BRAMANTE, Donato Lazzaro. Cancelleria, Rome, compl. (bgn. 1495)
              Literature   BEMBO, Pietro. *Gli Asolani*
              Painting   BELLINI, Giovanni. *Madonna of San Zaccaria* (S. Zaccaria, Venice)
                             BELLINI, Giovanni. *Portrait of the Doge Loredano* (Nat. Gal. Lond.)
                             RAPHAEL. *Tempi Madonna* (Munich)
Portugal Discoveries   ALMEIDA, Francisco de. Ceylon
Spain   Universities   Seville fnd.

SLAVONIC EUROPE

Russia   Architecture   Novo, Aloiso. Cathedral of the Archangels, Moscow (compl. 1509)

1506

CENTRAL EUROPE

Germany   Literature   BEBEL, Heinrich. *Facetiae*
              Painting   DÜRER, Albrecht. *Madonna with the Siskin* (Kais. Fried. Mus., Berlin)
                             DÜRER, Albrecht. *The Feast of the Rose Garlands* (Strahow, Prague)
              Philology   REUCHLIN, Johannes. *Rudimenta Hebraica*
              Universities   Frankfurt an der Oder, fnd.

[47]

LATIN EUROPE

Italy   Archaeology   Laocoön Group disc.

Architecture   PERUZZI, Baldassare.   Villa Farnesina, Rome, (compl. 1511)

Painting   FRANCIA; Francesco Raibolini.   Frescoes in S. Cecilia, Bologna

LEONARDO DA VINCI.   *Virgin of the Rocks* (compl. 1508; Nat. Gal. Lond.)

LEONARDO DA VINCI.   *Virgin and Child with St. Anne and the Infant St. John* (compl. c. 1510; Louvre)

RAPHAEL.   *Ansidei Madonna* (Nat. Gal. Lond.)

Sculpture   MICHELANGELO.   *Our Lady* (Bruges)

1507

BRITISH ISLES

Scotland   Literature   DUNBAR, William.   *Dance of the Seven Deadly Sins*

CENTRAL EUROPE

Germany   Geography   WALDSEEMUELLER, Martin (called Hylacomylus).   *Cosmographiae Introductio*

Jurisprudence   *Constitutio Criminalis Bambergensis* (" Mater Carolinae ")

Sculpture   STOSS, Veit.   *Angelic Salutation* (St. Lawrence, Nuremberg)

LATIN EUROPE

France   Printing   First Greek book printed in France (*Liber gnomagyricus*)

Italy   Painting   RAPHAEL.   *Entombment* (Borghese, Rome)

RAPHAEL.   *La Belle Jardinière* (Louvre)

RAPHAEL.   *Madonna del Granduca* (Pitti)

RAPHAEL.   *St. Catherine* (Nat. Gal. Lond.)

SLAVONIC EUROPE

Czechoslovakia   Architecture   Charles Bridge, Prague, compl. (bgn. 1357)

1508

BRITISH ISLES

Scotland   Printing   The Chepman and Myllar prints (earliest specimens of Scottish printing)

[48]

THE LOW COUNTRIES

Flanders   Painting   MATSYS; Quentin Massys. *Pietà* (Nat. Gal. Lond.)

CENTRAL EUROPE

Germany   Painting   DÜRER, Albrecht. *The Ten Thousand Martyrs* (Belvedere, Vienna)

Philology   TACITUS. *Annales*, Books I-VI, disc. in Monastery of Corvey

Theology   GEILER VON KAISERSBERG, Johann. *Predigten*

Switzerland   Architecture   Town Hall, Basle, bgn.

LATIN EUROPE

France   Jurisprudence   BUDÉ, Guillaume. *Annotationes ad Pandectas*

Italy   History   GUICCIARDINI, Francesco. *Storie Fiorentine* (compl. 1509)

Literature   ARIOSTO, Ludovico. *Cassaria*

Painting   CARPACCIO, Vittore. *Death of the Virgin* (Ferrara)

RAPHAEL. *Esterhazy Madonna* (Budapest)

SIGNORELLI, Luca. *Virgin and Saints* (Milan)

TITIAN. *The Tribute Money* (Dresden)

Philology   Ed. Prin. Lysias (Aldus, Venice)

Ed. Prin. Rhetores Graeci (Aldus, Venice)

Portugal   Discoveries   ALMEIDA, Francisco de. Laccadive Islands

Spain   Discoveries   Yucatan, by Juan Díaz de Solís and Vicente Yáñez Pinzón

Literature   MONTALVO, García Rodríguez de. *Amadís de Gaula* (Spanish version).

Universities   Alcalá de Henares fnd.

1509

BRITISH ISLES

England   Literature   HAWES, Stephen. *The Passetyme of Pleasure*

SKELTON, John. *Phylyppe Sparowe* (*circa*)

Sculpture   TORRIGIANO, Pietro. Tomb of King Henry VII (compl. 1517; Westminster Abbey)

Universities   St. John's College, Cambridge, fnd.

Brasenose College, Oxford, fnd.

Scotland   Literature   BARCLAY, Alexander. *The Shyp of Folys of the Worlde* (Pynson, London)

THE LOW COUNTRIES

Flanders	Painting	DAVID, Gerard. *Madonna with Angels and Saints* (Rouen)
		MATSYS; Quentin Massys. *Altarpiece of St. Anne* (Brussels)
Holland	Philosophy	ERASMUS. *Moriae Encomium*

CENTRAL EUROPE

Germany	Literature	TENGLER, Ulrich. *Laienspiegel*
	Painting	DÜRER, Albrecht. *Virgin and Child* (Basle)

LATIN EUROPE

Italy	Literature	ARIOSTO, Ludovico. *I Suppositi*
		Ed. Prin. Plutarch's *Opera Moralia* (Aldus, Venice)
	Painting	FRANCIA; Francesco Raibolini. *Baptism of Christ* (Dresden)
		LEONARDO DA VINCI. *St. John the Baptist* (compl. 1512; Louvre)
		RAPHAEL. Wall Paintings of the Stanza della Segnatura (compl. 1511; Vatican)
Portugal	Discoveries	Malacca Peninsula by Sequeira

1510

BRITISH ISLES

England	Biography	MORE, Thomas. *The Lyfe of Picus, Erle of Myrandula*
	Literature	*King Apolyn of Tyre* (Wynkyn de Worde)
		The Birth of Merlin (Wynkyn de Worde)
	Schools	COLET, John. St. Paul's School fnd.
Scotland	Theology	The Aberdeen Breviary (Chepman and Myllar, Edinburgh)

THE LOW COUNTRIES

Holland	Politics	ERASMUS. *Institutio Christiani Principis*
	Painting	LEYDEN, Lucas van. *The " Round " Passion* (engravings)

NORTHERN EUROPE

Denmark	Philology	PEDERSEN, Christjern. *Vocabularium*

CENTRAL EUROPE

Germany	Architecture	Halberstadt Cathedral compl.
	Painting	ALTDORFER, Albrecht. *Holy Family at the Fountain* (Kais. Fried. Mus., Berlin)
		GRUENEWALD, Matthias. Isenheim Altarpiece (Colmar)

Germany   Philosophy   AGRIPPA V. NETTESHEIM, Heinrich Cornelius.
                                 De Occulta Philosophia

LATIN EUROPE

Italy   Painting   RAPHAEL. *Virgin with the Diadem* (Louvre)
                                 TITIAN. *Sacred and Profane Love* (Borghese,
                                 Rome)

1511

BRITISH ISLES

England   Literature   *The History of King Ponthus* (Wynkyn de
                                 Worde)

THE LOW COUNTRIES

Flanders   Painting   MATSYS; Quentin Massys. *Lamentation of
                                 Christ* (Antwerp)
Holland   Philosophy   ERASMUS. *De Ratione Studii*

NORTHERN EUROPE

Denmark   History   PEDERSEN, Christjern. *Diurnale Roeskildense*

CENTRAL EUROPE

Germany   Painting   DÜRER, Albrecht. *Trinity* (Belvedere,
                                 Vienna)
                                 DÜRER, Albrecht. *" Little " Passion* (wood-
                                 cuts)
                                 DÜRER, Albrecht. *Life of the Virgin* (wood-
                                 cuts)
                   Philosophy   GEILER VON KAISERSBERG, Johann. *Navicula
                                 sive Speculum Fatuorum*

LATIN EUROPE

France   Literature   GRINGORE, Pierre. *Jeu du Prince des Sots*
Italy   Painting   RAPHAEL. Wall Paintings in the Stanza
                                 d'Eliodoro, Vatican bgn. (compl. 1514)

1512

BRITISH ISLES

England   Literature   HAWES, Stephen. *The Example of Vertu*
                                 The History of Helias, Knight of the Swan
                                 (Wynkyn de Worde)
Scotland   Universities St. Leonard's College, St. Andrews, fnd.

THE LOW COUNTRIES

Holland   Philology   ERASMUS. *De duplici Copia verborum ac
                                 rerum commentarii duo*

CENTRAL EUROPE

Germany   Literature   MURNER, Thomas. *Narrenbeschwoerung*
                         MURNER, Thomas. *Die Schelmenzunft*
                 Painting   DÜRER, Albrecht. *Virgin with the Pear* (Belvedere, Vienna)

LATIN EUROPE

Italy   Painting   SEBASTIANO DEL PIOMBO. *La Fornarina* (Uffizi)
                       MICHELANGELO. Sistine Chapel ceiling compl. (bgn. 1508)
                       RAPHAEL. *Madonna di Foligno* (Vatican)
                       SIGNORELLI, Luca. *Last Supper* (Cortona)
                 Philology   ALEANDER, Girolamo. *Lexicon Graeco-Latinum*
Spain   Discoveries   Florida by Ponce de León

ROMAN CATHOLIC CHURCH

Lateran Council (compl. 1517)

1513

BRITISH ISLES

Scotland   Literature   DOUGLAS, Gawin. *The XIII bukes of Eneados*

THE LOW COUNTRIES

Holland   Literature   ERASMUS. *Silva Carminum*

CENTRAL EUROPE

Germany   Geography   WALDSEEMUELLER, Martin ; Hylacomylus. *Tabulae Modernae*
                 Painting   DÜRER, Albrecht. *" Little " Passion* (on copper)
                       DÜRER, Albrecht. *The Knight, Death and the Devil* (engravings)
                       GRUENEWALD, Matthias. *Mocking of Christ* (University, Munich)
                 Politics   HUTTEN, Ulrich von. *Nemo*
                 Sculpture   RIEMENSCHNEIDER, Tilman. Emperor Henry II monument (Bamberg)
                       VISCHER, Peter. Statues of the Tomb of Emperor Maximilian (Innsbruck)

LATIN EUROPE

France   History   LEMAIRE DE BELGES, Jean. *Illustrations des Gaules et Singularitez de Troyes*

Italy	Literature	BIBBIENA, Bernardo. *La Calandria*
	Painting	RAPHAEL. *St. Cecilia* (compl. 1516, Bologna)
		RAPHAEL. Frescoes in S. Maria della Pace, Rome
	Philology	Ed. Prin. Pindar (Aldus, Venice)
		Ed. Prin. Plato in Greek (Aldus, Venice)
Portugal	Literature	VICENTE, Gil. *Auto da Sibilla Cassandra* (*circa*)
	Architecture	Salamanca new Cathedral bgn.
Spain	Discoveries	Pacific Ocean by Vasco Núñez de Balboa

1514

BRITISH ISLES

England	History	MORE, Thomas. History of Richard III
	Philology	LINACRE, Thomas. *De Emendata Structura Latini Sermonis*
Scotland	Literature	BARCLAY, Alexander. *Eclogues*

THE LOW COUNTRIES

| Flanders | Painting | MATSYS; Quentin Massys. *The Banker and his Wife* (Louvre) |

NORTHERN EUROPE

| Denmark | History | SAXO GRAMMATICUS, *Danorum Regum Heroumque Historiae* (ed. by Christjern Pedersen ; Badius, Paris) |

CENTRAL EUROPE

| Germany | Painting | DÜRER, Albrecht. *Melancholia* (engravings) |
| | | DÜRER, Albrecht. *St. Jerome in his Cell* (engravings) |

LATIN EUROPE

France	Archaeology	BUDÉ, Guillaume. *De Assè et Partibus Eius*
Italy	Architecture	Raphael app. architect of St. Peter's, Rome
	Painting	CORREGGIO, Antonio Allegri da. *Virgin of St. Francis* (Dresden)
		SARTO, Andrea del. *Nativity of the Virgin* (Annunziata, Florence)
	Politics	MACHIAVELLI, Niccolò. *Il Principe*
Spain	Theology	VIVES, Juan Luis. *Christi Jesu Triumphans*
		XIMÉNEZ DE CISNEROS, Francisco. The Complutensian Polyglot Bible (publ. 1520)

[53]

1515

BRITISH ISLES

England   Architecture   Hampton Court Palace bgn.

THE LOW COUNTRIES

Flanders   Architecture   St. Gommaire, Lierre, compl. (bgn. 1425)

NORTHERN EUROPE

Denmark   Theology   PEDERSEN, Christjern. *Ioertegns Postil*

CENTRAL EUROPE

Germany   Painting   DÜRER, Albrecht. *Emperor Maximilian's Prayer-Book* (pen-drawings; Albertina, Vienna)

                  Politics   *Epistolae Virorum Obscurorum*

LATIN EUROPE

France   Architecture   Château de Chenonceaux bgn. (compl. 1524)
                                 VIART, Charles. Château de Blois bgn. (compl. *c.* 1529)
                  Literature   MAROT, Clément. *Le Temple de Cupidon*
Italy   Painting   BELLINI, Giovanni. *Portrait of Fra Teodoro da Urbino* (Nat. Gal. Lond.)
                                 CARPACCIO, Vittore. *The Ten Thousand Martyrs* (Venice)
                                 RAPHAEL. *Portrait of Baldassare Castiglione* (Louvre)
                                 SIGNORELLI, Luca. *Virgin and Saints* (Nat. Gal. Lond.)
                                 TITIAN. *Noli me tangere* (Nat. Gal. Lond.)
                  Philology   Ed. Prin. Tacitus' Complete Works (Beroaldi, Rome)
Spain   Discoveries   Mexico by Juan de Grijalva

1516

BRITISH ISLES

England   Literature   *Nova Legenda Angliae* (Wynkyn de Worde)
                  History   FABYAN, Robert. *The New Cronycles of Englande and of Fraunce* (Pynson, London)
                  Philosophy and Politics } MORE, Thomas. *Utopia*
                  Universities   Corpus Christi College, Oxford, fnd.

THE LOW COUNTRIES

Holland	Theology	ERASMUS. *Novum Instrumentum* (New Testament in Greek and Latin; pr. at Basle by Froben)

CENTRAL EUROPE

Germany	Literature	BRANT, Sebastian. *Klagspigel*
	Painting	DÜRER, Albrecht. *Portrait of Michael Wohlgemuth* (Munich)
		BALDUNG, Hans, called Grien. Freiburg Altarpiece (Cath., Freiburg)
	Sculpture	RIEMENSCHNEIDER, Tilman. Monument of Abbot Trithemius (Würzburg)
	Theology	*Theologia Deutsch* (asc. to Martin Luther)

LATIN EUROPE

France	Architecture	Azay-le-Rideau Château bgn. (compl. 1524)
Italy	Literature	ARIOSTO, Ludovico. *Orlando Furioso*
	Painting	LOTTO, Lorenzo. *The Adoration* (Bergamo)
		RAPHAEL. *Madonna di S. Sisto* (Dresden)
	Philology	Ed. Prin. Pausanias (Aedes Aldi, Venice)
		Ed. Prin. Xenophon's Complete Works (Giunta, Florence)
	Philosophy	POMPONATIUS, Petrus; Pietro Pomponazzi. *Tractatus de Immortalitate Animae*
	Sculpture	MICHELANGELO. *Moses* (S. Pietro in Vincoli, Rome)
Portugal	Literature	RESENDE, Garcia de. *Cancionéiro Geral*
Spain	Discoveries	La Plata River by Juan Díaz de Solís

1517

BRITISH ISLES

England	Literature	SKELTON, John. *Magnyfycence* (*circa*)
Scotland	Literature	DUNBAR, William. *Orisone* bgn. (compl. 1518)

CENTRAL EUROPE

Germany	Literature	SACHS, Hans. *Hofgesind Veneris* (Sachs' earliest play)
		ANON. *Theuerdanck* (Schönsperger, Nuremberg)
	Painting	BALDUNG, Hans, called Grien. *Woman and Death* (Basle)
	Theology	LUTHER, Martin. Ninety-Five Theses
		REUCHLIN, Johann. *De Arte Cabbalistica*

LATIN EUROPE

France	Architecture	Choir of Saint-Etienne-du-Mont, Paris (compl. 1538; Nave bgn. 1540; Façade blt. 1610)
Italy	Architecture	SCARPAGNINO and LOMBARDO, Pietro. Scuola San Rocco, Venice, bgn. (compl. 1547)
	Literature	FOLENGO, Teofilo. *Baldus*
		FOLENGO, Teofilo. *Liber Macaronicus*
	Painting	ROMANO, Giulio. *Lo Spasimo* (some pts. by Raphael; Prado, Madrid)
		RAPHAEL. Wall Paintings of the Stanza dell' Incendio (Vatican)
		SARTO, Andrea del. *Madonna delle Arpie* (Uffizi)
	Philology	Ed. Prin. Plutarch's Lives (Giunta, Florence)
Spain	Literature	TORRES NAHARRO, Bartolomé. *Propaladia*

1518

BRITISH ISLES

England	Academies	Royal College of Physicians, London, fnd.
Scotland	Schools	Royal High School, Edinburgh, fnd.

THE LOW COUNTRIES

Flanders	Architecture	Notre-Dame, Antwerp, compl. (bgn. 1352)
Holland	Painting	LEYDEN, Lucas van. *The Temptation* (engravings)

CENTRAL EUROPE

Germany	Painting	DÜRER, Albrecht. *The Great Cannon* (etchings)
		DÜRER, Albrecht. *Portrait of Emperor Maximilian* (woodcuts; Belvedere, Vienna)
		DÜRER, Albrecht. *Virgin crowned by Angels* (woodcuts)
	Philology	MELANCHTHON, Philipp. *Institutiones Linguae Graecae*
	Theology	LUTHER, Martin. *Von Ablass und Gnade*

LATIN EUROPE

France	Universities	Collège de France fnd.
Italy	Painting	PERUGINO; Pietro Vanuzzi. *St. Sebastian* (Perugia)
		RAPHAEL. *Portrait of Pope Leo X* (Pitti)
		RAPHAEL. *St. Michael and the Devil* (Louvre)
		TITIAN. *Assumption of the Virgin* (Venice)
Spain	Philosophy	VIVES, Juan Luis. *De Initiis, Sectis et Laudibus Philosophiae*

1519

BRITISH ISLES

England

Architecture	St. George's Chapel, Windsor Castle, compl. (bgn. 1473)
Literature	SKELTON, John. *Colyn Cloute*

CENTRAL EUROPE

Germany

Literature	MURNER, Thomas. *Die Geuchmatt* *Tyll Ulenspigel*
Painting	DÜRER, Albrecht. *St. Anthony* (engravings) GRUENEWALD, Matthias. *Stuppach Madonna* (Stuppach)
Sculpture	VISCHER, Peter. Shrine of St. Sebald (bgn. *c.* 1508; Nuremberg)

LATIN EUROPE

Italy

Painting	PIOMBO, Sebastiano del. *Resurrection of Lazarus* (Nat. Gal. Lond.)

Spain

Discoveries	CORTÉS, Hernán, landing in Mexico

1520

CENTRAL EUROPE

Germany

Politics	HUTTEN, Ulrich von. *Vadiscus* LUTHER, Martin. *An den Christlichen Adel Teutscher Nation ...* LUTHER, Martin. *De Captivitate Babylonica ...* LUTHER, Martin. *Von der Freiheit eines Christenmenschen ...*
Theology	LUTHER, Martin. *Von den guten Werken*

LATIN EUROPE

France

Architecture	Saint-Maclou, Rouen, compl. (bgn. 1432)
Libraries	Bibliothèque Royale (Nationale) Paris, fnd.

Italy

Academies	Academy of Sciences, Padua, fnd.
Literature	ARIOSTO, Ludovico. *Il Negromante* MORLINI. *Novellae*
Painting	RAPHAEL. *The Transfiguration* (Vatican)
Philosophy	POMPONATIUS, Petrus; Pietro Pomponazzi. *De Fato, Libero Arbitrio, Praedestinatione, Providentia Dei*

Portugal

Discoveries	Magellan Strait by Fernão Magelhães

Spain

Painting	FERNÁNDEZ, Alexo. *La Virgen de los Conquistadores* (*circa*; Seville)

[57]

1521

BRITISH ISLES

England	Printing	First Cambridge pr. by John Siberch (Bullock, Henry, *Oratio habita Cantabrigiae . . . ad Card. Wolsaeum*)

CENTRAL EUROPE

Germany	Church	Diet of Worms
	Politics	HUTTEN, Ulrich von. *Gespraechbuechlein*
	Theology	LUTHER, Martin. *Das Magnificat verteutscht*
		LUTHER, Martin. *Vom Missbrauch der Messe*
		MELANCHTHON, Philipp. *Loci Communes*

LATIN EUROPE

France	Literature	*Le Violier des Histoires Romaines* (French version of *Gesta Romanorum*)
Italy	Painting	CORREGGIO, Antonio Allegri da. Frescoes in S. Giovanni, Parma, bgn. (compl. 1524)
		LOTTO, Lorenzo. *Virgin and Saints* (Bergamo)
		TITIAN. *Bacchanal* (Prado, Madrid)
	Sculpture	MICHELANGELO. *Christ with the Cross* (Rome)
	Warfare	MACHIAVELLI, Niccolò. *Sette Libri dell'Arte della Guerra*
Portugal	Discoveries	Philippine Islands by Fernão Magelhães

1522

BRITISH ISLES

England	Theatre	Interlude of the World and the Child
Scotland	Education	BARCLAY, Alexander. *Mirrour of good maners* (Pynson, London)

THE LOW COUNTRIES

Holland	Education	ERASMUS. *Colloquia*

CENTRAL EUROPE

Germany	Literature	PAULI, Johannes. *Schimpff und Ernst*
	Painting	HOLBEIN, Hans, the Younger. *The Solothurn Madonna* (Solothurn)
	Politics	MURNER, Thomas. *Von dem Grossen Lutherischen Narren . . .*
	Theology	LUTHER, Martin. *Das New Testament*

[58]

LATIN EUROPE

Italy	Painting	PERUGINO ; Pietro Vanuzzi. *The Transfiguration* (Perugia)
	Philology	ALCIATI, Andrea. *Emblematum Libellus*
Spain	Discoveries	The Bermudas by Juan Bermúdez

1523

BRITISH ISLES

England	Agriculture	FITZHERBERT, Anthony. *The Boke of Husbandrie*
	History	BOURCHIER, John, Lord Berners. Froissart's Chronicles, trans. bgn. (compl. 1525; Pynson, London)
	Philology	LINACRE, Thomas. *Rudimenta Grammatices*
	Politics	SKELTON, John. *Why come ye nat to courte?*

CENTRAL EUROPE

Germany	Painting	DÜRER, Albrecht. *Portrait of the " Great" Cardinal* (engravings)
		HOLBEIN, Hans, the Younger. *Portrait of Erasmus* (Louvre)
		HOLBEIN, Hans, the Younger. *Alphabet of the Dance of Death* (drawings)
	Politics	SACHS, Hans. *Die Wittenbergisch Nachtigall*
	Sculpture	STOSS, Veit. *Adoration of the Shepherds* (Bamberg)
	Theology	LUTHER, Martin. *Das Alt Testament*, Pt. I

LATIN EUROPE

Italy	Literature	MACHIAVELLI, Niccolò. *Mandragola*
	Painting	TITIAN. *Bacchus and Ariadne* (Nat. Gal. Lond.)
		TITIAN. *Flora* (Uffizi)
		TITIAN. *Entombment of Christ* (Louvre)
	Sculpture	MICHELANGELO. Sculptures in the Medici Chapel, Florence
Portugal	Literature	VICENTE, Gil. *Ignez Pereira*

1524

THE LOW COUNTRIES

Holland	Philosophy	ERASMUS. *De Libero Arbitrio*

CENTRAL EUROPE

Germany	Geography	APIANUS, Petrus; Peter Bienwitz. *Cosmographia*

Germany	Literature	LUTHER, Martin. *Geystliche gesangk Buechleyn*
	Painting	DÜRER, Albrecht. *Portrait of Frederick the Wise, Elector of Saxony* (engravings; Kais. Fried. Mus., Berlin)
		DÜRER, Albrecht. *Portrait of Willibald Pirkheimer* (engravings)
		GRUENEWALD, Matthias. *St. Erasmus and St. Maurice* (Munich)
	Schools	LUTHER, Martin. *An die Rathsherrn aller Staedte deutschen Lands, dass sie christliche Schulen aufrichten und erhalten sollen*
		First Protestant *Gymnasium*, Madgeburg, fnd.
	Theology	MELANCHTHON, Philipp. *Summa Doctrinae Lutheri*

LATIN EUROPE

France	History	COMMINES, Philippe de. *Mémoires*
Italy	Architecture	MICHELANGELO. Bibliotheca Laurenziana, Florence, bgn. (compl. 1526)
	Literature	TRISSINO, Giovanni Giorgio. *Sofonisba*
	Sculpture	MICHELANGELO. *Madonna* bgn. (compl. 1532; S. Lorenzo, Florence)
Spain	Architecture	San Esteban, Salamanca, bgn. (compl. 1610)

ROMAN CATHOLIC CHURCH

Order of the Theatines fnd.

1525

BRITISH ISLES

| England | Theology | TYNDALE, William. *New Testament* (Quentell, Cologne, and Schoeffer, Worms) |

THE LOW COUNTRIES

| Flanders | Architecture | Maison du Roy, Brussels, compl. |

CENTRAL EUROPE

Germany	Aesthetics	DÜRER, Albrecht. *Underweysung der Messung* . . .
	Philology	MELANCHTHON, Philipp. *Grammatica Latina*
	Sculpture	VISCHER, Peter. Tomb of Cardinal Albrecht of Brandenburg (Coll. Church, Aschaffenburg)
	Theology	LUTHER, Martin. *De Servo Arbitrio*
Switzerland	Theology	ZWINGLI, Ulrich. *De vera et falsa Religione*

LATIN EUROPE

Italy	Academies	Accademia degli Intronati, Siena, fnd.
	Literature	BEMBO, Pietro. *Prose della Volgar Lingua*
		RUCELLAI, Giovanni. *Rosmunda*
	Painting	CORREGGIO, Antonio Allegri da. Frescoes in Parma Cathedral bgn. (compl. 1530)
		SARTO, Andrea del. *Madonna del Sacco* (Annunziata, Florence)
		SODOMA; Giovanni Antonio Bazzi. Decoration of the Chapel of St. Catherine, Siena

SLAVONIC EUROPE

Czechoslovakia	Architecture	St. Barbara Cathedral, Kutná Hora, compl. (bgn. 1380)

1526

BRITISH ISLES

England	Theology	TYNDALE, William. Prologue to the Epistle of St. Paul to the Romans

THE LOW COUNTRIES

Flanders	Architecture	Notre-Dame, Huy, compl. (bgn. 1311)
Holland	Painting	LEYDEN, Lucas van. *Last Judgment* (Leyden)

CENTRAL EUROPE

Germany	Church	First Diet of Speyer (Spires)
	Painting	ALTDORFER, Albrecht. *Suzanna bathing* (Munich)
		DÜRER, Albrecht. *Four Apostles* (Munich)
		DÜRER, Albrecht. *Portrait of Hieronymus Holzschuher* (Kais. Fried. Mus., Berlin)
		HOLBEIN, Hans, the Younger. *Virgin of Burgomaster Meyer* (Darmstadt)

LATIN EUROPE

France	Architecture	NEPVEU, Pierre (called Trinqueau). Chambord Château bgn.
Italy	Literature	FOLENGO, Teofilo. *Orlandino*
		SANNAZARO, Jacopo. *De Partu Virginis*
	Painting	TITIAN. *Pesaro Madonna* (Venice)
Portugal	Discoveries	New Guinea by Enrique de Meneses
Spain	Discoveries	Peru by Francisco Pizarro
	Politics	VICTORIA, Francisco de. *De Indis, de Jure Belli, de Potestate civili*

[61]

1527

BRITISH ISLES

England   Literature   TYNDALE, William. *Parable of the wycked Mammon*

Scotland   History   BOËCE, Hector. *Scotorum Historiae*

THE LOW COUNTRIES

Flanders   Architecture   Oudenarde Town Hall bgn. (compl. 1535)

CENTRAL EUROPE

Germany   Theology   MELANCHTHON, Philipp. *Libellus Visitatorius*

    Universities   Marburg fnd.

    Warfare   DÜRER, Albrecht. *Etliche Unterricht von Bevestigung der Statt . . .*

LATIN EUROPE

France   Libraries   Lyons fnd.

Italy   Literature   FOLENGO, Teofilo. *Chaos del Triperuno*

    Poetics   VIDA, Marco Girolamo. *De Arte Poetica*

Spain   Architecture   DE RIAÑO, Diego, and GARUZA, Martín. Seville City Hall bgn. (compl. 1532)

1528

BRITISH ISLES

England   Theology   TYNDALE, William. *The Obedience of a Christen Man*

THE LOW COUNTRIES

Holland   Philology   ERASMUS. *Ciceronianus*

                   ERASMUS. *De Recta Latini Graecique Sermonis Pronuntiatione*

CENTRAL EUROPE

Germany   Aesthetics   DÜRER, Albrecht. *Vier Buecher von menschlicher Proportion*

    Painting   GRUENEWALD, Matthias. *Lamentation over the body of Christ* (*circa*; Aschaffenburg)

LATIN EUROPE

France   Architecture   Fontainebleau Château bgn.

    Geography   FERNEL, Jean. First modern attempt to measure a Geographical Degree

Italy	Literature	ARIOSTO, Ludovico. *La Lena*
		CASTIGLIONE, Baldassare. *Il Cortegiano* (first pr.; written 1514)
	Painting	CORREGGIO, Antonio Allegri da. *Adoration of the Shepherds* (Milan)
	Philology	Ed. Prin. Epictetus (Aedes Aldi, Venice)

1529

BRITISH ISLES

England	Education	COLET, John. *De pueris ... instituendis*
Scotland	Literature	LINDSAY, David. *The Complaynt to the King*

THE LOW COUNTRIES

Holland	Education	ERASMUS. *De pueris statim et liberaliter ... instituendis*

CENTRAL EUROPE

Germany	Architecture	Minster, Ulm, compl. (bgn. 1377)
	Church	Second Diet of Speyer (Spires)
	Painting	ALTDORFER, Albrecht. *Battle of Arbela* (Munich)
	Politics	HUTTEN, Ulrich von. *Arminius*
	Theology	LUTHER, Martin. *Catechism*

LATIN EUROPE

France	Literature	JANNEQUIN. *Les Cris de Paris*
		TORY, Geoffroy. *Champ Fleury*
	Philology	BUDÉ, Guillaume. *Commentarii Linguae Graecae*
Italy	Painting	LUINI, Bernardino. *The Passion* (Lugano)
Spain	Discoveries	California by Bezerro and Juan de Grijalva
	Literature	GUEVARA, Antonio de. *Libro dureo de Marco Aurelio*
	Politics	VIVES, Juan Luis. *De Concordia et Discordia in humano Genere*

1530

BRITISH ISLES

England	Theology	TYNDALE, William. *The Practyse of Prelates*
		TYNDALE, William. *Pentateuch* (Hans Luft, Marlborough in the lande of Hesse; Marburg)

NORTHERN EUROPE

Sweden	Literature	PETRI, Olaus. *Ndgre gudhelige vijsor* (Certain Divine Songs)

[63]

CENTRAL EUROPE

Germany	Church	*Confessio Augustana*
	Education	LUTHER, Martin. *Sermon an die Prediger, dass sie die Leute ermahnen ihre Kinder zur Schule zu halten*
	Painting	BALDUNG, Hans, called Grien. *Virgin* (Vienna)
	Philology	LUTHER, Martin. *Sendbrief vom Dolmetschen*
Switzerland	Theology	ZWINGLI, Ulrich. *Fidei Ratio ad Carolum V*

LATIN EUROPE

France	Philology	BUDÉ, Guillaume. *De Philologia*
		CORDIER, Mathurin. *De corrupti Sermonis emendatione apud Gallos ... libellus*
	Typography	GARAMOND, Claude, est. as type-founder at Paris
Italy	Literature	BEMBO, Pietro. *Rime*
		FRACASTORO, Girolamo. *Syphilidis Libri III*
	Painting	CORREGGIO, Antonio Allegri da. *Leda* (Kais. Fried. Mus., Berlin)
		CORREGGIO, Antonio Allegri da. *Nativity* (Dresden)
		TITIAN. *St. Peter Martyr* (SS. Giovanni e Paolo, Venice)

1531

BRITISH ISLES

England	Education	ELYOT, Thomas. *The Boke named the Governour* (Berthelet, London)

THE LOW COUNTRIES

Holland	Economics	Amsterdam Exchange fnd.

CENTRAL EUROPE

Germany	Church	Schmalkaldic League fnd.
	Philosophy	AGRIPPA VON NETTESHEIM, Heinrich Cornelius. *De Vanitate ... Scientiarum*
	Theology	MELANCHTHON, Philipp. *Apologia*
Switzerland	Theology	ZWINGLI, Ulrich. *Christianae Fidei ... Explanatio*

LATIN EUROPE

France	Literature	MARGUERITE, Queen of Navarre. *Le Miroir de l'Ame Pêcheresse*
Spain	Philosophy	VIVES, Juan Luis. *De Disciplinis*

HUNGARY

	Universities	Debreczen fnd.

[64]

1532

THE LOW COUNTRIES

Holland Philology ERASMUS. Ed. of Terence

CENTRAL EUROPE

Germany Church Peace of Nuremberg
Jurisprudence *Constitutio Criminalis Carolina* (*Peinliche Halsgerichtsordnung*)
Painting CRANACH, Lucas, the Elder. *Portrait of Melanchthon* (Dresden)
HOLBEIN, Hans, the Younger. *Portrait of the Merchant Georg Gisze* (Kais. Fried. Mus., Berlin)

Switzerland Philology Ed. Prin. Eleven Plays of Aristophanes (Cratander, Basle)

LATIN EUROPE

France Architecture LEMERCIER, L'Aîné, Pierre, and DA CORTONA, Domenico. Saint-Eustache, Paris, bgn, (compl. 1589)
Literature MAROT, Clément. *L'Adolescence Clémentine*
RABELAIS, François. *Pantagruel*
Philology ESTIENNE, Robert. *Dictionarium, seu linguae latinae Thesaurus*
Italy Architecture PERUZZI, Baldassare. Palazzo Massimi, Rome, bgn. (compl. 1536)
SANSOVINO, Jacopo. Palazzo Cornaro, Venice, bgn.
History MACHIAVELLI, Niccolò. *Istorie Fiorentine* (posth.)
Painting TITIAN. *Portrait of Charles V with his Dog* (Prado, Madrid)

1533

BRITISH ISLES

England Literature HEYWOOD, John. *Play of the Wether*

CENTRAL EUROPE

Germany Mathematics REGIOMONTANUS, Johann Mueller. *De Triangulis omnimodis Libri V* (first pr.; written 1463)
Painting HOLBEIN, Hans, the Younger. *The Ambassadors* (Nat. Gal. Lond.)
HOLBEIN, Hans, the Younger. *The Falconer* (Hague)

LATIN EUROPE

France	Architecture	DA CORTONA, Domenico. Hôtel de Ville, Paris, bgn.
	Discoveries	Canadian coast, first landing by Jacques Cartier
Italy	Literature	ALAMANNI, Ludovico. *Opere Toscane*
Spain	Discoveries	Chile by Diego de Almagro
	Universities	Granada fnd.

1534

BRITISH ISLES

England	History	VERGIL, Polydore. *Historia Anglica*
	Literature	BOURCHIER, John, Lord Berners. *The Boke of Duke Huon of Burdeux*
		ELYOT, Thomas. *The Castel of Helth*

NORTHERN EUROPE

Iceland	Printing	Breviarium Holense (first book pr. in Iceland)

LATIN EUROPE

France	Literature	RABELAIS, François. *Gargantua*
Italy	Academies	Accademia degli Infiammati, Padua, fnd.
	Architecture	MICHELANGELO and SANGALLO, Antonio. Palazzo Farnese, Rome, bgn. (compl. 1580)
		SANSOVINO, Jacopo. San Francesco della Vigna, Venice, bgn. (compl. 1562)
	Literature	ARETINO, Pietro. *Ragionamenti*, Pt. I
Spain	Colonization	Cuzco entered by Francisco Pizarro
	Philology	VALDÉS, Juan de. *Diálogo de la Lengua*
	Theology	SERVET, Miguel. *De Trinitatis Erroribus*

1535

BRITISH ISLES

England	Church	Act of Supremacy
	Literature	BOURCHIER, John, Lord Berners. *The Golden Boke of Marcus Aurelius* (trans. from Antonio de Guevara)
	Theology	COVERDALE, Miles. *Biblia, the Bible . . . translated out of the Doutche and Latyn into English* (Van Meteren, Antwerp)

CENTRAL EUROPE

Germany	Architecture	Heilbronn Town Hall bgn.
Switzerland	Theology	ROBERT, Pierre (Olivétan) and DE VINGLE, Paul. First French Protestant Bible iss. at Neuchâtel (Bible of the Sword)

LATIN EUROPE

France   Literature   Scève, Maurice de. *La déplorable Fin de Flamète*

                Theology   Calvin, Jean. *Institutio Christianae Religionis*

Italy   Literature   Vida, Marco Girolamo. *Christiados Libri VI*

                Painting   Titian. *La Bella* (Pitti)

Spain   Colonization   Buenos Ayres fnd. by Pedro de Mendoza

                               Lima and Truxillo fnd. by Francisco Pizarro

                History   Hernández de Oviedo, Gonzalo. *Historia general y natural de las Indias*

1536

BRITISH ISLES

England   Church   The Ten Articles

CENTRAL EUROPE

Germany   Medicine   Paracelsus; Theophrastus Bombastus von Hohenheim. *Grosse Chirurgie*

Switzerland   Theology   *Confessio Helvetica Prior*

LATIN EUROPE

France   Philology   Dolet, Etienne. *Commentarii Linguae Latinae* bgn. (compl. 1538)

Italy   Architecture   Sansovino, Jacopo. Libreria Vecchia, Venice, bgn. (compl. 1553)

                               Zecca, Venice, bgn. (compl. 1584)

SLAVONIC EUROPE

Czechoslovakia   Architecture   Belvedere, Prague, bgn. (compl. 1590)

1537

BRITISH ISLES

England   Theology   *The Institution of a Christen Man* (The Bishops' Book)

                               Coverdale, Miles. *Biblia* . . . (2nd ed.; Nycolson, Southwark)

                               Matthew, Thomas; John Rogers. *The Byble* (Van Meteren, Antwerp)

Scotland   Universities   St. Mary's College, St. Andrews, fnd.

CENTRAL EUROPE

Germany   Painting   Holbein, Hans, the Younger. *Portrait of Lady Jane Seymour* (Belvedere, Vienna)

Germany	Painting	HOLBEIN, Hans, the Younger. *Portrait of Sir Richard Southwell* (Uffizi)
		HOLBEIN, Hans, the Younger. *Portrait of the Sieur de Morette* (Dresden)
	Schools	*Gymnasium*, Strasbourg, fnd.

LATIN EUROPE

France	Literature	DES PÉRIERS, Bonaventure. *Cymbalum Mundi*
Italy	Mathematics	FONTANA, Niccolò, called Tartaglia. *Nova Scienza*
	Schools	Conservatorio di S. Maria di Loretto, Naples, fnd.
Portugal	Astronomy	NUÑEZ, Pedro. *Tratado da Sphera*

1538

BRITISH ISLES

England	Literature	BALE, John. *God's Promises* (*The chefe promyses of God*)
		BALE, John. *Johan Baptystes preachynge in the Wyldernesse*
		BALE, John. *The Temptacyon of our Lorde*

THE LOW COUNTRIES

| Flanders | Medicine | VESALIUS, Andreas. *Tabulae Anatomicae* |

CENTRAL EUROPE

Germany	Education	STURM, Johannes. *De Litterarum Ludis recte aperiendis*
	Painting	HOLBEIN, Hans, the Younger. *Portrait of Christina, Duchess of Milan* (Nat. Gal. Lond.)
		HOLBEIN, Hans, the Younger. *Icones Historiarum Veteris Testamenti* (woodcuts)
		HOLBEIN, Hans, the Younger. *Icones Mortis* (woodcuts)
	Theology	LUTHER, Martin. *Schmalkaldische Artikel*

LATIN EUROPE

Italy	Literature	COLONNA, Vittoria. *Rime*
	Painting	TITIAN. *Venus of Urbino* (Uffizi)
Spain	Aesthetics	HOLLANDA, Francisco de. *Tractado de Pintura Antigua*
	Philosophy	VIVES, Juan Luis. *De Anima et Vita*

1539

BRITISH ISLES

England	Church	Statute of the Six Articles
	Theology	*The Byble in Englyshe* (The " Great Bible "; 2nd ed. with Thomas Cranmer's Preface; 1540)

CENTRAL EUROPE

Germany	Painting	HOLBEIN, Hans, the Younger. *Portrait of Anne of Cleves* (Louvre)

LATIN EUROPE

France	Architecture	Château of Saint-Germain-en-Laye bgn. (compl. 1544)
	Jurisprudence	Edict of Villers-Cotterets (official Acts of Law to be pron. in French)
	Literature	MAROT, Clément. *Les Cantiques de la Paix*
	Universities	Nîmes fnd.
Spain	Literature	GUEVARA, Antonio de. *Menosprecio de la Corte y Alabanza de la Aldea*

1540

BRITISH ISLES

England	Literature	COVERDALE, Miles. *Ghostly Psalms*
	Politics	ELYOT, Thomas. *The Image of Governance* (Berthelet, London)
Scotland	Literature	LINDSAY, David. *Ane Pleasant Satyre of the Thrie Estaits*

CENTRAL EUROPE

Germany	Astronomy	RHAETICUS, Georg Joachim. *Narratio de Revolutionibus Copernici*

LATIN EUROPE

France	Literature	HERBERAY, Nicolas de, Seigneur des Essarts. *Le Premier Livre d'Amadis de Gaule*
	Philology	DOLET, Etienne. *La Manière de bien traduire d'une Langue en autre*
Italy	Academies	Accademia Rossana, Naples, fnd.
	Architecture	LIPPI, Annibale. Villa Medici, Rome, bgn.
		MICHELANGELO. Piazza del Campidoglio, Rome (outline made)
		SANSOVINO, Jacopo. Loggetta del Campanile, Venice, bgn.
	Metallurgy	BIRINGUCCIO, Vanuccio. *De la Pirotechnia*
	Painting	TITIAN. *Presentation of the Virgin* (Venice)
	Universities	Macerata fnd.
Spain	Architecture	Alcázar, Toledo, bgn.
	Discoveries	Mississippi River by Hernández de Soto

[69]

ROMAN CATHOLIC CHURCH

LOYOLA's Compania Jesu confirmed by
Pope Paul III

1541

THE LOW COUNTRIES

Holland	Literature	JOHANNES SECUNDUS; Jan Everaerds. *Basia* (posth.)

CENTRAL EUROPE

Germany	Church	Diet of Regensburg (Ratisbon)
	Mathematics	REGIOMONTANUS, Johann Mueller. *Compositio Tabularum Sinuum*
	Politics	LUTHER, Martin. *Wider Hans Worst*
Switzerland	Botany	GESNER, Konrad. *Enchiridion Historiae Plantarum*
	Church	Calvin settles at Geneva *Catechismus Ecclesiae Genevensis*

LATIN EUROPE

Italy	Literature	BERNI, Francesco. *Orlando Innamorato*
	Painting	MICHELANGELO. *Last Judgment* (Sistine Chapel, Rome)
Spain	Discoveries	Amazon River by Francisco de Orellana

1542

BRITISH ISLES

England	Universities	Magdalene College, Cambridge, fnd.

CENTRAL EUROPE

Germany	Botany	FUCHS, Leonhard. *Historia Stirpium*

LATIN EUROPE

France	Literature	MAROT, Clément. *L'Enfer*
	Philology	DOLET, Etienne. Cicero's *Ad Familiares* and *Tusculanae Disputationes* I and II (Fr. version)
		HEROET, Antoine. *Androgyne* (partial translation of Plato's Symposium into Fr. verse)
Italy	Academies	Academia Vitruviana, Rome, fnd.
	Philosophy	CARDANO, Girolamo. *De propria Vita*
Portugal	Discoveries	Japan by De Mota
	Geography	NUÑEZ, Pedro. *De Crepusculis*

ROMAN CATHOLIC CHURCH

Holy Office fnd.

1543

BRITISH ISLES

England   Theology   *The Necessary Doctrine and Erudition of a Christen Man* (The King's Book)

THE LOW COUNTRIES

Flanders   Medicine   VESALIUS, Andreas. *De humani Corporis Fabrica*

CENTRAL EUROPE

Germany   Schools   Fuerstenschulen, Schulpforta, Grimma, Meissen, fnd.

LATIN EUROPE

France   Literature   MAROT, Clément. *Les Pseaumes de David*
    Philosophy   RAMUS, Petrus ; Pierre de la Ramée. *Animadversiones in Dialecticam Aristotelis*
    Theology   CALVIN, Jean. *Traité des Reliques*
Italy   Literature   ALAMANNI, Ludovico. *La Coltivazione*
    Painting   TITIAN. *Ecce Homo* (Belvedere, Vienna)
Spain   Literature   BOSCÁN, Juan, and GARCILASO DE LA VEGA. *Las Obras de Boscán y algunas de Garcilaso de la Vega*
    Theology   VIVES, Juan Luis. *De Veritate Fidei Christianae*

SLAVONIC EUROPE

Poland   Astronomy   COPERNICUS, Nicolaus. *De Revolutionibus Orbium Coelestium*

1544

CENTRAL EUROPE

Germany   Geography   MUENSTER, Sebastian. *Cosmographia*
    Mathematics   STIFEL, Michael. *Arithmetica Integra*
    Universities   Koenigsberg (E. Prussia) fnd.
Switzerland   Philology   Ed. Prin. Flavius Josephus (Froben, Basle)

LATIN EUROPE

France   Literature   DES PÉRIERS, Bonaventure. *Nouvelles Récréations*
    DOLET, Etienne. *Le Second Enfer*
    SCÈVE, Maurice. *Délie*

[71]

1545

BRITISH ISLES

England	Literature	ELYOT, Thomas. *The Defence of good Women* (Berthelet, London)
	Sport	ASCHAM, Roger. *Toxophilus* (Whitchurch, London)

THE LOW COUNTRIES

Flanders	Music	DES PRÈS, Josquin. *Vingt et quatre Chansons* . . .

CENTRAL EUROPE

Switzerland	Bibliography	GESNER, Konrad. *Bibliotheca Universalis* (compl. 1555)

LATIN EUROPE

France	Medicine	PARÉ, Ambroise. *La Manière de traicter les Playes*
	Painting	CLOUET, François. *Portrait of King Francis I on Horseback* (? Florence)
Italy	Architecture	PALLADIO, Andrea. Basilica, Vicenza, bgn. (compl. 1549)
	Botany	First Botanical Garden est. at Padua
	Mathematics	CARDANO, Girolamo. *Ars Magna*
	Painting	BRONZINO; Angelo Allori. Frescoes in the Chapel of Eleanor of Toledo bgn. (compl. 1564; Palazzo Vecchio, Florence)
		LOTTO, Lorenzo. *Pietà* (Milan)
		TITIAN. *Portrait of Pietro Aretino* (Pitti)
	Philology	Ed. Prin. Euripides' *Electra*, ed. by Piero Vettori
Spain	Literature	*Cancionero de Romances* bgn. (compl. 1550)
	Theology	ALCÁNTARA, Pedro de. *De Oratione et Meditatione* (Spanish version 1588)

ROMAN CATHOLIC CHURCH

Council of Trent bgn. (end. 1563)

1546

BRITISH ISLES

England	Universities	Christ Church College, Oxford, fnd.

CENTRAL EUROPE

Germany	Literature	SACHS, Hans. *Griselda* (Comedy)
		SACHS, Hans. *Lisabetha* (Tragedy)
	Painting	CRANACH, Lucas, the Elder. *Fons Juventutis* (Kais. Fried. Mus., Berlin)

LATIN EUROPE

France	Architecture	LESCOT, Pierre. Louvre, Paris, bgn.
	Philology	Plato's *Ion*, first Fr. trans.
Italy	Literature	ARIOSTO, Ludovico. *Satire* (posth.)
	Medicine	FRACASTORO, Girolamo. *De Morbis contagiosis*
	Painting	TINTORETTO; Jacopo Robusti. Frescoes in S. Maria dell' Orto, Venice

ROMAN CATHOLIC CHURCH

Burning of Etienne Dolet at Paris, for heresy
First Index Expurgatorius

1547

BRITISH ISLES

England	Theology	*Homilies* (Whitchurch, London)
	Universities	Trinity College, Cambridge, fnd.

LATIN EUROPE

France	Literature	AMYOT, Jacques. *L'Histoire Aethiopique* (Théagène et Chariclée)
		MARGUERITE, Queen of Navarre. *Marguerites*
		PELETIER, Jacques. *Les Œuvres Poétiques*
	Philology	Plato's *Crito*, first Fr. trans.
	Politics	BUDÉ, Guillaume. *De l'Institution du Prince*
Italy	Architecture	MICHELANGELO app. architect of St. Peter's, Rome
	Literature	TRISSINO, Giovanni Giorgio. *L'Italia liberata dai Goti* bgn. (compl. 1548)
Spain	Painting	CAMPAÑA, Pedro de; Peter de Kempeneer. *Deposition from the Cross* bgn. (compl. 1548; Cathedral, Seville)
	Politics	SEPÚLVEDA, Juan Ginés. *Democrates alter, sive de justis belli causis apud Indos* (*circa*)

1548

BRITISH ISLES

England	Biography	BALE, John. *Illustrium Majoris Britanniae Scriptorum . . . Summarium* (Overton, Ipswich)

CENTRAL EUROPE

Germany	Church	The " Interim "

LATIN EUROPE

France	Literature	BEZA; Théodore de Bèze. *Poemata Juvenilia*
Italy	Literature	ALAMANNI, Ludovico. *Girone il Cortese*
		FIRENZUOLA, Agnolo. *Ragionamenti*
	Painting	TINTORETTO; Jacopo Robusti. *Miracle of St. Mark* (Venice)
		TITIAN. *Portrait of Emperor Charles V* (Prado, Madrid)
	Universities	Messina fnd.
Spain	Theology	LOYOLA, Iñigo de (St. Ignatius). *Exercitia Spiritualia*

1549

BRITISH ISLES

England	Church	*The Booke of Common Praier Noted* (Music by John Merbecke)

CENTRAL EUROPE

Germany	History	HERBERSTEIN, Siegmund von. *Rerum Moscovitarum Commentarii*
	Literature	DEDEKIND, Friedrich. *Grobianus*
		SACHS, Hans. *Comedie vom reichen sterbenden Menschen*

LATIN EUROPE

France	Literature	DU BELLAY, Joachim. *Olive*
		JODELLE, Etienne. *Erreurs amoureuses*
	Philology	DU BELLAY, Joachim. *La Défense et Illustration de la Langue Française*
Italy	Architecture	LIGORIO, Pirro. Villa d'Este, Tivoli, bgn.
	Medicine	First Anatomical Theatre est., Padua

1550

BRITISH ISLES

England	Literature	Ed. Prin. *The Vision of Piers Plowman* (Crowley, London)
	Theology	CRANMER, Thomas. *Defence of the true and catholic Doctrine of the Sacrament of the Body and Blood of Christ* (Wolfe, London)
		GARDINER, Stephen. *Explication and Assertion of the true catholic Faith*

NORTHERN EUROPE

Denmark	Theology	Christian III's Bible (ed. Christjern Pedersen)

CENTRAL EUROPE

Germany   Mathematics   RIESE, Adam. *Rechnung nach der Lenge auf der Linichen und Feder*

Palaeontology   HERBERSTEIN, Siegmund von. *De Natura Fossilium*

Theology   OSIANDER, Andreas. *De Justificatione*

LATIN EUROPE

France   Literature   RONSARD, Pierre de. *Odes*

Italy   Academies   Accademia degli Innominati, Parma, fnd.

Architecture   BAROZZI, Giacomo, called il Vignola. "Villa di Papa Giulio," Rome, bgn.

History of Art   VASARI, Giorgio. *Le Vite de' più eccellenti Pittori*

Literature   STRAPAROLA, Giovan-Francesco. *Le tredici piacevoli Notti* bgn. (compl. 1553)

Painting   BRONZINO; Angelo Allori. *Portrait of Lucrezia Panciatichi* (Uffizi)

TITIAN. *Portrait of King Philip II of Spain in armour* (Prado, Madrid)

Philosophy   CARDANO, Girolamo. *De Subtilitate*

Spain   Architecture   Casa de la Infanta, Zaragoza, compl.

SLAVONIC EUROPE

Poland   Architecture   DE QUADRO, Giovanni Battista. Poznan Town Hall

History   BIELSKI, Marcin. *Kronika Swiata* (The Sacred Chronicle)

1551

BRITISH ISLES

England   Mathematics   RECORDE, Robert. *The Pathway to Knowledge* (Wolfe, London)

Philosophy   WILSON, Thomas. *The Arte of Logike*

CENTRAL EUROPE

Austria   Schools   Jesuit College, Vienna, fnd.

Germany   Literature   SACHS, Hans. *Der boes Rauch—Das heiss Eisen*

Theology   OSIANDER, Andreas. *De Unico Mediatore Jesu Christo*

Switzerland   Theology   Geneva English Bible

Zoology   GESNER, Konrad. *Historia Animalium* bgn. (compl. 1587)

LATIN EUROPE

France   Sculpture   GOUJON, Jean. *Diane chasseresse* (Louvre; date uncertain)

Italy   Aesthetics   Ed. Prin. Leonardo da Vinci's *Trattato della Pittura*

        Literature   GRAZZINI, Antonio Francesco. *La Gelosia*

ROMAN CATHOLIC CHURCH

Collegium Romanum est.

SLAVONIC EUROPE

Poland   Politics   FRYCZ-MODRZEWSKI. *De Re Publica emendanda*

1552

BRITISH ISLES

England   Schools   Shrewsbury School fnd.

        Zoology   WOTTON, Edward. *De Differentiis Animalium*

CENTRAL EUROPE

Germany   Theology   MELANCHTHON, Philipp. *Examen Ordinandorum*

LATIN EUROPE

France   Architecture   DELORME, Philibert. Anet Château bgn. (compl. 1559)

        Literature   JODELLE, Etienne. *Cléopâtre captive*

                      JODELLE, Etienne. *La Rencontre*

                      RONSARD, Pierre de. *Les Amours*

        Theology   CALVIN, Jean. *De aeterna Dei Praedestinatione*

Italy   Architecture   ALESSI, Galeazzo. S. Maria in Carignano, Genoa, bgn. (compl. 1603)

        Literature   FIRENZUOLA, Agnolo. Prose Works

        Medicine   EUSTACHIO, Bartolommeo. *Tabulae Anatomicae*

        Painting   BRONZINO; Angelo Allori. *Christ in Limbo* (S. Croce, Florence)

Portugal   Literature   BARROS, João de. *Asia*, Pt. I

Spain   History   CASAS, Bartolomé de las. *Brevissima Relación de la Destruyción de las Indias*

                      LÓPEZ DE GÓMARA, Francisco. *Historia general de las Indias*

ROMAN CATHOLIC CHURCH

Collegium Germanicum, Rome, est.

1553

BRITISH ISLES

England	Church	King Edward VI's Catechism
	Literature	UDALL, Nicholas. *Ralph Roister Doister*
	Philosophy	WILSON, Thomas. *The Arte of Rhetorique* (Grafton, London)

CENTRAL EUROPE

Germany	Literature	SACHS, Hans. *Tristrant und Isolde*

LATIN EUROPE

Spain	History	CIEZA DE LEÓN, Pedro. *Primera Parte de la Crónica del Perú*
	Jurisprudence	SOTO, Domingo de. *De Justicia et Jure*
	Theology	SERVET, Miguel. *Christianismi Restitutio*
	Universities	Lima (Peru) fnd.

1554

BRITISH ISLES

Scotland	Politics	BUCHANAN, George. *Jephthes*

THE LOW COUNTRIES

Flanders	Painting	BRUEGHEL, Pieter, the Elder. *Fall of Icarus* (compl. 1555; Brussels)

NORTHERN EUROPE

Sweden	History	MAGNUS, Johannes. *De omnibus Gothorum Suecorumque Regibus . . .*

LATIN EUROPE

France	Architecture	Arras Belfry compl. (bgn. 1463)
	Medicine	FERNEL, Jean. *Universa Medicina*
	Philology	Ed. Prin. Anacreon (Estienne, Paris)
	Theology	CALVIN, Jean. *Defensio orthodoxae Fidei*
Italy	Literature	BANDELLO, Matteo. *Novelle* bgn. (compl. 1573)
	Painting	TITIAN. *Danae* (Prado, Madrid)
		TITIAN. *Venus and Adonis* (New York ?)
	Sculpture	CELLINI, Benvenuto. *Perseus* (Florence)
Portugal	Colonization	São Paolo (Brazil) fnd.
Spain	Literature	*La Vida de Lazarillo de Tormes*
	Theology	GRANADA, Luis de. *Libro de la Oración y Meditación*

[77]

SLAVONIC EUROPE

Russia   Architecture   St. Basil Cathedral (Vassily Blazhennoy), Moscow, bgn. (compl. 1560)

1555

BRITISH ISLES

England   Architecture   Gray's Inn Hall, London, bgn. (compl. 1560)
     Church   *De Heretico Comburendo*; re-enactment of Statute. Burning of Latimer
     Discoveries   Novaya Zemlya by Bourrough
     English Moscovy Company fnd.
     Universities   St. John's College, Oxford, fnd.
     Trinity College, Oxford, fnd.

THE LOW COUNTRIES

Flanders   Printing   PLANTIN, Christophe. Est. of press, Antwerp. First " Plantin ": *La Institutione di una Fanciulla nata nobilmente*

NORTHERN EUROPE

Sweden   History   MAGNUS, Olaus. *Historia Gentium Septentrionalium*

CENTRAL EUROPE

Germany   Literature   WICKRAM, Joerg. *Rollwagenbuechlein*
     Painting   CRANACH, Lucas, the Elder, and Lucas, the Younger. Altarpiece at Weimar
     Theology   CANISIUS, Petrus. *Summa Doctrinae Christianae*

LATIN EUROPE

France   Literature   LABÉ, Louise. *Œuvres*
     PELETIER, Jacques. *L'Amour des Amours*
     Occultism   NOSTRADAMUS, Michel de. *Centuries*
     Philosophy   RAMUS, Petrus. *Dialectique*
     Zoology   BELON, Pierre. *L'Histoire et la Nature des Oyseaux*
Italy   Architecture   BAROZZI, Giacomo, called il Vignola. Palazzo Caprarola, Rome, bgn. (compl. 1559)

1556

BRITISH ISLES

England   Church   Burning of Cranmer

CENTRAL EUROPE

Germany	Metallurgy	AGRICOLA; Georg Landmann. *De Re Metallica*
	Schools	Jesuit College, Ingolstadt, fnd.

LATIN EUROPE

Italy	Architecture	PALLADIO, Andrea. S. Giorgio Maggiore, Venice, bgn. (compl. 1610 by Vincenzo Scamozzi)
	Mathematics	FONTANA, Niccolò, called Tartaglia. *Trattato di Numeri e Misure*
	Philosophy	CARDANO, Girolamo. *De Varietate Rerum*

SLAVONIC EUROPE

Poland	Printing	First Polish Bible pr. in Cracow

1557

BRITISH ISLES

England	Literature	SURREY, Henry Howard, Earl of. Translation of Books II and IV of the Aeneid (first English blank verse) Tottel's Miscellany
	Mathematics	RECORDE, Robert. *The Whetstone of Witte* (Kyngston, London)

CENTRAL EUROPE

Germany	Literature	SACHS, Hans. *Das Narrenschneiden* WICKRAM, Joerg. *Der Goldfaden*

ROMAN CATHOLIC CHURCH

First Index Librorum Prohibitorum

1558

CENTRAL EUROPE

Germany	Literature	SACHS, Hans. *Collected Poems*, Pts. I-III (Pt. IV, 1578; Pt. V, 1579)
	Universities	Jena fnd.

LATIN EUROPE

France	Literature	DU BELLAY, Joachim. *Les Regrets*
Italy	Physics	PORTA, Giovanni Battista della. *Magia Naturalis*

ROMAN CATHOLIC CHURCH

Congregation of the Oratorians, Italy, fnd.

1559

BRITISH ISLES

England	Literature	SACKVILLE, Richard, and others. *Myrroure for Magistrates*

CENTRAL EUROPE

Germany	Architecture	Ottheinrichsbau, Heidelberg, compl.
	History	*Historia Ecclesiae Christi* bgn. (compl. 1574; the " Magdeburg Centuries ")
	Schools	Jesuit College, Munich, fnd.
Switzerland	Academies	Academy of Geneva fnd.

LATIN EUROPE

France	Church	First Synod of the French Protestant Church
	Literature	AMYOT, Jacques. *Daphnis et Chloé*
		AMYOT, Jacques. *Les Vies des hommes illustres grecs et romains* bgn. (compl. 1574)
		MARGUERITE, Queen of Navarre. *Heptaméron*
	Theology	*Confessio Gallicana*
Italy	Aesthetics	BAROZZI, Giacomo, called il Vignola. *Regola delle cinque Ordini d'Architettura* (compl. 1565)
	Painting	TITIAN. *Entombment* (Prado, Madrid)
Spain	Literature	MONTEMAYOR, Jorge de. *Los siete Libros de la Diana*

1560

BRITISH ISLES

England	Schools	Westminster School fnd.
Scotland	Theology	KNOX, John. *Treatise on Predestination*
		Church of Scotland established

LATIN EUROPE

France	Literature	RONSARD, Pierre de. *Oeuvres*
Italy	Academies	Academia Secretorum Naturae, Naples, fnd.
	Museums	Uffizi Gallery, Florence, fnd.
	Painting	TINTORETTO; Jacopo Robusti. *Glorification of St. Roch* (Venice)

1561

BRITISH ISLES

England	Literature	NORTON, Thomas, and SACKVILLE, Thomas. *Tragedy of Gorboduc*
	Schools	Merchant Taylors' School, London, fnd.

THE LOW COUNTRIES

Flanders   Architecture   Antwerp City Hall bgn. (compl. 1565)
               Church   *Confessio Belgica*

CENTRAL EUROPE

Germany   Astronomy   Observatory of Cassel est.

LATIN EUROPE

France   Literature   GRÉVIN, Jacques. *César*
Italy   History   GUICCIARDINI, Francesco. *Storia d'Italia* (posth. -1564)
        Medicine   FALLOPPIO, Gabriele. *Observationes Anatomicae*
        Painting   TINTORETTO; Jacopo Robusti. *The Marriage in Cana* (S. Maria della Salute, Venice)
        Poetics   SCALIGER, Julius Caesar. *Poetices Libri septem*

1562

BRITISH ISLES

England   Architecture   Hall of the Middle Temple, London, bgn. (compl. 1572).

THE LOW COUNTRIES

Flanders   Painting   BRUEGHEL, Pieter, The Elder. *Dulle Griet* (Antwerp)

CENTRAL EUROPE

Germany   Church   The " Heidelberg Catechism "

LATIN EUROPE

France   Painting   CLOUET, François. *Portrait of Pierre Cutte* (Louvre)
        Universities   Douai (later Lille) fnd.
Italy   Architecture   PALLADIO, Andrea. Façade of S. Francesco della Vigna, Venice, bgn.
        Painting   PAOLO VERONESE; Paolo Cagliari. *The Marriage in Cana* (Louvre)
Spain   Biography   TERESA DE JESÚS, Teresa Sánchez de Cepeda Davila y Ahumada. *Libro de su Vida* bgn. (compl. 1566)
        History   ZURITA, Gerónimo de. *Los Anales de la Corona de Aragón* bgn. (compl. 1579)

[81]

1563

BRITISH ISLES

England   Biography   FOXE, John. *Book of Martyrs* (Day, London)

LATIN EUROPE

Italy   Architecture   MICHELANGELO. S. Maria degli Angeli, Rome, planned

Spain   Architecture   DE TOLEDO, Juan. El Escorial planned

1564

CENTRAL EUROPE

Germany   Universities   Braunsberg fnd.

LATIN EUROPE

France   Architecture   DELORME, Philibert. The Tuileries (Central Pavilion), Paris, bgn.

Italy   Architecture   LUGARO, Rocco, and ALESSI, Galeazzo. Palazzo Doria (now Municipio), Genoa, bgn.

                                     MICHELANGELO, plan by. Palazzo dei Conservatori, Rome, bgn. (compl. 1568)

      Painting   TINTORETTO; Jacopo Robusti. *Portrait of Jacopo Soranzo* (Venice)

Spain   Theology   TERESA DE JESÚS. *Camino de Perfección* bgn. (compl. 1567)

ROMAN CATHOLIC CHURCH

Professio Fidei Tridentinae

SLAVONIC EUROPE

Czechoslovakia   Theology   BLAHOSLAV, Jan. Czech New Testament (Bible of Kralice)

Russia   Printing   First book pr. in Russia (*Apostol*, pr. by Ivan Feodorov and Peter Timofeiev, Moscow)

1565

BRITISH ISLES

England   Architecture   Gate of Honour, Caius College, Cambridge, bgn. (compl. 1574)

      History   STOW, John. *Summarie of Englyshe Chronicles* (Marsh, London)

[82]

THE LOW COUNTRIES

Flanders	Painting	BRUEGHEL, Pieter, the Elder. *Hunters in the Snow* (Vienna)
		BRUEGHEL, Pieter, the Elder. *Return of the Herds* (Vienna)
Holland	Architecture	The Hague City Hall

CENTRAL EUROPE

| Germany | Literature | *Spiel von Frau Jutten* |

LATIN EUROPE

France	Poetics	RONSARD, Pierre de. *Abrégé de l'Art Poétique Français*
	Theology	BEZA; Théodore de Bèze. *Novum Testamentum*
Italy	Literature	CINTHIO, Giovanni Battista Giraldi. *Hecatommithi*
	Painting	TINTORETTO; Jacopo Robusti. *Crucifixion* (Venice)
	Philosophy	TELESIO, Bernardino. *De Rerum Natura juxta propria Principia*
Spain	Theatre	Confradia de la Sagrada Pasión fnd.

1566

BRITISH ISLES

England	Literature	GASCOIGNE, George. *The Supposes*
		GASCOIGNE, George. *Jocasta*
		PAINTER, William. *The Palace of Pleasure* bgn. (compl. 1567; Denham, London)
	Poetics	PUTTENHAM, George. *The Arte of English Poesie*

CENTRAL EUROPE

| Switzerland | Theology | *Confessio Helvetica Posterior* |

LATIN EUROPE

France	History	ESTIENNE, Henri. *Apologie pour Hérodote*
Italy	Societies	Congregazione dei Musici di Roma fnd. (Academy since 1839)
	Painting	VERONESE; Paolo Cagliari. *The Family of Darius before Alexander* (Nat. Gal. Lond.)
Spain	Theology	GRANADA, Luis de. *Guía de Pecadores* bgn. (compl. 1569)

ROMAN CATHOLIC CHURCH

Catechismus Romanus

1567

BRITISH ISLES

England	Schools	Rugby School fnd. by Lawrence Sheriff

THE LOW COUNTRIES

Flanders	Painting	BRUEGHEL, Pieter, the Elder. *Land of Cockayne* (Munich)

LATIN EUROPE

France	Architecture	DELORME, Philibert. *Le premier Tome de l'Architecture*
Italy	Music	PALESTRINA, Giovanni Pierluigi da. *Missa Papae Marcelli* (comp. 1562-63)
Spain	Discoveries	Solomon Islands by Alvaro Mendana

1568

BRITISH ISLES

England	Theology	*The Holie Bible* (The Bishops' Bible; Jugge, London)

THE LOW COUNTRIES

Flanders	Painting	BRUEGHEL, Pieter, the Elder. *The Blind Men* (Naples)
Holland	Literature	MARNIX VAN SANT ALDEGONDE, Philip van. *De Biënkorf der H. Roomsche Kercke.*

LATIN EUROPE

Italy	Architecture	Il Gesú, Rome, bgn. Plan by Vignola (compl. 1632)

ROMAN CATHOLIC CHURCH

Breviarium Romanum

1569

THE LOW COUNTRIES

Holland	Geography	MERCATOR; Gerard Kremer. *Nova et aucta Orbis Terrae Descriptio*

LATIN EUROPE

France	Painting	CLOUET, François. *Portrait of King Charles IX* (? Vienna)
	Schools	English School, Douai, est. Jesuit College, Lyons, est.

Spain   Literature   ERCILLA, Alonso de. *La Araucana*

Theology   ARIAS MONTANO, Benito. Polyglot Bible pr. by Christophe Plantin, Antwerp (compl. 1572)

1570

BRITISH ISLES

England   Education   ASCHAM, Roger. *The Scholemaster* (Daye, London)

THE LOW COUNTRIES

Holland   Geography   ORTELIUS, Abraham. *Theatrum Orbis Terrarum*

LATIN EUROPE

Italy   Architecture   PALLADIO, Andrea. *Quattro Libri dell'Architettura*

Mathematics   CARDANUS, Girolamo. *Opus novum de Proportionibus Numerorum*

Theatre   A "Pagliaccio" in the troupe of Juan Ganasso, first recorded mention

1571

BRITISH ISLES

England   Schools   Harrow School fnd. by John Lyon

Universities   Jesus College, Oxford, fnd.

LATIN EUROPE

France   Church   Synod of La Rochelle

Painting   CLOUET, François. *Portrait of Elisabeth of Austria* (Louvre)

Theatre   First Italian Comedians come to Paris

Italy   Libraries   Bibliotheca Mediceo-Laurenziana, Florence, opened

Spain   History   HURTADO DE MENDOZA, Diego. *Guerra de Granada* bgn. (compl. 1575)

1572

BRITISH ISLES

England   Societies   Society of Antiquaries fnd.

CENTRAL EUROPE

Germany   Architecture   Town Hall, Rothenburg ob der Tauber, bgn. (compl. 1590)

LATIN EUROPE

France	Literature	RONSARD, Pierre de. *La Franciade*
	Philology	ESTIENNE, Henri. *Thesaurus Graecae Linguae* (-1573)
		Ed. Prin. Plutarch's Opera Omnia (Estienne, Paris)
	Universities	Nancy—Pont-à-Mousson fnd.
Italy	Painting	VERONESE, Paolo. *The Feast in the House of Levi* (Venice)
Portugal	Literature	CAMÕES, Luis de. *Os Lusiadas*

1573

BRITISH ISLES

England	Literature	GASCOIGNE, George. *A Hundreth sundrie Floures* ... (Smith, London)

THE LOW COUNTRIES

Flanders	Music	ORLANDO DI LASSO; Roland Delattre. *Patrocinium Musices* bgn. (compl. 1576)

NORTHERN EUROPE

Denmark	Astronomy	BRAHE, Tycho. *De nova Stella* ...

CENTRAL EUROPE

Germany	Literature	FISCHART, Johann. *Floeh Haz*

LATIN EUROPE

France	Literature	DESPORTES, Philippe. *Premières Œuvres*
Italy	Literature	TASSO, Torquato. *Aminta*
	Painting	TITIAN. *Pietà* (Venice)
Spain	Theology	TERESA DE JESÚS. *Libro de las Fundaciones*

1574

BRITISH ISLES

England	Mathematics	DEE, John. *Euclides Anglice*

CENTRAL EUROPE

Switzerland	Universities	Bern fnd.

LATIN EUROPE

Italy	Architecture	FONTANA, Domenico. Palazzo del Quirinale, Rome, bgn.
		VASARI, Giorgio. Palazzo degli Uffizi, Florence, compl. (bgn. 1560)
	Painting	TITIAN. *Battle of Lepanto* bgn. (compl. 1575; Prado, Madrid)

1575

BRITISH ISLES

England Literature GASCOIGNE, George. *The Posies*
GASCOIGNE, George. *Complaint of Philomene* (bgn. 1562)
GASCOIGNE, George. *The Glasse of Government*
Music BYRD, William, and TALLIS, Thomas. *Cantiones Sacrae* (Vautroller, London)

THE LOW COUNTRIES

Holland Philology CANTER, Willem. *Syntagma de Ratione emendendi Graecos Auctores*
LIPSIUS, Justus. Ed. *Tacitus*
Universities Leyden fnd.

CENTRAL EUROPE

Germany Literature FISCHART, Johann. *Gargantua (Affentheurliche Naupengeheurliche˙ Geschichtsklitterung)*
Universities Altdorf fnd.

LATIN EUROPE

France Biography BEZA; Théodore de Bèze. *Vita Calvini*
Theology *Bibliotheca Veterum Patrum* bgn.
Italy Architecture SCAMOZZI, Vincenzo. S. Giorgio Maggiore, Venice, compl.
Mathematics MAUROLYCUS, Franciscus. *Arithmeticorum Libri II*
Spain Architecture Palace and Gardens, Aranjuéz, bgn.
History MORALES, Ambrosio de. *Las Antigüedades de las Ciudades de España* bgn. (compl. 1577)
Philosophy HUARTE, Juan. *Examen de Ingenios para las Ciencias*

SLAVONIC EUROPE

Czechoslovakia Church *Confessio Bohemica*

1576

BRITISH ISLES

England Architecture SMITHSON, Robert. Hardwick Hall, Derbyshire, bgn. (compl. 1597)
Discoveries Frobisher Bay by Martin Frobisher
Literature GASCOIGNE, George. *The Steele Glas* (Smith, London)
The Paradise of Dainty Devices

[87]

England Theatre First Play House in London opened (The Theatre, Finsbury Field, Shoreditch, erected by James Burbage, and first Blackfriars Theatre, erected by Richard Farrant)

NORTHERN EUROPE

Denmark Astronomy Tycho Brahe's Observatory, Uraniborg, est.

CENTRAL EUROPE

Germany Literature FISCHART, Johann. *Das Glueckhafft Schiff von Zuerich*
  Universities Helmstedt fnd.

LATIN EUROPE

France Politics BODIN, Jean. *Les Six Livres de la République*
Italy Architecture PALLADIO, Andrea. Il Redentore, Venice, bgn.
Spain Music VICTORIA, Tomás Luis de. *Liber Primus* (Psalms, Masses, Magnificat)

SLAVONIC EUROPE

Poland Universities Warsaw fnd.

1577

BRITISH ISLES

England History HOLINSHED, Ralph. *Chronicles of England, Scotland, and Ireland* (Harrison, London)
  Navigation DEE, John. *The Art of Navigation* (Daye, London)

NORTHERN EUROPE

Denmark Architecture Kronborg Castle bgn. (compl. 1581)

CENTRAL EUROPE

Germany Church *Formula Concordiae*

LATIN EUROPE

France Jurisprudence CUJAS, Jacques. *Animadversiones et Observationes*
Italy Painting TINTORETTO; Jacopo Robusti. Frescoes in the Scuola San Rocco, Venice, bgn. (compl. 1581)

Spain	Painting	EL GRECO; Domenico Theotocopuli. *Assumption of the Virgin* (Chicago) EL GRECO; Domenico Theotocopuli. Altarpiece of San Domingo el Antiguo (Madrid)
	Theology	TERESA DE JESÚS. *Las Moradas o Castillo interior*

1578

BRITISH ISLES

England	Literature	LYLY, John. *Euphues. The Anatomy of Wit* (Cawood, London)
Scotland	Politics	BUCHANAN, George. *Baptistes*

THE LOW COUNTRIES

Holland	Geography	MERCATOR; Gerard Kremer. *Tabulae Geographicae*

CENTRAL EUROPE

Germany	Literature	FISCHART, Johann. *Philosophisch Ehzuchtbuechlein* FRISCHLIN, Nicodemus. *Susanna*

LATIN EUROPE

France	Politics	LA BOËTIE, Etienne de. *Le Contr'un, ou Discours de la Servitude volontaire* (posth.)
	Pottery	Fayence Factory, Nevers, fnd.
Spain	Theology	JUAN DE AVILA, San. *Epistolario espiritual para todos Estados*

SLAVONIC EUROPE

Poland	Universities	Vilna fnd.

1579

BRITISH ISLES

England	Literature	SPENSER, Edmund. *The Shepheardes Calender*
Scotland	Politics	BUCHANAN, George. *De Jure Regni apud Scotos*

CENTRAL EUROPE

Germany	Literature	FRISCHLIN, Nicodemus. *Hildegardis Magna*

LATIN EUROPE

France	Literature	DU BARTAS, Guillaume de Saluste. *Commentaires sur la sepmaine de la création du monde*

France	Mathematics	VIETA, François Viète. *Canon Mathematicus*
	Politics	DU PLESSIS-MORNAY, Philippe. *Vindiciae contra Tyrannos* (authorship uncertain)
Italy	Literature	TASSO, Torquato. *Scelta di Rime*
	Painting	BAROCCI, Federigo. *Madonna del Popolo* (Pitti)
Spain	Painting	EL GRECO; Domenico Theotocopuli. *El Espolio* (Toledo).
		EL GRECO; Domenico Theotocopuli. *Crucifixion* (Louvre)

1580

BRITISH ISLES

England	Discoveries	The globe circumnavigated by Francis Drake (bgn. 1577)
	Literature	LYLY, John. *Euphues and his England*
Scotland	Libraries	Edinburgh University Library fnd.

CENTRAL EUROPE

| Germany | Politics | FISCHART, Johann. *Das Jesuiterhuetlein* |

LATIN EUROPE

France	Literature	MONTAIGNE, Michel de. *Essais* (Millanges, Bordeaux)
	Philology	TURNÈBE, Adrien. *Adversaria*
	Theology	BODIN, Jean. *Démonomanie*
Italy	Architecture	Teatro Olimpico, Vicenza (plan by Andrea Palladio; built by Vincenzo Scamozzi, compl. 1584)
Spain	History	DÍAZ DEL CASTILLO, Bernal. *Historia verdadera de la Conquista de la Nueva España*
	Painting	EL GRECO; Domenico Theotocopuli. *Martyrdom of St. Maurice* (Prado, Madrid)
		EL GRECO; Domenico Theotocopuli. *The Dream of King Philip II* (*circa*; Escorial)

SLAVONIC EUROPE

| Poland | Literature | KOCHANOWSKI, Jan. *Treny* (Songs of Sorrow) |

1581

BRITISH ISLES

| England | Philology | SENECA. *His tenne Tragedies translated into Englysh* (Marsh, London) |

CENTRAL EUROPE

Germany   Literature   FRISCHLIN, Nicodemus. *Dido*

LATIN EUROPE

Italy   Literature   TASSO, Torquato. *La Gerusalemme Liberata*

    Theology   BELLARMIN, Roberto Francesco Romolo. *Disputationes de Controversiis Christianae Fidei adversus huius Temporis Haereticos* bgn. (compl. 1593)

SLAVONIC EUROPE

Czechoslovakia   Universities   Olmuetz (Olomouc) fnd.

Russia   Printing   First Slavonic Bible pr., Ostrovo (Volhynia

1582

BRITISH ISLES

Scotland   History   BUCHANAN, George. *Rerum Scoticarum Historia* (Arbuthnot, Edinburgh)

    Universities   Edinburgh fnd.

THE LOW COUNTRIES

Holland   Libraries   Utrecht Library (now University Library), fnd.

LATIN EUROPE

Italy   Academies   Accademia della Crusca fnd.

    Philosophy   BRUNO, Giordano. *Il Candelaio*

Spain   Literature   HERRERA, Fernando de. *Algunas Obras*

ROMAN CATHOLIC CHURCH

    BULL: *Inter Gravissimas* (Institution of the Gregorian Calendar)

1583

BRITISH ISLES

England   Literature   PEELE, George. *Arraignement of Paris* (first acting; pr. 1584)

THE LOW COUNTRIES

Flanders   Sculpture   GIAN DA BOLOGNA; Jean de Boulogne. *Rape of the Sabines* (Florence)

| Holland | Chronology | SCALIGER, Joseph Justus. *De Emendatione Temporum* |
| | Printing | Louis Elzevir's Press est. at Leyden (first "Elzevir": *Drusii Ebraicarum Quaestionum ac Responsionum Libri duo*) |

CENTRAL EUROPE

| Germany | Architecture | St. Michael's Church, Munich, bgn. (compl. 1597) |

LATIN EUROPE

France	Jurisprudence	GODEFROY, Denis. *Corpus Juris Civilis* (ed.)
Italy	Botany	CESALPINO, Andrea. *De Plantis Libri XVI*
	Literature	TASSO, Torquato. *Il Padre di Famiglia*
	Physics	GALILEI, Galileo. Discovery of the Principle of the Pendulum
Spain	Literature	LEÓN, Luis de. *La perfecta Casada*
	Theology	LEÓN, Luis de. *Los Nombres de Cristo* bgn. (compl. 1595)

1584

BRITISH ISLES

England	Literature	GREENE, Robert. *The Mirror of Modesty*
	Universities	Emmanuel College, Cambridge, fnd.
Scotland	History	KNOX, John. *History of the Reformation of Religion within the Realme of Scotland*
	Occultism	SCOT, Reginald. *The Discoveries of Witchcraft*

THE LOW COUNTRIES

| Holland | Universities | Franeker fnd. |

CENTRAL EUROPE

| Germany | Literature | FRISCHLIN, Nicodemus. *Julius Redivivus* |

LATIN EUROPE

France	Education	SAINTE-MARTHE, Scévole de. *Paedotrophia*
Italy	Architecture	SCAMOZZI, Vincenzo. Procuratie Nuove, Venice, bgn.
	Philosophy	BRUNO, Giordano. *De la Causa, Principio ed Uno*
		BRUNO, Giordano. *La Cena de le Ceneri*
		BRUNO, Giordano. *Spaccio de la Bestia trionfante*
	Politics	GENTILIS, Albericus. *De Legationibus*
Spain	Architecture	DE HERRERA, Juan. El Escorial compl. (*see* 1563)

1585

THE LOW COUNTRIES

Flanders   Mathematics   STEVIN, Simon. *Practique d'Arithmétique*
Holland   Navigation   WAGHENAER. *Spiegel der Zeevaart*

LATIN EUROPE

Italy   Academies   Academy of the Caracci, Bologna, fnd.
     Philosophy   BRUNO, Giordano. *Eroici Furori*
     Sculpture   DELLA PORTA, Giacomo. Fontana delle Tartarughe, Rome, constr.
Spain   Literature   CERVANTES SAAVEDRA, Miguel de. *Galatea*
     Music   VICTORIA, Tomás Luis de. *Officium Hebdomadae Sanctae*

1586

BRITISH ISLES

England   History   CAMDEN, William. *Britannia* (Newbery, London)
     Literature   LYLY, John. *Endymion* (first acting; pr. 1591)

THE LOW COUNTRIES

Flanders   Mathematics   STEVIN, Simon. *La Disme*

CENTRAL EUROPE

Austria   Universities   Graz fnd.
Germany   Theatre   First performance of English Comedians in Germany (Dresden)

LATIN EUROPE

France   Politics   PASQUIER, Etienne. *Lettres*
Italy   Architecture   FONTANA, Domenico. Palazzo del Laterano, Rome, bgn.
Spain   Painting   EL GRECO; Domenico Theotocopuli. *Burial of the Count of Orgaz* (Toledo)

SLAVONIC EUROPE

Russia   Colonization   Voronezh fnd.

1587

BRITISH ISLES

England   Literature   MARLOWE, Christopher. *Tamburlaine the Great* (first acting; pr. 1590)

THE LOW COUNTRIES

Holland	Geography	ORTELIUS, Abraham. *Thesaurus Geographicus*

CENTRAL EUROPE

Germany	Literature	*Historia von D. Johann Fausten . . .*

LATIN EUROPE

France	Literature	MALHERBE, François. *Les Larmes de Saint Pierre*
Italy	Literature	TASSO, Torquato. *Il Re Torrismondo*

SLAVONIC EUROPE

Russia	Colonization	Tobolsk fnd.

1588

BRITISH ISLES

England	Discoveries	Davis Strait by John Davis
	Literature	KYD, Thomas. *The Spanish Tragedie* (first acting; pr. 1594)
		MARLOWE, Christopher. *The tragical history of Doctor Faustus* (first acting ; pr. 1604)
		ANON. *The Troublesome Reigne of King John* (first acting; pr. 1591)
	Music	BYRD, William. *Psalmes, Sonets and Songs of Sadnes and Pietie.*
Wales	Theology	First Welsh Bible (Bishop Morgan's Bible)

THE LOW COUNTRIES

Holland	Politics	*Geusen Lieden Boexken*

LATIN EUROPE

Italy	Architecture	DA PONTE, Antonio. Rialto Bridge, Venice, bgn. (compl. 1591)
	Jurisprudence	GENTILIS, Albericus. *De Jure Belli Commentatio Prima*
	Painting	BAROCCI, Federigo. *Madonna of the Rosary* (compl. 1591; Sinigaglia)
		CARACCI, Annibale. *Assumption of the Virgin* (Dresden)
	Philosophy	BRUNO, Giordano. *Acrotismus*
Spain	Theology	MALÓN DE CHAIDE, Pedro. *Libro de la Conversión de la Magdalena*

ROMAN CATHOLIC CHURCH

Annales Ecclesiastici issued (compl. 1856; first ed. Caesar Baronius)

1589

BRITISH ISLES

England	Literature	GREENE, Robert.. *Friar Bacon and Friar Bungay* (first acting; pr. 1594)
		MARLOWE, Christopher. *The Rich Jew of Malta* (first acting (?); pr. 1633)
		PEELE, George. *Tale of Troy*
	Music	BYRD, William. *Songs of sundrie Natures* ...
		BYRD, William. *Liber Primus Sacrarum Cantionum* (Pt. II: 1591)

CENTRAL EUROPE

Germany	Schools	Collegium Illustre, Tuebingen, fnd.

LATIN EUROPE

Italy	Literature	MARINO, Giovanni Battista. *Canzone de' Baci*
	Music	PALESTRINA, Giovanni Pierluigi da. *Hymni totius Anni*

SLAVONIC EUROPE

Russia	Academies	Kiev Academy fnd.

1590

BRITISH ISLES

England	Literature	LODGE, Thomas. *Rosalynde*
		MARLOWE, Christopher. *Edward II* (first acting; pr. 1594)
		SIDNEY, Sir Philip. *The Countesse of Pembrokes Arcadia* (posth.; Ponsonbie, London)
		SPENSER, Edmund. *The Faerie Queene* (Ponsonbie, London)

THE LOW COUNTRIES

Holland	Physics	Microscope invented by Zacharias Jansen

LATIN EUROPE

France	Architecture	Amboise Palace
Italy	Literature	GUARINI, Giovanni-Battista. *Il Pastor Fido*
	Painting	TINTORETTO; Jacopo Robusti. *The Paradise* (Venice)
Spain	History	ACOSTA, José de. *Historia natural y moral de las Indias*
	Universities	Madrid fnd.

[95]

1591

BRITISH ISLES

England	Literature	GREENE, Robert. *Orlando Furioso*
		PEELE, George. *The Battell of Alcazar* (first acting (?); pr. 1594)
		SHAKESPEARE. *The Comedy of Errors* (first acting ?)
		SIDNEY, Sir Philip. *Astrophel and Stella* (posth.)
Ireland	Universities	Trinity College, Dublin, fnd.

CENTRAL EUROPE

Germany	Music	HASSLER, Hans Leo von. *Cantiones Sacrae*

LATIN EUROPE

France	Mathematics	VIETA; François Viète. *In Artem analyticem Isagoge*
Italy	Architecture	OLIVIERI, Pietro Paolo, Carlo RAINALDI and MADERNA. S. Andrea della Valle, Rome, bgn. (compl. 1607)
	Philosophy	BRUNO, Giordano. *De Monade, Numero et Figura*
		BRUNO, Giordano. *De Triplici Minimo*
		CAMPANELLA, Tommaso. *Philosophia Sensibus demonstrata*

1592

BRITISH ISLES

England	Literature	GREENE, Robert. *The Scottish Historie of James IV* (first acting; pr. 1599)
		LODGE, Thomas. *Phillis*
		LYLY, John. *Galatea*
		NASH, Thomas. *Summer's Last Will and Testament* (first acting; pr. 1600)
		SHAKESPEARE. *Henry VI*, Pt. I (first acting?)
		Shakespeare-Apocrypha. *Arden of Feversham*

LATIN EUROPE

France	History	MONLUC, Blaise de. *Commentaires*
Spain	History	MARIANA, Juan de. *Historiae de Rebus Hispaniae*

1593

BRITISH ISLES

England   Architecture   Neville's Court, Trinity College, Cambridge, bgn.

Literature   LYLY, John. *The Woman in the Moon* (first acting; pr. 1597)
MARLOWE, Christopher. *The Massacre of Paris*
SHAKESPEARE. *Venus and Adonis* (Field, London)

LATIN EUROPE

Italy   Literature   TASSO, Torquato. *La Gerusalemme Conquistata*

SLAVONIC EUROPE

Russia   Colonization   Beresov fnd.

1594

BRITISH ISLES

England   Literature   DRAYTON, Michael. *Ideas Mirrour. Amours*
LODGE, Thomas. *Marius and Sylla*
LYLY, John. *Mother Bombie* (first pr.; acted earlier)
MARLOWE, Christopher. *Dido, Queen of Carthage* (compl. by Nash)
NASH, Thomas. *The Unfortunate Traveller*
SHAKESPEARE. *Lucrece* (Field, London)
SHAKESPEARE. *Henry VI.* Pt. II (first pr; acted earlier as *The Contention of York and Lancaster*)
SHAKESPEARE. *Titus Andronicus*

Music   MORLEY, Thomas. *Madrigalls to Foure Voyces* . . .

Politics   HOOKER, Richard. *Laws of Ecclesiastical Polity*, Pt. I (Windet, London)

THE LOW COUNTRIES

Holland   Geography   MERCATOR; Gerard Kremer. *Atlas*

LATIN EUROPE

France   Church   Jesuits expelled from France (re-admitted 1603; re-expelled 1764)

Politics   *Satyre Ménippée*

Italy   Music   PERI, Jacopo, and RINUCCINI, Ottavio. *Dafne* (first opera. First public performance, 1597)

1595

BRITISH ISLES

England Literature PEELE, George. *The Old Wives Tale* (first pr.; acted earlier)
SHAKESPEARE. *Henry VI*, Pt. III (first pr.; acted earlier as *The Contention of York and Lancaster*)
Shakespeare-Apocrypha. *Locrine*
SPENSER, Edmund. *Colin Clouts come Home againe* (Ponsonbie, London)
SPENSER, Edmund. *Amoretti. Epithalamium* (Ponsonbie, London)

CENTRAL EUROPE

Germany Chemistry LIBAVIUS, Andreas. *Alchymia Collecta*
Literature ROLLENHAGEN, Georg. *Froschmeuseler*

LATIN EUROPE

Spain Literature PÉREZ DE HITA, Ginés. *Las Guerras civiles de Granada* bgn. (compl. 1604)
Theology RIBADENEYRA, Pedro de. *Tratado de la Religión y Virtudes que deve tener el Príncipe Cristiano*

1596

BRITISH ISLES

England History RALEIGH, Walter. *The Discoverie . . . of Guiana* (Robinson, London)
Schools Gresham College, London, fnd.
Universities Sidney Sussex College, Cambridge, fnd.

THE LOW COUNTRIES

Holland Discoveries Spitzbergen by Barentz

CENTRAL EUROPE

Germany Astronomy KEPLER, Johannes. *Mysterium Cosmographicum*
Mathematics RHAETICUS, Georg Joachim. *Opus Palatinum*

LATIN EUROPE

Italy Painting CARACCI, Annibale. Frescoes in the Galleria Farnese, Rome, bgn. (compl. 1607)
Spain Architecture Collegiate Church, Manresa (bgn. 1328)
Theology VALERA, Cipriano de. *El Testamento Nuevo* (transl. by Cassiodoro de Reina; rev. by Cipriano de Valera)

1597

BRITISH ISLES

England   Literature   SHAKESPEARE. *Richard II* (first pr.; Wise, London; acted earlier)

SHAKESPEARE. *Richard III* (first pr.; Wise, London; acted earlier)

SHAKESPEARE. *Romeo and Juliet* (first pr.; acted earlier)

Music   DOWLAND, John. *The first Booke of Songes or Ayres*

MORLEY, Thomas. *A Plaine and Easie Introduction to Practicall Musick*

Philosophy   BACON, Francis. *Essaies* (Windet for Hooper, London)

CENTRAL EUROPE

Germany   Literature   *Das Lalenbuch*

LATIN EUROPE

Italy   Medicine   TAGLIACOZZI, Gasparo. *De Curtorum Chirurgia per Insitionem*

Painting   CARAVAGGIO, Michelangelo da. Frescoes in S. Luigi dei Francesi, Rome, bgn. (compl. 1598)

Physics   GALILEI, Galileo. Thermometer invented

SLAVONIC EUROPE

Poland   Architecture   St. Peter's Cathedral, Cracow, bgn.

History   BIELSKI, Marcin. *Kronika Polska*

1598

BRITISH ISLES

England   History   HAKLUYT, Richard. *The Principal Navigations . . . of the English nation* (compl. ed.; Bishop, Newberie and Barker, London; compl. 1600)

Libraries   Bodleian Library, Oxford, fnd.

Literature   JONSON, Ben. *Every Man in his Humour* (first acting; pr. 1601)

SHAKESPEARE. *King Henry IV*. Pt. I (Wise, London)

SHAKESPEARE. *Love's Labour's Lost* (first pr.; acted earlier)

Shakespeare-Apocrypha. *Mucedorus* (first pr.)

Music   WILBYE, John. *First Set of English Madrigals*

Topography   STOW, John. *Survey of London* (Wolfe, London)

THE LOW COUNTRIES

Holland Geography ORTELIUS, Abraham. *Veteris Geographiae Tabulae*

CENTRAL EUROPE

Germany Literature *Die Schiltbuerger*

LATIN EUROPE

France Church Edict of Nantes
 Literature CHARRON, Pierre. *Les trois Vérités*
Italy Jurisprudence GENTILIS, Albericus. *De Jure Belli Libri tres*
 Painting CARAVAGGIO, Michelangelo da. *The Entombment* (Vatican)
Spain Literature VEGA CARPIO, Lope Félix de. *Arcadia*
 VEGA CARPIO, Lope Félix de. *La Dragontea*
 Politics PÉREZ, Antonio. *Relaciones*

1599

BRITISH ISLES

England Colonization Canada Company fnd.
 Literature PEELE, George. *The Love of King David . . .* (first pr.)
 SHAKESPEARE. *Julius Caesar* (first acting ?)
 The Passionate Pilgrim (attributed to Shakespeare; William Jaggard, London)
 Theatre Globe Theatre, Southwark, opened

LATIN EUROPE

Italy Zoology ALDROVANDI, Ulisse. *Ornithologia* bgn. (compl. 1603)
Spain Literature ALEMÁN, Mateo. *Guzmán de Alfarache*
 Politics MARIANA, Juan de. *De Rege et Regis Institutione*

1600

BRITISH ISLES

England Architecture HOLD, Thomas. Merton College Library, Oxford, bgn. (compl. 1624)
 Colonization East India Company fnd.
 Literature DEKKER, Thomas. *Comedy of Old Fortunatus*
 DEKKER, Thomas. *The Shoemaker's Holiday*
 SHAKESPEARE. *King Henry IV.* Pt. II (first pr.; acted earlier)

England	Literature	SHAKESPEARE. *King Henry V* (first pr.)
		SHAKESPEARE. *Midsummer Night's Dream* (first pr.; acted earlier)
		SHAKESPEARE. *Much Ado about Nothing* (first pr.; acted earlier)
		SHAKESPEARE. *The Merchant of Venice* (first pr.; acted earlier)
		Shakespeare-Apocrypha. *Sir John Oldcastle* (first pr.)
	Music	MORLEY, Thomas. *The First Book of Ayres*
	Physics	GILBERT, William. *De Magnete* ...

THE LOW COUNTRIES

| Holland | Universities | Harderwijk fnd. |

LATIN EUROPE

France	Economy	SERRES, Olivier de. *Théâtre de l'Agriculture et Ménage des Champs*
Italy	Architecture	FONTANA, Domenico. Royàl Palace, Naples, bgn. (compl. 1641)
	Music	CACCINI, Giulio. *Il Rapimento di Cefalo*
		CAVALIERI, Emilio de'. *La Rappresentazione di Anima e di Corpo*
		PERI, Jacopo. *Euridice*
Spain	Painting	EL GRECO; Domenico Theotocopuli. *Portrait of the Grand Inqusitor* bgn. (compl. 1601; New York)
	Theology	JUAN DE LOS ANGELES. *Lucha espiritual y amorosa entre Dios y el Alma*

1601

BRITISH ISLES

England	Literature	JONSON, Ben. *Cynthia's Revels*
		LYLY, John. *Love's Metamorphosis*
Ireland	Libraries	Trinity College Library, Dublin, fnd.

THE LOW COUNTRIES

| Holland | Colonization | Dutch East India Company fnd. |

NORTHERN EUROPE

| Denmark | Architecture | Frederiksborg Palace bgn. (compl. 1625) |
| | Astronomy | BRAHE, Tycho. *Astronomiae instauratae Mechanica* |

CENTRAL EUROPE

| Germany | Music | HASSLER, Hans Leo von. *Lustgarten Neuer Teutscher Gesaenge* |

LATIN EUROPE

France	Literature	HARDY, Alexandre. *Les . . . Amours de Théagène et Chariclée*
	Philosophy	CHARRON, Pierre. *De la Sagesse*
Portugal	Discoveries	Australian Continent by Godinho de Eredia (first landing)
Spain	History	MARIANA, Juan de. *Historia general de España*

1602

BRITISH ISLES

England	Libraries	Oxford. Inauguration of the Bodleian
	Literature	DEKKER, Thomas. *Satiro-mastix*
		SHAKESPEARE. *Hamlet* (first acting ?; first Quarto, 1603; second Quarto, 1604)
		SHAKESPEARE. *The Merry Wives of Windsor* (first pr. ; acted earlier)
		Shakespeare-Apocrypha. *Thomas, Lord Cromwell* (first pr.)

NORTHERN EUROPE

Denmark	Astronomy	BRAHE, Tycho. *Astronomiae instauratae Progymnasmata*

LATIN EUROPE

France	Politics	PASQUIER, Etienne. *Le Catéchisme des Jésuites*
Italy	Literature	MARINO, Giovanni Battista. *Rime* (compl. 1614)
	Music	CACCINI, Giulio. *L'Euridice*
	Zoology	ALDROVANDI, Ulisse. *De Animalibus Insectis Libri VII*

1603

BRITISH ISLES

England	Literature	HEYWOOD, Thomas. *A Woman killed with Kindness*
		JONSON, Ben. *Sejanus* (first acting; pr. 1605)
		SHAKESPEARE. *Troilus and Cressida* (first acting; pr. 1609)
	Medicine	LODGE, Thomas. *Treatise of the Plague*
Scotland	Politics	BARCLAY, John. *Euphormionis Satyricon*

LATIN EUROPE

France	Discoveries	CHAMPLAIN, Samuel. *Des Sauvages, ou Voyages de Samuel Champlain*
	Literature	DESPORTES, Philippe. *Psaumes*

Spain	Painting	EL GRECO; Domenico Theotocopuli. Paintings in the Hospital de la Caridad, Illescas (compl. 1606)

1604

BRITISH ISLES

England	Church	Hampton Court Conference
	Literature	DEKKER, Thomas. *The Honest Whore* (first pr.; acted earlier)
		MARSTON, John. *The Malcontent* (first pr.; acted earlier)
		SHAKESPEARE. *Othello* (first acting; pr. 1622)
		SHAKESPEARE. *Measure for Measure* (first acting; pr. 1622)
	Societies	Incorporation of the Musicians' Society of London

THE LOW COUNTRIES

Flanders	Music	ORLANDO DI LASSO; Roland Delattre. *Magnum Opus Musicum*
	Painting	RUBENS, Peter Paul. *Baptism of Christ* (Antwerp)

CENTRAL EUROPE

Germany	Mathematics	KEPLER, Johann. *Paralipomena ad Vitellionem*

LATIN EUROPE

France	History	THUANUS; Jacques-Auguste de Thou. *Historiarum . . . libri cxxxviii* (compl. 1614)
Spain	History	SANDOVAL, Prudencio de. *Historia de la Vida y Hechos del Emperador Carlos V*
	Literature	VEGA CARPIO, Lope Félix de. *Rimas*
		VEGA CARPIO, Lope Félix de. *El Peregrino en su Patria*

SLAVONIC EUROPE

Russia	Colonization	Tomsk fnd.

1605

BRITISH ISLES

England	Literature	CHAPMAN, George, JONSON, Ben, and MARSTON, John. *Eastward-Hoe*
		JONSON, Ben. *Volpone* (first acting; pr. 1607)
		Shakespeare-Apocrypha. *The London Prodigal* (first pr.)

[103]

| England | Music | DOWLAND, John. *Lachrymae, or Seven Teares* |
| | Philosophy | BACON, Francis. *Of the proficience and advancement of Learning* |

CENTRAL EUROPE

| Germany | Botany | Botanical Garden, Giessen, fnd. |
| | Theology | ARND, Johann. *Das wahre Christentum* |

LATIN EUROPE

France	Technics	Canal de Briare bgn. (compl. 1642)
Italy	Architecture	MADERNA, Carlo. Façade, St. Peter's, Rome, bgn. (compl. 1612)
Spain	Literature	CERVANTES SAAVEDRA, Miguel de. *Don Quixote*, Pt. I
	Music	VICTORIA, Tomás Luis de. *Officium Defunctorum*
	Philosophy	SUÁREZ, Francisco. *Disputationes metaphysicae*

1606

BRITISH ISLES

| England | Literature | SHAKESPEARE. *King Lear* (first acting; pr. 1608) |

THE LOW COUNTRIES

Flanders	Painting	RUBENS, Peter Paul. *The Circumcision* (S. Ambrogio, Genoa)
		RUBENS, Peter Paul. Wall-Paintings in S. Maria in Vallicella, Rome
Holland	Discoveries	Australian coast by Willem Janszoon
	History	SCALIGER, Joseph Justus. *Thesaurus Temporum*

CENTRAL EUROPE

| Germany | Colonization | Mannheim fnd. |

LATIN EUROPE

| Spain | Discoveries | Torres Strait and New Hebrides, by Luis Vaz de Torres |

1607

BRITISH ISLES

| England | Architecture | THORPE, John. Holland House, Kensington, bgn. |
| | Literature | DEKKER, Thomas, and WEBSTER, John. *Westward-Hoe* |

England	Literature	SHAKESPEARE. *Macbeth* (first acting ?)
		SHAKESPEARE. *Timon of Athens* (first acting?)
		WEBSTER, John. *The White Devil* (first acting; pr. 1612)
	Music	BYRD, William. *Gradualia*

CENTRAL EUROPE

Germany	Architecture	Friedrichsbau, Heidelberg, compl.
	Universities	Giessen fnd.

LATIN EUROPE

France	Literature	HARDY, Alexandre. *Coriolan*
	Philology	SAUMAIZE, Claude de. Greek Anthology disc. at Heidelberg
Italy	Music	MONTEVERDI, Claudio. *Orfeo*

1608

BRITISH ISLES

England	Literature	DEKKER, Thomas. *The Honest Whore*, Pt. II (first acting; pr. 1630)
		SHAKESPEARE. *Antony and Cleopatra* (first acting)
		Shakespeare-Apocrypha. *The Merry Devil of Edmonton*
		Shakespeare - Apocrypha. *A Yorkshire Tragedy*

THE LOW COUNTRIES

Holland	Physics	LIPPERSHEY, Hans. Inv. of telescope

CENTRAL EUROPE

Germany	Architecture	Wolffenbuettel, Marienkirche bgn. (compl. 1623)
	Church	Protestant Union fnd.

LATIN EUROPE

France	Colonization	CHAMPLAIN, Samuel. Quebec fnd.
	Church	Reformation of Port-Royal-des-Champs by Angelica Arnauld
	Literature	REGNIER, Mathurin. *Satyres* (1613)
Italy	Music	MONTEVERDI, Claudio. *Arianna*

1609

BRITISH ISLES

England	Colonization	Virginia Company fnd.
	Discoveries	HUDSON, Henry. Disc. Hudson and Delaware Rivers

England	Literature	BEAUMONT, Francis, and FLETCHER, John. *Philaster*
		DEKKER, Thomas. *The Guls Hornbook*
		SHAKESPEARE. *Sonnets* (G. Eld for J. Thorpe, London)
		SHAKESPEARE (?). *Pericles* (first pr.)
	Philosophy	BACON, Francis. *De Sapientia Veterum* (Barker, London)

THE LOW COUNTRIES

Flanders	Painting	RUBENS, Peter Paul. *Adoration of the Magi* (Prado, Madrid)
Holland	Politics	GROTIUS, Hugo. *Mare Liberum*

CENTRAL EUROPE

Germany	Architecture	WOLFF, Jacob, the Elder. Pellerhaus, Nuremberg, compl.
	Astronomy	KEPLER, Johann. *Astronomia Nova de Motibus Stellae Martis*
	Church	Catholic League fnd.
	Press	CAROLUS, Johann. First newspaper ed. by, at Strasbourg

LATIN EUROPE

France	Theology	SALES, Francois de. *Introduction à la Vie dévote*
Italy	Academies	Accademia de' Lincei, Rome fnd.
	Astronomy	GALILEI, Galileo. Disc. satellites of Jupiter
	Libraries	Ambrosian Library, Milan, fnd.
	Painting	RENI, Guido. *Aurora* (Rospigliosi Gal., Rome)
Spain	Colonisation	Paraguay. Estab. of Spanish Jesuits
	History	GARCILASO DE LA VEGA, El Inca. *Comentarios Reales* bgn. (compl. 1617)
	Literature	VEGA CARPIO, Lope Félix de. *Jerusalén conquistada*
	Painting	EL GRECO ; Domenico Theotocopuli. *View and Plan of Toledo* (Casa del Greco, Toledo)
	Poetics	VEGA CARPIO, Lope Félix de. *Arte nuevo de hacer Comedias*

1610

BRITISH ISLES

England	Discoveries	Hudson Bay by Henry Hudson
	Literature	JONSON, Ben. *The Alchymist* (first acting; pr. 1612)
		SHAKESPEARE. *Cymbeline* (first acting)
	Theology	DONNE, John. *Pseudo-Martyr*
	Universities	Wadham College, Oxford, fnd. (Statutes, 1612)

THE LOW COUNTRIES

Holland Colonization Cape Town fnd.

NORTHERN EUROPE

Sweden Literature ASTEROPHERUS, Magnus Olai. *Tisbe* (first Swedish comedy; acted at Arboga)

CENTRAL EUROPE

Germany Astronomy KEPLER, Johann. *Narratio de observatis a se quattuor Jovis Satellitibus*

LATIN EUROPE

France Literature D'URFÉE, Honoré. *L'Astrée*
  Theology The Douai English Bible
Italy Astronomy GALILEI, Galileo. *Sidereus Nuncius*
  Literature MARINO, Giovanni-Battista. *La Strage degli Innocenti*
  Politics BELLARMIN, Roberto Francesco Romolo. *De Potestate Summi Pontificis in rebus temporalibus*

1611

BRITISH ISLES

England Literature CHAPMAN, George. *The Iliads of Homer*
    DONNE, John. *Anatomie of the Worlde*
    JONSON, Ben. *Catilina*
    MIDDLETON, Thomas. *The Roaring Girl*
    SHAKESPEARE. *The Winter's Tale* (first acting)
    TOURNEUR, Cyril. *The Atheist's Tragedy*
  Music BYRD, William. *Parthenia* (with John Bull and Orlando Gibbons)
    BYRD, William. *Psalmes, Songs and Sonnets*
  Theology Authorized Version of the Bible, (King James's Bible; Parker, London)

NORTHERN EUROPE

Sweden Literature MESSENIUS, Johannes. *Disa* (first acting)

CENTRAL EUROPE

Germany Physics KEPLER, Johann. *Dioptrice*
    KEPLER, Johann. Inv. Astronomical Telescope

LATIN EUROPE

France   Church   Oratorian Congregation fnd. in France
            Colonization CHAMPLAIN, Samuel de, fnd. Mont Royal
                          (Montreal)
Spain   Universities Manila (Philippines) fnd.

1612

BRITISH ISLES

England   Church   First Baptist Church in England estab.,
                          London
            Literature   FIELD, Nathaniel. *A Woman is a Weather-*
                          cock
                          SHAKESPEARE. *The Tempest* (first acting)
            Music   GIBBONS, Orlando. *The first Set of Madri-*
                          gals and Mottets in 5 Parts
            Theatre   HEYWOOD, Thomas. *Apology for Actors*

NORTHERN EUROPE

Sweden   Literature   MESSENIUS, Johannes. *Signill* (first acting)

CENTRAL EUROPE

Germany   Theology   BOEHME, Jacob. *Aurora oder Morgenroete*
                          im Aufgang (first pr. 1634)

LATIN EUROPE

France   Literature   HARDY, Alexandre. *La Force du Sang*
Italy   Philology   Della Crusca Academy, Vocabulary
Spain   Literature   VEGA CARPIO, Lope Félix de. *Los Pastores*
                          de Belén
            Philosophy   SUÁREZ, Francisco. *Tractatus de Legibus ac*
                          Deo Legislatore
            Politics   MÁRQUEZ, Juan. *El Gobernador Cristiano*

1613

BRITISH ISLES

England   Architecture HOLD, Thomas. Oxford Bodleian Library
                          bgn. (compl. 1618)
            Literature   BEAUMONT, Francis, and FLETCHER, John.
                          Knight of the Burning Pestle (first pr.;
                          acted earlier)
                          DRAYTON, Michael. *Polyolbion* (18 Songs;
                          complete edition in 1622)
                          SHAKESPEARE. *King Henry VIII* (first
                          acting ?)

LATIN EUROPE

Spain	Literature	CERVANTES SAAVEDRA, Miguel de. *Novelas exemplares*
		GÓNGORA, Luis de. *Soledades* (circa)
		GÓNGORA, Luis de. *Fábula de Polifemo y Galatea*
		VEGA CARPIO, Lope Félix de. *La Dama boba*
	Theology	SUÁREZ, Francisco. *Defensio Fidei Catholicae*
	Universities	Córdoba (Argentina) fnd.

1614

BRITISH ISLES

England	Architecture	JONES, Inigo. Chilham Castle, Kent, bgn. (compl. 1616)
	History	RALEIGH, Walter. *The History of the World* (Burre, London)
	Literature	CHAPMAN, George. *The Odysseys of Homer*
		JONSON, Ben. *Bartholomew Fair* (first acting; pr. 1640)
Scotland	Mathematics	NAPIER, John. *Mirifici Logarithmorum Canonis Descriptio*

THE LOW COUNTRIES

Flanders	Painting	RUBENS, Peter Paul. *Deposition from the Cross* (Antwerp)
Holland	Universities	Groningen fnd.

CENTRAL EUROPE

Austria	Architecture	SOLARI, Antonio. Salzburg Cathedral bgn. (compl. 1680)
Germany	Architecture	RIDINGER, Georg. Aschaffenburg Palace compl.

LATIN EUROPE

France	Theology	CASAUBON, Isaac. *De Rebus sacris et ecclesiasticis Exercitationes*
		SALES, François de. *Traité de l'Amour de Dieu*
Italy	Music	FRESCOBALDI, Girolamo. *Toccate . . . di Cembalo*
	Painting	DOMENICHINO; Domenico Zampieri. *Communion of St. Jerome* (Vatican)
		RENI, Guido. *Pietà.* (Bologna; compl. 1616)
Portugal	Travels	PINTO, Fernão Mendes. *Peregrinaçam* (posth.)

Spain	Literature	CERVANTES SAAVEDRA, Miguel de. *El Viaje del Parnaso*
		VEGA CARPIO, Lope Félix de. *Peribáñez y el Comendador de Ocaña* (circa)
	Sculpture	MONTAÑÉS, Juan Martínez. Crucifix "de los Cálices" (Seville)

SLAVONIC EUROPE

Czechoslovakia	Architecture	SCAMOZZI, Vincenzo. Prague, façade of the Hradschin blt.
	History	Ed. Prin. of Johannes Longinus (Jan Dlugosz, 1450-1480), *Historia Polonica*

1615

BRITISH ISLES

England	History	CAMDEN, William. *Annales* (Pt. I, compl. 1625; Pt. II, 1627; Pt. III, 1629)
	Medicine	HARVEY, William. First lectures on circulation of blood (compl. 1616)
Scotland	Mathematics	NAPIER, John. *Rabdologiae, seu Numerationis per Virgulas, libri duo*

THE LOW COUNTRIES

Flanders	Painting	RUBENS, Peter Paul. *Abduction of the Daughters of Leucippus* (Munich)

CENTRAL EUROPE

Germany	Architecture	HOLL, Elias. Augsburg City Hall bgn. (compl. 1620)
	Mathematics	KEPLER, Johann. *Nova Stereometria Doliorum*
	Music	PRAETORIUS, Michael. *Syntagma Musicum*
	Press	*Frankfurter Journal* bgn.
	Theology	ARND, Johann. *Postille*

LATIN EUROPE

France	Architecture	DE BROSSE, Salomon. Paris, Palais du Luxembourg bgn. (compl. 1624)
Italy	Architecture	Rome, Villa Borghese compl.
		SCAMOZZI, Vincenzo. *Idea dell'Architettura Universale*
Portugal	Discoveries	Blue Nile sources disc. by Pedro Paëz
Spain	Literature	CERVANTES SAAVEDRA, Miguel de. *Don Quixote*, Pt. II
		CERVANTES SAAVEDRA, Miguel de. *Ocho Comedias*

1616

BRITISH ISLES

England   Church   First Congregational Church fnd. at Southwark

Discoveries   William Baffin disc. Baffin Bay

Walter Raleigh, expedition to Guiana

Literature   JONSON, Ben. *The Divell is an Asse* (first acting; pr. 1631)

WEBSTER, John. *The Duchess of Malfi* (first acting; pr. 1623)

THE LOW COUNTRIES

Flanders   Painting   RUBENS, Peter Paul. *Last Judgment* (Munich)

RUBENS, Peter Paul. *The Lion Hunt* (Munich)

Press   *Nieuwe Tijdinghen* bgn. at Antwerp

Holland   Discoveries   Australia west coast disc. by Dirk Hartogszoon

Cape Horn disc. by Le Maire and William Schouten

Painting   HALS, Frans. *Banquet of the officers of St. George's Shooting Company* (Haarlem)

LATIN EUROPE

France   History   AUBIGNÉ, Théodore-Agrippa d'. *Histoire Universelle* (compl. 1620)

Literature   AUBIGNÉ, Théodore-Agrippa d'. *Les Tragiques*

Italy   Sculpture   BERNINI, Giovanni Lorenzo. *Apollo and Daphne* (Rome)

Spain   Literature   CERVANTES SAAVEDRA, Miguel de. *Los Trabajos de Persiles y Sigismunda*

1617

BRITISH ISLES

England   Architecture   JONES, Inigo. Lincoln's Inn Chapel, London, bgn. (compl. 1623)

JONES, Inigo. Queen's House at Greenwich bgn. (compl. 1635)

History   SELDEN, John. *The History of Tythes*

CENTRAL EUROPE

Germany   Societies   "Fruchtbringende Gesellschaft," Weimar, fnd.

LATIN EUROPE

France	Painting	CALLOT, Jacques. *Capricci* (engravings)
Italy	Painting	DOMENICHINO; Domenico Zampieri. *Legend of St. Cecilia* (S. Luigi, Rome)
Spain	Literature	VEGA CARPIO, Lope Félix de. *Comedias*, Pt. I
		VILLEGAS, Esteban Manuel de. *Poesías eróticas o amatorias*

1618

BRITISH ISLES

England	Colonization	English African Company fnd.
	Mathematics	BRIGGS, Henry. *Logarithmorum Chilias Prima*

THE LOW COUNTRIES

Holland	Literature	CATS, Jacobus. *Maechden-plicht of te Ampt der Jonkvrouwen* (Emblemata)

CENTRAL EUROPE

Germany	Astronomy	KEPLER, Johann. *Epitome Astronomiae Copernicae*
	History	*Theatrum Europaeum* (compl. 1738)
	Literature	WECKHRLIN, Georg Rudolph. *Oden und Gesaenge*

LATIN EUROPE

France	Literature	RACAN, Honoré de Bueil, Marquis de. *Bergeries*
Spain	Literature	CASTRO, Guillén de. *Las Mocedades del Cid*
		ESPINEL, Vicente. *Vida del Escudero Marcos Obregón*
		VEGA CARPIO, Lope Félix de. *Fuente Ovejuna* (before 1618)
	Theology	JUAN DE LA CRUZ. *Obras espirituales*

1619

BRITISH ISLES

England	Architecture	JONES, Inigo. Banqueting House, Whitehall, bgn. (compl. 1622)
	Mathematics	LYLE, Henry. *Decimall Arithmeticke* (first explanation of decimal notation)
	Schools	Dulwich College and Library fnd.

THE LOW COUNTRIES

Flanders	Painting	VAN DYCK, Anthony. *Portrait of Cornelis van der Geest* (Nat. Gal. Lond.)

Holland	Colonization	Batavia fnd.
	Philosophy	GROTIUS, Hugo. *De Veritate Religionis Christianae*

CENTRAL EUROPE

Germany	Academies	Rostock, first Academy of Natural Science fnd.
	Astronomy	KEPLER, Johann. *De Cometis*
		KEPLER, Johann. *Harmonice Mundi*
	Education	Weimar, first compulsory education of children
	Theology	BOEHME, Jacob. *Von den drei Principien des Goettlichen Lebens*

LATIN EUROPE

Spain	History	CABRERA DE CÓRDOBA, Luis. *Felipe Segundo, Rey de España*
	Painting	VELÁZQUEZ, Diego de Silva. *Adoration of the Magi* (Prado, Madrid)

1620

BRITISH ISLES

England	Colonization	New Plymouth fnd. by Pilgrim Fathers
	Philosophy	BACON, Francis. *Novum Organum*

THE LOW COUNTRIES

Flanders	Painting	RUBENS, Peter Paul. *Chapeau de Paille* (Nat. Gal. Lond.)
		RUBENS, Peter Paul. *Fall of the Damned* (Munich)
		VAN DYCK, Anthony. *St. Sebastian* (Munich)

LATIN EUROPE

France	Painting	CALLOT, Jacques. The Impruneta etching
Italy	Literature	MARINO, Giovanni-Battista. *La Zampogna*
	Philosophy	CAMPANELLA, Tommaso. *De Sensu Rerum et Magia*
	Universities	Sassari fnd.

1621

BRITISH ISLES

England	Literature	BURTON, Robert. *The Anatomy of Melancholy* (Lichfield and Short for Cripps, Oxford)
	Politics	BACON, Francis. *Nova Atlantis*
Scotland	Politics	BARCLAY, John. *Argenis*

THE LOW COUNTRIES

Holland   Colonization Dutch West India Company fnd.

CENTRAL EUROPE

Germany   Literature   OPITZ, Martin. *Trostgedichte*
                   Theology   BOEHME, Jacob. *De Signatura Rerum*
                   Universities Rintelen fnd.
                                 Strasbourg fnd.

SLAVONIC EUROPE

Czechoslovakia Architecture SPEZZA, Andrea. Waldstein Palace, Prague,
                                 bgn. (compl. 1628)

LATIN EUROPE

France   Literature   MAIRET, Jean de. *Sylvie*
Spain   Literature   CASTRO, Guillén de. *Comedias*, Pt. I
                                 VEGA CARPIO, Lope Félix de. *Filomena*
                   Painting   VELÁZQUEZ, Diego de Silva. *Christ in the
                                 House of Martha* (Nat. Gal. Lond.)

1622

BRITISH ISLES

England   Botany   Oxford Botanical Garden estab.
                   History   BACON, Francis. *The History of the Reign
                                 of King Henry the Seventh*
                   Literature   DEKKER, Thomas, and MASSINGER, Philip.
                                 The Virgin Martyr

THE LOW COUNTRIES

Flanders   Painting   VAN DYCK, Anthony. *Portrait of Cardinal
                                 Bentivoglio* (Pitti, Florence)

CENTRAL EUROPE

Germany   Theology   BOEHME, Jacob. *Vom uebersinnlichen Leben*

LATIN EUROPE

France   Literature   SOREL, Charles. *Francion*
Italy   Literature   TASSONI, Alessandro. *La Secchia Rapita*
                   Medicine   ASELLI, Gasparo. *De Lactibus* (discovery of
                                 mesenteric glands and lacteal vessels)

ROMAN CATHOLIC CHURCH

                   Canonization of Iñigo de Loyola (St.
                   Ignatius)
                   Congregatio de Propaganda Fide fnd.
                   Archbishopric of Paris estab.

1623

BRITISH ISLES

England	Literature	MASSINGER, Philip. *The Duke of Milan* (first pr.; acted earlier)
		MASSINGER, Philip. *The Bondman* (first acting; pr. 1624)
		SHAKESPEARE. *Comedies, Histories, and Tragedies* (The "First Folio," Isaac Jaggard and Edward Blount, London)
		WEBSTER, John. *The Devil's Law-Case* (first pr.; acted earlier)
	Philosophy	BACON, Francis. *De Dignitate et Augmentis Scientiarum*

THE LOW COUNTRIES

Flanders	Painting	RUBENS, Peter Paul. *Portrait of the Painter* (Windsor)

CENTRAL EUROPE

Austria	Universities	Salzburg fnd.
Germany	Theology	BOEHME, Jacob. *Mysterium Magnum*
Switzerland	Botany	BAUHIN, Gaspard. *Pinax Theatri Botanici*

LATIN EUROPE

France	Literature	DE VIAU, Théophile. *Le Parnasse Satirique*
Italy	Astronomy	GALILEI, Galileo. *Il Saggiatore*
	Literature	MARINO, Giovanni Battista. *Adone*
		MICHELANGELO. *Rime* (posth.)
	Painting	DOMENICHINO; Domenico Zampieri. Frescoes in S. Andrea della Valle, Rome (compl. 1628)
	Politics	CAMPANELLA, Tommaso. *Civitas Solis*
Spain	History	MONCADA, Francisco de. *Expedición de los Catalanes y Aragoneses contra Turcos y Griegos*

1624

BRITISH ISLES

England	Literature	MASSINGER, Philip. *The Renegado* (first acting; pr. 1637)
	Mathematics	BRIGGS, Henry. *Arithmetica Logarithmica* (Jones, London)
	Universities	Pembroke College, Oxford, fnd.
Wales	Philosophy	HERBERT, Edward; Lord Herbert of Cherbury. *De Veritate*

THE LOW COUNTRIES

Holland	Painting	HALS, Frans. *The Laughing Cavalier* (Wall. Coll. Lond.)
	Philology	*Novum Testamentum Graecum*, ed. Elzevir, at Leyden

CENTRAL EUROPE

Germany	Literature	OPITZ, Martin. *Teutsche Poemata*
	Poetics	OPITZ, Martin. *Buch von der Deutschen Poeterey*

LATIN EUROPE

France	Literature	HARDY, Alexandre. *Théâtre* (compl. 1628)
	Philosophy	BALZAC, Jean de. *Lettres*
		GASSENDI, Pierre. *Exercitationes paradoxicae adversus Aristoteleos*
Italy	Music	MONTEVERDI, Claudio. *Combattimento di Tancredi e Clorinda*
Spain	Literature	TIRSO DE MOLINA; Fray Gabriel Téllez. *Los Cigarrales de Toledo*
		TIRSO DE MOLINA; Fray Gabriel Téllez. *El Condenado por Desconfiado*
		TIRSO DE MOLINA; Fray Gabriel Téllez. *El Burlador de Sevilla y Convidado de Piedra*

1625

BRITISH ISLES

England	Colonization	Barbados, British colony estab.
	Literature	JONSON, Ben. *The Staple of News* (first acting; pr. 1631)
		MASSINGER, Philip. *A New Way to pay old Debts* (first acting; pr. 1632)
	Press	*Mercurius Britannicus* fnd.

THE LOW COUNTRIES

Flanders	Painting	RUBENS, Peter Paul. *History of Maria de' Medici* (Louvre)
		RUBENS, Peter Paul. *Assumption of the Virgin* (Antwerp Cath.)
Holland	Jurisprudence	GROTIUS, Hugo. *De Jure Belli ac Pacis*

CENTRAL EUROPE

Germany	Music	SCHUETZ, Heinrich. *Cantiones Sacrae*

LATIN EUROPE

France   Colonization   Cayenne fnd.

            Literature   GOMBAULD, Jean Augier de Lussac. *Amaranthe*

Spain   Painting   ZURBARÁN, Francisco de. *History of St. Peter* (Seville Cath.)

1626

BRITISH ISLES

England   Architecture   JONES, Inigo. York House Water Gate, London, blt.

            Literature   DONNE, John. *Devotions upon emergent Occasions*

                               MASSINGER, Philip. *The Roman Actor* (first acting; pr. 1629)

                               SHIRLEY, James. *The Maid's Revenge* (first acting; pr. 1639)

                               SHIRLEY, James. *The Wedding* (first acting; pr. 1629)

THE LOW COUNTRIES

Holland   Colonization   New Amsterdam (New York) fnd.

            Painting   REMBRANDT. *Tobias and his Wife* (Amsterdam)

LATIN EUROPE

France   Botany   Paris, Jardin des Plantes, fnd.

            Colonization   French West African Company fnd.

                               French Company for the Islands of America fnd.

Italy   Architecture   Rome, S. Ignazio bgn. (compl. 1675; Zampieri and Grassi, Façade by Alessandro Algardi)

Spain   Literature   QUEVEDO, Francisco Gómez de. *Vida del Buscón*

            Politics   QUEVEDO, Francisco Gómez de. *Política de Dios*

ROMAN CATHOLIC CHURCH

            Collegium de Propaganda Fide, Rome, fnd.

1627

BRITISH ISLES

England   Colonization   Boston (New England) fnd.

            Literature   MASSINGER, Philip. *The Great Duke of Florence* (first acting; pr. 1635)

            Chemistry   BACON, Francis. *Sylva Sylvarum*

THE LOW COUNTRIES

Flanders	Painting	RUBENS, Peter Paul. *Portrait of Sir Anthony van Dyck* (Windsor)
Holland	Painting	HALS, Frans. *Banquet of the officers of St. Andrew's Shooting Company* (Haarlem) REMBRANDT. *St. Paul in Prison* (Stuttgart)

CENTRAL EUROPE

Germany	Astronomy	KEPLER, Johann. *Tabulae Rudolphinae*
	Music	SCHUETZ, Heinrich. *Daphne* (first German Opera; performed at Torgau)

LATIN EUROPE

Spain	Literature	VEGA CARPIO, Lope Félix de. *La Corona Trágica* QUEVEDO, Francisco Gómez de. *Sueños* TIRSO DE MOLINA; Fray Gabriel Téllez. *Comedias*
	Theology	ESCOBAR Y MENDOZA, Antonio. *Summula Casuum Conscientiae*

1628

BRITISH ISLES

England	History	THUCYDIDES. *Eight Books of the Peloponnesian War ... interpreted by Thomas Hobbes*
	Medicine	HARVEY, William. *Exercitatio Anatomica de Motu Cordis et Sanguinis in Animalibus*

LATIN EUROPE

Spain	Literature	RÍUZ DE ALARCÓN, Juan. *La verdad sospechosa*

SLAVONIC EUROPE

Russia	Colonization	Krasnoyarsk fnd.

1629

BRITISH ISLES

England	Literature	FORD, John. *The Lover's Melancholy* MASSINGER, Philip. *The Picture*
	Theatre	First public appearance of (French) actresses in England

CENTRAL EUROPE

Germany	Church	Edict of Restitution against German Protestants
	Music	SCHUETZ, Heinrich. *Sinfoniae Sacrae*

LATIN EUROPE

France	Architecture	Paris, Palais Royal bgn. (compl. 1636; Jacques Lemercier)
	Literature	CORNEILLE, Pierre. *Mélite* (first performance; first pr. 1633)
		MAIRET, Jean de. *Silvanire*
		MAIRET, Jean dc. *Sophonisbe*
Italy	Architecture	BERNINI, Giovanni Lorenzo. Portico of St. Peter's, Rome, bgn. (compl. 1667)
Spain	Literature	CALDERÓN DE LA BARCA, Pedro. *El Príncipe constante*
		CALDERÓN DE LA BARCA, Pedro. *La Dama duende*
	Painting	VELÁZQUEZ, Diego de Silva. *The Drinkers (Los Borrachos).* (Prado, Madrid)

1630

BRITISH ISLES

England	Literature	FORD, John. *Love's Sacrifice* (first acting; pr. 1633)
Wales	Theology	First popular Welsh Bible

THE LOW COUNTRIES

Flanders	Painting	RUBENS, Peter Paul. *The Blessings of Peace* (Nat. Gal. Lond.)
Holland	Painting	HALS, Frans. *The Gipsy Girl* (Louvre)
		REMBRANDT. *Portrait of his Mother* (etchings)

LATIN EUROPE

France	Literature	MALHERBE, François. *Œuvres*
	Painting	POUSSIN, Nicolas. *Triumphs of Flora* (Louvre)
Italy	Music	FRESCOBALDI, Girolamo. *Arie Musicale*
Spain	Painting	VELÁZQUEZ, Diego de Silva. *Forge of Vulcan* (Prado, Madrid)

1631

BRITISH ISLES

England	Architecture	JONES, Inigo. Covent Garden Piazza, London, designed

England   Literature   CHAPMAN, George. *Caesar and Pompey* (first pr.; acted earlier)
HEYWOOD, Thomas. *The Fair Maid of the West* (first pr.; acted earlier)
SHIRLEY, James. *The Traitor* (first acting; pr. 1635)

Mathematics   HARRIOT, Thomas. *Artis analyticae praxis ad aequationes Algebraicas nova methodo resolvendas*

THE LOW COUNTRIES

Flanders   Painting   VAN DYCK, Anthony. *Elevation of the Cross* (Notre-Dame, Courtrai)
Holland   Painting   REMBRANDT. *Holy Family* (Munich)
REMBRANDT. *Presentation in the Temple* (Hague)

CENTRAL EUROPE

Germany   Jurisprudence SPEE, Friedrich von. *Cautio Criminalis*

LATIN EUROPE

France   Politics   BALZAC, Jean de. *Le Prince*
     Press   *Gazette de France* fnd.
Italy   Architecture   LONGHENA, Baldassare. S. Maria della Salute, Venice, bgn.
Spain   Literature   LEÓN, Luis de. *Poesías* (posth.)
VEGA CARPIO, Lope Félix de. *El Castigo sin Venganza*
VEGA CARPIO, Lope Félix de. *La Moza de Cántaro* bgn. (compl. 1632)

Painting   ZURBARÁN, Francisco de. *Apotheosis of St. Thomas Aquinas* (bgn. 1625; Seville)

SLAVONIC EUROPE

Czechoslovakia   Philology   COMENIUS, Johan Amos. *Janua Linguarum reserata*

1632

BRITISH ISLES

England   Colonization   Maryland fnd. by Lord Baltimore
     Literature   MASSINGER, Philip. *The Maid of Honour*
MILTON, John. *L'Allegro* and *Il Penseroso*
SHAKESPEARE. The " Second Folio " (Thos. Cotes for Robert Allot, London)
Scotland   Church   The Bishopric of Edinburgh fnd.

THE LOW COUNTRIES

Flanders	Painting	RUBENS, Peter Paul. *St. Ildefons Altarpiece* (Belvedere, Vienna)
		VAN DYCK, Anthony. *Portrait of Francisco de Moncada* (Louvre)
		VAN DYCK, Anthony. *Charles I and His Family* (" The Great Piece "). (Windsor)
Holland	Astronomy	Leyden Observatory estab.
	Literature	CATS, Jakobus. *Spiegel van den ouden en nieuwen Tydt*
	Painting	REMBRANDT. *Anatomy Class of Dr. Tulp* (Hague)
	Universities	Amsterdam fnd.

NORTHERN EUROPE

Sweden	Universities	Swedish University of Dorpat (Tartu) fnd.

LATIN EUROPE

France	Painting	CALLOT, Jacques. *Les petites Misères de la Guerre* (engravings)
Italy	Architecture	Rome, Il Gesù compl. (bgn. 1568 by Vignola)
	Astronomy	GALILEI, Galileo. *Dialogo . . . sopra i due massimi Sistemi del Mondo . . .*
Spain	Literature	CALDERÓN DE LA BARCA, Pedro. *La Vida es Sueño* (compl. 1635)
		VEGA CARPIO, Lope Félix de. *La Dorotea*
	Painting	RIBERA, José Antonio de. *Trinity* (Escorial)
		VELÁZQUEZ, Diego de Silva. *Portrait of King Philip IV of Spain* (Nat. Gal. Lond.)

SLAVONIC EUROPE

Russia	Colonization	Yakutsk fnd.

1633

BRITISH ISLES

England	Literature	DONNE, John. *Poems*
		FLETCHER, Phineas. *The Purple Island*
		FORD, John. *The Broken Heart*
		FORD, John. *'Tis Pity she's a Whore* (first pr.; acted earlier)
		HERBERT, George. *The Temple* (Buck and Daniel, Cambridge)
		SHIRLEY, James. *The Young Admiral* (first acting; pr. 1637)
	Theatre	PRYNNE, William. *Histrio-mastix*

THE LOW COUNTRIES

Flanders	Painting	VAN DYCK, Anthony. *Charles I on a grey Horse* (Windsor Castle)
Holland	Architecture	CAMPEN, Jacob van, and POST, Pieter. Mauritshuis, at the Hague, bgn.
	Painting	REMBRANDT. *Portrait of Saskia* (Cassel)
		REMBRANDT. *Saskia in a Hat* (Dresden)
		REMBRANDT. *Descent from the Cross* (etchings)

LATIN EUROPE

France	Painting	CALLOT, Jacques. *Les Grandes Misères de la Guerre* (engravings)
Italy	Physics	TORRICELLI, Evangelista, and VIVIANI, Vincenzo. Invention of barometer
	Politics	CAMPANELLA, Tommaso. *Monarchia Messiae*
	Sculpture	BERNINI, Giovanni Lorenzo. Tabernacle of St. Peter's, Rome
Spain	Literature	CALDERÓN DE LA BARCA, Pedro. *La Devoción de la Cruz* (before 1633)
	Painting	RIBERA, José Antonio de. *Jacob's Dream* (Prado, Madrid)

1634

BRITISH ISLES

England	Literature	CAREW, Thomas. *Coelum Britannicum*
		FORD, John. *Perkin Warbeck*
		MILTON, John. *Comus* (first acting; pr. 1637)
		Shakespeare-Apocrypha. *The two noble Kinsmen* (ascribed to Shakespeare and John Fletcher; first pr.)
		SHIRLEY, James. *The Gamester* (first acting; pr. 1637)

THE LOW COUNTRIES

Holland	Painting	REMBRANDT. *Descent from the Cross* (Leningrad)
		REMBRANDT. *Incredulity of St. Thomas* (Berlin)
		REMBRANDT. *Portrait of the Painter as an Officer* (Hague)
		REMBRANDT. *The Jewish Bride* (Leningrad)
		REMBRANDT. *Portrait of the Painter in a Casque* (Cassel)
	Universities	Utrecht fnd.

CENTRAL EUROPE

Germany Astronomy KEPLER, Johann. *Somnium de Astronomia Lunari*
  Poetics OPITZ, Martin. *Prosodia Germanica*
  Theatre First Oberammergau Passion-Play

LATIN EUROPE

Italy Literature BASILE, Giovanni Battista. *Lo Cunto de li Cunti*, Pt. I
Spain Literature GÓNGORA, Luis de. *Delicias del Parnaso*
  VEGA CARPIO, Lope Félix de. *Rimas humanas y divinas* (incl. *La Gatomaquia*)

1635

BRITISH ISLES

England Colonization Boston Grammar School fnd. (first Latin Grammar School in Brit. N. America)
  Politics SELDEN, John. *Mare Clausum*

THE LOW COUNTRIES

Flanders Painting RUBENS, Peter Paul. *Rape of the Sabines* (Nat. Gal. Lond.)
  VAN DYCK, Anthony. *Children of Charles I* (Windsor Castle and Turin)
Holland Painting REMBRANDT. *Rembrandt and Saskia at Table* (Dresden)
  REMBRANDT. *Samson threatening his Father-in-law* (Berlin)
  REMBRANDT. *The Sacrifice of Abraham* (Leningrad)
  REMBRANDT. *St. John in the Wilderness* (Berlin)
  Philology VOSSIUS, Gerard Jan. *Aristarchus, sive de Arte Grammatica*

CENTRAL EUROPE

Switzerland History MERIAN, Matthaeus. *Theatrum Europaeum* (compl. 1738)

LATIN EUROPE

France Academies Académie Française fnd.
  Architecture LEMERCIER, Jacques. Church of the Sorbonne, Paris, bgn. (compl. 1659)
  Colonization French Settlements in Guadeloupe and Martinique fnd.
  Literature CORNEILLE, Pierre. *Médée* (first perf.; first pr. 1639)

[123]

| Spain | Literature | TIRSO DE MOLINA; Fray Gabriel Téllez. *Don Gil de las Calzas verdes*
VEGO CARPIO, Lope Félix de. *El mejor Alcalde, el Rey* (before 1635)
VEGA CARPIO, Lope Félix de. *El Caballero de Olmedo* (before 1635) |
| | Painting | RIBERA, José Antonio de. *Immaculate Conception* (Salamanca)
VELÁZQUEZ, Diego de Silva. *Surrender of Breda* (*Las Lanzas*; Prado, Madrid) |

HUNGARY

| Universities | Budapest fnd. |

1636

BRITISH ISLES

| England | Literature | MASSINGER, Philip. *The Bashful Lover* (first acting; pr. 1635) |

THE LOW COUNTRIES

| Flanders | Painting | VAN DYCK, Anthony. *Charles I on horseback* (Nat. Gal. Lond.)
VAN DYCK, Anthony. *Children of Charles I* (Dresden) |
| Holland | Painting | REMBRANDT. *Danae* (Leningrad)
REMBRANDT. *Samson overwhelmed by Philistines* (Frankfurt-on-Main) |

CENTRAL EUROPE

| Germany | Music | SCHUETZ, Heinrich. *Geistliche Concerte*, Pt. I |

LATIN EUROPE

France	Literature	CORNEILLE, Pierre. *Le Cid* (first perf.; first pr. 1637)
	Mathematics	FERMAT, Pierre de. *Methodus ad disquirendum Maximum et Minimum*
Italy	Architecture	BORROMINI, Francesco. S. Giovanni in Laterano, Rome, recons. bgn. (compl. 1649)

1637

BRITISH ISLES

| England | Literature | KING, Henry. *Poems*
MILTON, John. *Lycidas* |

THE LOW COUNTRIES

Flanders	Painting	VAN DYCK, Anthony. *Children of Charles I* (Windsor Castle)
Holland	Literature	VONDEL, Joost van den. *Gijsbrecht van Aemstel*
	Painting	REMBRANDT. *Portrait of himself as a Polish Nobleman* (The " Sobieski "; Leningrad)
	Theology	*Staatenbibel*

CENTRAL EUROPE

Germany	Literature	DACH, Simon. *Anke von Tharaw*
		GRYPHIUS, Andreas. *Sonnete*

LATIN EUROPE

France	Astronomy	DESCARTES, René. *Les Météores*
	Mathematics	DESCARTES, René. *La Géométrie*
		FERMAT, Pierre de. Disc. " Last Theorem "
	Philosophy	DESCARTES, René. *Discours de la Méthode*
	Physics	DESCARTES, René. *La Dioptrique*
Italy	Theatre	First European Opera House opened at S. Cassiano, Venice
Spain	Literature	CALDERÓN DE LA BARCA, Pedro. *El Mágico Prodigioso*
	Painting	RIBERA, José Antonio de. *Pietà* (S. Martino, Naples)

SLAVONIC EUROPE

Czechoslovakia	Education	COMENIUS, Johan Amos. *Porta Sapientiae reserata*

1638

BRITISH ISLES

England	Architecture	JONES, Inigo. New Lodge, Hyde Park, blt.
	Astronomy	WILKINS, John. *The Discovery of a World in the Moon*
Scotland	Church	The Glasgow meeting of the General Assembly of the Church of Scotland

THE LOW COUNTRIES

Flanders	Painting	JORDAENS, Jacob. *Twelfth Night* (*circa*; Leningrad)
		RUBENS, Peter Paul. *The Brazen Serpent* (Nat. Gal. Lond.)
Holland	Painting	REMBRANDT. *Noli me tangere* (Nat. Gal. Lond.)
		REMBRANDT. *Wedding of Samson* (Dresden)

NORTHERN EUROPE

Sweden   Colonization   Swedish Colony on the Delaware River fnd.

CENTRAL EUROPE

Germany   Literature   LOGAU, Friedrich von. *Erstes Hundert Teutscher Reimensprueche*

LATIN EUROPE

France   History   SULLY, Maximilien de Béthune, Duc de. *Mémoires*, Pts. I and II

    Painting   POUSSIN, Nicolas. *Bacchanalian Festival* (compl. 1639; Nat. Gal. Lond.)

Italy   Physics   GALILEI, Galileo. *Dialoghi delle Nuove Scienze*

Spain   Painting   RIBERA, José Antonio de. *Twelve Prophets, Moses and Elias* bgn. (compl. 1643; Naples)

1639.

BRITISH ISLES

England   Colonization   Madras fnd.

    History   FULLER, Thomas. *The Historie of the Holy Warre* (Buck, Cambridge)

    Literature   FORD, John. *The Lady's Trial*

THE LOW COUNTRIES

Flanders   Painting   RUBENS, Peter Paul. *Judgment of Paris* (Prado, Madrid)

Holland   Painting   REMBRANDT. *Portrait of Jan Six* (Cassel)

LATIN EUROPE

France   Painting   CLAUDE LORRAIN; Claude Gelée. *Ancient Port of Messina* (Louvre)

    CLAUDE LORRAIN; Claude Gelée. *La Danse au Village* (Louvre)

1640

BRITISH ISLES

England   Colonization   Cambridge, Massachusetts Bay. Bay Psalm Book pr. (first surviving book pr. in Brit. North America)

    Jurisprudence   SELDEN, John. *De Jure Naturali et Gentium juxta Disciplinam Hebraeorum*

    Politics   HOBBES, Thomas. *De Corpore Politico*

THE LOW COUNTRIES

Flanders	Painting	VAN DYCK, Anthony. *Cupid and Psyche* (Hampton Court)
Holland	Painting	REMBRANDT. *Portrait of himself* (Nat. Gal. Lond.)
	Theology	JANSEN, Cornelius. *Augustinus*

CENTRAL EUROPE

Germany	Literature	MOSCHEROSCH, Johann Michael. *Wunderbahre Satyrische Gesichte verteutscht durch Philander von Sittewalt* (first dated ed., 1642)

LATIN EUROPE

France	Literature	CORNEILLE, Pierre. *Cinna* (first perf.; first pr. 1643)
		CORNEILLE, Pierre. *Horace* (first perf.; first pr. 1641)
Italy	Literature	MARINO, Giovanni Battista. *Calloandro Fidele*
	Sculpture	BERNINI, Giovanni Lorenzo. Fontana del Tritone, Rome, blt.
Spain	Literature	CALDERÓN DE LA BARCA, Pedro. *Comedias*
	Painting	VELÁZQUEZ, Diego de Silva. *Portrait of Pope Innocent X* (Palazzo Doria, Rome)
	Politics	GRACIÁN, Baltasar. *El Político*
		SAAVEDRA FAJARDO, Diego. *Idea de un Príncipe político Cristiano*

1641

BRITISH ISLES

England	Literature	SHIRLEY, James. *The Cardinal* (first acting; pr. 1652)

THE LOW COUNTRIES

Flanders	Painting	VAN DYCK, Anthony. *Portrait of Prince William of Orange* (Amsterdam)
Holland	Painting	REMBRANDT. *Saskia* (Dresden)
		REMBRANDT. *Descent from the Cross* (etchings)

LATIN EUROPE

France	Philosophy	DESCARTES, René. *Meditationes de prima Philosophia*
Italy	Architecture	BORROMINI, Francesco. San Carlo alle Quattro Fontane, Rome, bgn. (compl. 1667)
Spain	Literature	VÉLEZ DE GUEVARA, Luis. *El Diablo Cojuelo*

SLAVONIC EUROPE

Czechoslovakia Education COMENIUS, Johan Amos. *Via Lucis*

1642

BRITISH ISLES

England Literature BROWNE, Thomas. *Religio Medici*
         Politics FULLER, Thomas. *The Holy State*
                HOBBES, Thomas. *De Cive*

THE LOW COUNTRIES

Holland Discoveries New Zealand and Tasmania disc. by Abel
                Tasman
         Painting REMBRANDT. *The Night Watch* (Amster-
                dam)
                REMBRANDT. *The Three Trees* (etchings)

CENTRAL EUROPE

Germany Literature FLEMMING, Paul. *Teutsche Poemata*
Switzerland Geography MERIAN, Matthaeus. *Topographia* (compl.
                1688)

LATIN EUROPE

France Architecture MANSART, François. Château at Maisons-
                Laffitte bgn. (compl. 1650)
         Astronomy GASSENDI, Pierre. *De apparente Magni-
                tudine Solis . . .*
         Literature CORNEILLE, Pierre. *Polyeucte* (first perf.;
                first pr. 1643)
         Painting LE NAIN, Louis. *The Forge* (Louvre)
Italy Architecture BORROMINI, Francesco. St. Ivo, Rome, bgn.
                (compl. 1660)
Spain Philosophy GRACIÁN, Baltasar. *Agudeza y Arte de
                Ingenio* (compl. 1648)

1643

BRITISH ISLES

England Press *Mercurius Civicus* (first illus. London period-
                ical)

THE LOW COUNTRIES

Holland History *Acta Sanctorum* bgn. (compl. 1867)

NORTHERN EUROPE

Norway Literature The Edda discovered by Bishop Sveinson
Sweden Press *Ordinarie Post Tidende* bgn., Stockholm

CENTRAL EUROPE

Germany	Literature	MOSCHEROSCH, Johann Michael. *Epigrammata*

LATIN EUROPE

France	Education	" Petites Ecoles " estab. Port-Royal
	Literature	CORNEILLE, Pierre. *La Mort de Pompée* (first perf.; first pr. 1644)
	Philosophy	GASSENDI, Pierre. *Disquisitiones Anticartesianae*
	Theology	ARNAULD, Antoine. *De la fréquente Communion*

SLAVONIC EUROPE

Czechoslovakia	Physics	COMENIUS, Johan Amos. *Physicae . . . Synopsis*

EASTERN ORTHODOX CHURCH

Orthodox Confession of the Catholic and Apostolic Eastern Church

1644

BRITISH ISLES

England	Education	MILTON, John. *Of Education*
	Politics	MILTON, John. *Areopagitica. A Speech to the Parliament of England for the Liberty of unlicensed Printing*

THE LOW COUNTRIES

Holland	Literature	VONDEL, Joost van den. *Verscheide Gedichten*
	Painting	REMBRANDT. *The Woman taken in Adultery* (Nat. Gal. Lond.)

CENTRAL EUROPE

Germany	Societies	Nuremberg, " Gesellschaft der Schaefer an der Pegnitz " fnd.

LATIN EUROPE

France	Literature	CORNEILLE, Pierre. *Rodogune* (first perf.; first pr. 1647)
	Painting	CLAUDE LORRAIN; Claude Gelée. *Echo and Narcissus* (Nat. Gal. Lond.)
		CLAUDE LORRAIN; Claude Gelée. *Seaport at Sunset* (Nat. Gal. Lond.)
	Philosophy	DESCARTES, René. *Principia Philosophiae*
	Pottery	Rouen Pottery Factory fnd.

[129]

Italy	Mathematics	TORRICELLI, Evangelista. *Opera Geometrica*
	Sculpture	BERNINI, Giovanni Lorenzo. Statue of St. Teresa (S. Maria della Vittoria, Rome; compl. 1646)
Spain	Literature	CALDERÓN DE LA BARCA, Pedro. *El Alcalde de Zalamea*
	Painting	VELÁZQUEZ, Diego de Silva. *The Lady with the Fan* (compl. 1649; Wallace Coll.)
	Politics	QUEVEDO, Francisco Gómez de. *Vida de Marco Bruto*
	Theology	ESCOBAR Y MENDOZA, Antonio de. *Liber Theologiae Moralis*

1645

BRITISH ISLES

England	Literature	MILTON, John. *Poems*
Wales	Theology	HERBERT, Edward; Lord Herbert of Cherbury. *De Religione Gentilium*

THE LOW COUNTRIES

Holland	Philology	VOSSIUS, Gerard Jan. *De Vitiis Sermonis*

CENTRAL EUROPE

Germany	Literature	ZESEN, Philipp von. *Die Adriatische Rosamund*
	Music	SCHUETZ, Heinrich. *Die Sieben Worte Christi am Kreuz*

LATIN EUROPE

France	Architecture	MANSART, François. Church of Val-de-Grâce at Paris bgn. (compl. 1650; dome painted by Pierre Mignard)
	Astronomy	GASSENDI, Pierre. *Institutio Astronomica*
	Literature	AUBIGNAC, François-Hédelin d'. *Zénobie*
		CORNEILLE, Pierre. *Théodore* (first perf.; first pr. 1646)
		ROTROU, Jean. *La Sœur*
		SCARRON, Paul. *Jodelet*
	Painting	LE SUEUR, Eustache. *La Vie de Saint Bruno* (compl. 1648; Louvre)
	Politics	SALMASIUS; Claude de Saumaize. *De Primatu Papae*
Italy	Zoology	SEVERINO, Marco Aurelio. *Zootomia Democritea*
Spain	History	MELO, Francisco Manuel de. *Historia de los Movimientos y Separación de Cataluña*
	Literature	CALDERÓN DE LA BARCA, Pedro. *El gran Teatro del Mundo* (circa)

1646

BRITISH ISLES

England	Literature	CRASHAW, Richard. *Steps to the Temple* SUCKLING, Sir John. *Fragmenta aurea* (posth.)

THE LOW COUNTRIES

Holland	Painting	POTTER, Paul. *The Farm* (Munich)

LATIN EUROPE

France	Architecture	LEVAU and others. Church of Saint-Sulpice, Paris, fnd. (built from 1655-1777)
	Literature	ROTROU, Jean. *Saint Genest*
	Mathematics	VIETA; François Viète. *Opera Mathematica*
	Painting	CLAUDE LORRAIN; Claude Gelée. *Seaport at Sunset* (Louvre)
	Theatre	Supposed perf. of the first French opera (*Akébar, Roi du Mogol*) at Carpentras; text and score lost; first verified French opera, *Pomone*, by Robert Cambert (*see* 1671)

1647

BRITISH ISLES

England	Religion	Society of Friends (Quakers) fnd. by George Fox
	Theology	TAYLOR, Jeremy. *Liberty of Prophesying*

THE LOW COUNTRIES

Holland	Painting	POTTER, Paul. *The Bull* (Hague) REMBRANDT. *Holy Family* (Cassel)

NORTHERN EUROPE

Sweden	Colonization	Swedish African Company fnd.

LATIN EUROPE

France	Literature	ROTROU, Jean. *Venceslas*
	Painting	CLAUDE LORRAIN; Claude Gelée. *The Flight into Egypt* (Leningrad) MIGNARD, Pierre. *Portrait of Molière* (*circa*; Chantilly)
Italy	Mathematics	CAVALIERI, Bonaventura. *Exercitationes Geometricae*
Spain	Philosophy	GRACIÁN, Baltasar. *Oráculo manual*

[131]

1648

BRITISH ISLES

England	Literature	DONNE, John. *Biathanatos* (posth.)
		HERRICK, Robert. *Hesperides*
	Theology	Westminster Catechism

THE LOW COUNTRIES

Holland	Architecture	CAMPEN, Jacob van. Palace at Amsterdam bgn. (compl. 1655)
	Medicine	HELMONT, Jan Baptista van. *Ortus Medicinae*
	Painting	REMBRANDT. *The Samaritan* (Louvre)

LATIN EUROPE

France	Academies	Académie Royale de Peinture et de Sculpture, Paris, fnd.
	Literature	SCARRON, Paul. *Le Virgile Travesti*
		SCUDÉRY, Madeleine de. *Artamène* (compl. 1653)
	Painting	CLAUDE LORRAIN; Claude Gelée. *The Queen of Sheba visiting Solomon* (Nat. Gal. Lond.)
		POUSSIN, Nicolas. *Rebecca at the Fountain* (Louvre)

1649

BRITISH ISLES

England	History	HERBERT, Edward; Lord Herbert of Cherbury. *Life of Henry VIII*
	Literature	LOVELACE, Richard. *Lucasta*
	Politics	*Eikon Basilike* (ascribed to Charles I but claimed by John Gauden, Bishop of Worcester)
		MILTON, John. *Eikonoklastes*
	Societies	Society for the Propagation of the Gospel in New England (first British Missionary Society) fnd.

THE LOW COUNTRIES

| Holland | Architecture | Hague, Nieuwekerk bgn. (compl. 1656) |
| | Painting | REMBRANDT. *The Hundred-Guilder Piece* (etchings) |

CENTRAL EUROPE

| Germany | Literature | SPEE, Friedrich von. *Trutznachtigall* |

LATIN EUROPE

France	Painting	POUSSIN, Nicolas. *Judgment of Solomon* (Louvre)
	Philosophy	DESCARTES, René. *Les Passions de l'Ame*
	Politics	SALMASIUS; Claude de Saumaize. *Defensio Regia pro Carolo I*
Spain	Painting	MURILLO, Bartolomé Esteban. *St. Anthony of Padua* (Berlin)

1650

BRITISH ISLES

England	History	FULLER, Thomas. *A Pisgah - Sight of Palestine*
	Politics	MILTON, John. *Pro Populo Anglicano Defensio*
	Theology	BAXTER, Richard. *The Saints' Everlasting Rest*
		TAYLOR, Jeremy. *Holy Living*
	Universities	Harvard University, Cambridge (Mass.), fnd.
Wales	Literature	VAUGHAN, Henry. *Silex Scintillans*, Pt. I (Pt. II, 1656)

THE LOW COUNTRIES

Flanders	Architecture	HESIUS, Paul. Church of St. Michael, Louvain, bgn. (compl. 1666)
Holland	Painting	HALS, Frans. *Hille Bobbe* (*The Witch*) (Kais. Fried. Mus., Berlin)

CENTRAL EUROPE

Germany	Literature	GRYPHIUS, Andreas. *Teutsche Reim-Gedichte*
	Physics	GUERICKE, Otto von. Inv. air-pump
	Poetics	VONDEL, Joost van den. *Aanleidinge ter Nederduitsche dichtkunste*

LATIN EUROPE

France	Literature	CORNEILLE, Pierre. *Don Sancho d'Aragon*
		CORNEILLE, Pierre. *Andromède* (first perf.; first pr. 1651)
		VOITURE, Vincent. *Œuvres.*
	Music	DESCARTES, René. *Compendium Musicae*
Italy	Architecture	Palace of Isola Bella in Lago Maggiore bgn.
		LONGHENA, Baldassare. Palazzo Rezzonico, Venice, bgn. (compl. 1680)
Spain	Literature	ROJAS ZORRILLA, Francisco de. *Del rey abajo, ninguno*

[133]

Spain Painting CARREÑO DE MIRANDA, Juan. *Portrait of Alessandro del Borro* (Berlin)
RIBERA, José Antonio de. *Adoration of the Shepherds* (Louvre)
VELÁZQUEZ, Diego de Silva. *Portrait of Juan de Pareja* (Earl of Radnor's Coll.)

1651

BRITISH ISLES

England Biology HARVEY, William. *Exercitatio de Generatione Animalium*
Politics HOBBES, Thomas. *Leviathan*
Theology TAYLOR, Jeremy. *Sermons* (compl. 1655)
TAYLOR, Jeremy. *Holy Dying*

THE LOW COUNTRIES

Holland Painting REMBRANDT. *Noli me tangere* (Brunswick)

LATIN EUROPE

France Literature CORNEILLE, Pierre. *Nicomède*
SCARRON, Paul. *Le Roman Comique* (compl. 1657)
Painting POUSSIN, Nicolas. *The Holy Family* (Louvre)
Spain Painting RIBERA, José Antonio. *Communion of the Apostles* (Naples)

1652

BRITISH ISLES

England Literature DAVENANT, Sir William. *Gondibert*

THE LOW COUNTRIES

Flanders Painting TENIERS, David. *Fair* (Brussels)
Holland Painting REMBRANDT. *Portrait of Hendrickje Stoffels* (Louvre)

NORTHERN EUROPE

Sweden Medicine BARTHOLIN, Barthel. *De Lacteis Thoracicis*
RUDBECK, Olaf. *De Circulatione Sanguinis*

LATIN EUROPE

France Literature BALZAC, Jean de. *Socrate Chrétien*
Spain Theology ESCOBAR Y MENDOZA, Antonio. *Universae Theologiae Moralis Problemata*

SLAVONIC EUROPE

Russia Colonization Irkutsk fnd.

1653

BRITISH ISLES

England	Libraries	Manchester Endowed Library fnd.
	Literature	SHIRLEY, James. *The Court Secret* (first pr.; acted later)
		WALTON, Izaak. *The Compleat Angler* (Part II by Charles Cotton)

THE LOW COUNTRIES

Holland	Painting	METSU, Gabriel. *Woman taken in Adultery* (Louvre)
		REMBRANDT. *The Three Crosses* (etchings)

NORTHERN EUROPE

Sweden	Medicine	RUDBECK, Olaf. *Nova Exercitatio Anatomica*

LATIN EUROPE

France	Architecture	LEMERCIER, Jacques. Church of Saint-Roch, Paris, bgn. (compl. 1736)
	Literature	CYRANO DE BERGERAC, Savinien. *La Mort d'Agrippina*
Italy	Architecture	BORROMINI, Francesco. Church of S. Agnese, Rome, bgn. (compl. 1657)
Spain	Philosophy	GRACIÁN, Baltasar. *El Criticón*

1654

BRITISH ISLES

England	Medicine	GLISSON, Francis. *Anatomia hepatis*
	Politics	MILTON, John. *Pro Populo Anglicano Defensio Secunda*
	Theology	WALTON, Bryan. *Biblia Sacra Polyglotta* (compl. 1657)

THE LOW COUNTRIES

Holland	Literature	VONDEL, Joost van den. *Lucifer*
	Painting	REMBRANDT. *Hendrickje Stoffels as Bathsheba* (Louvre)
		REMBRANDT. *Descent from the Cross by Torchlight* (etchings)
		RUISDAEL, Jacob van. *Castle of Bentheim* (Amsterdam)

CENTRAL EUROPE

Germany	Literature	LOGAU, Friedrich von. *Teutsche Sinngedichte Drei Tausend*
	Pharmacology	GLAUBER, Johann Rudolph. *Pharmacopeia Spagyrica* (compl. 1668)

[135]

LATIN EUROPE

France	Literature	SCUDÉRY, Madeleine de. *Clélie* (compl. 1660)
	Mathematics	PASCAL, Blaise. *Traité du Triangle arithmétique* (publ. 1665)
		Correspondence between Blaise Pascal and Pierre de Fermat on Probability
Spain	Literature	MORETO, Agustín. *El Desdén con el Desdén*
		MORETO, Agustín. *El lindo Don Diego*
		MORETO, Agustín. *El valiente Justiciero*

SLAVONIC EUROPE

Czechoslovakia	Education	COMENIUS, Johan Amos. *Orbis Sensualium Pictus* (first pr. 1658)

1655

BRITISH ISLES

England	History	FULLER, Thomas. *The Church History of Britain*
	Mathematics	WALLIS, John. *Tractatus de Sectionibus Conicis*
	Politics	HOBBES, Thomas. *Letters upon Liberty and Necessity*

THE LOW COUNTRIES

Holland	Painting	MAES, Nicolas. *The Idle Servant* (Nat. Gal. Lond.)
		REMBRANDT. *Man in Armour* (Glasgow)
		REMBRANDT. *The "large" Ecce Homo* (etchings)
		REMBRANDT. *The Sacrifice of Abraham* (etchings)
		TERBORCH, Gerard. *The Consultation* (Berlin)

LATIN EUROPE

France	Astronomy	GASSENDI, Pierre. *De Rebus Coelestibus*
Italy	Architecture	CORTONA, Pietro da. S. Maria della Pace, Rome, bgn. (compl. 1657)
Spain	Painting	MURILLO, Bartolomé Esteban. *St. Isidor* (Seville)

1656

BRITISH ISLES

England	Literature	COWLEY, Abraham. *Poems*
	Mathematics	WALLIS, John. *Arithmetica Infinitorum*

England   Medicine   WHARTON, Thomas. *Adenographia sive Glandularum totius Corporis Descriptio*

    Politics   HARRINGTON, James. *The Commonwealth of Oceana*

    Theatre   London, first English opera perf. at Sir William Davenant's Theatre (*Siege of Rhodes*, Sir William Davenant)

THE LOW COUNTRIES

Holland   Painting   REMBRANDT. *Blessing of Abraham* (Cassel)

    REMBRANDT. *St. John the Baptist preaching in the Wilderness* (Berlin)

    VERMEER VAN DELFT, Jan. *Conversation* (Dresden)

    Physics   HUYGENS, Christian. Inv. pendulum-clock

NORTHERN EUROPE

Denmark   Astronomy   Copenhagen, Astronomical Tower blt.

CENTRAL EUROPE

Germany   Chemistry   GLAUBER, Johann Rudolph. *Miraculum Mundi*

LATIN EUROPE

France   Architecture   BRUANT, Liberal. Hôpital de la Salpêtrière, Paris, bgn. (compl. 1668)

    Literature   CYRANO DE BERGERAC, Savinien. *Le Pédant Joué.*

    MOLIÈRE. *Le Dépit amoureux* (first perf.; first pr. 1663)

Italy   Academies   Accademia degli Arcadi, Rome, fnd.

Spain   Painting   MURILLO, Bartolomé Esteban. *St. Anthony of Padua* (Seville)

    VELÁZQUEZ, Diego de Silva. *The Minions* (*Las Meninas*). (Madrid)

1657

BRITISH ISLES

England   Universities   Durham (re-fnd. 1832)

CENTRAL EUROPE

Germany   Literature   ANGELUS SILESIUS, Johann Scheffler. *Cherubinischer Wandersmann*

LATIN EUROPE

France   Philosophy   PASCAL, Blaise. *Lettres Provinciales* (*Lettres de Louis Montalte à un Provincial de ses amis . . .*)

    Theatre   AUBIGNAC, François-Hédelin d'. *Pratique du Théâtre*

Italy	Academies	Accademia del Cimento fnd.
Spain	Painting	VELÁZQUEZ, Diego de Silva. *Las Hilanderas* (Prado, Madrid)

SLAVONIC EUROPE

Czechoslovakia	Education	COMENIUS, Johan Amos. *Opera Didactica Omnia* (cont. *Didactica Magna*, written in Czech, 1628-1632)

1658

BRITISH ISLES

England	Church	The Savoy Synod
	Literature	BROWNE, Thomas. *Hydriotaphia*
		BROWNE, Thomas. *The Garden of Cyrus*
		DRYDEN, John. *Heroic Stanzas*
		HOBBES, Thomas. *De Homine*

THE LOW COUNTRIES

Holland	Medicine	SWAMMERDAM, Jan. Discovery of red blood corpuscles
	Painting	DE HOOCH, Pieter. *Dutch Courtyard* (Nat. Gal. Lond.)
		REMBRANDT. *Portrait of Nicolas Bruyning* (Cassel)
		REMBRANDT. *Jesus and the Samaritan Woman* (etchings)

CENTRAL EUROPE

Germany	Literature	GRYPHIUS, Andreas. *Absurda Comica oder Herr Peter Squentz*
		GRYPHIUS, Andreas. *Cardenio und Celinde*
	Medicine	KIRCHER, Athanasius. *Scrutinium Pestis*

LATIN EUROPE

France	Painting	CLAUDE LORRAIN; Claude Gelée. *David in the Cave of Adullam* (Nat. Gal. Lond.)
	Philosophy	GASSENDI, Pierre. *Syntagma Philosophorum*
	Societies	Société des Missions Etrangères fnd.
Spain	Aesthetics	VELÁZQUEZ, Diego de Silva. *Memoria de las Pinturas*
	Painting	VELÁZQUEZ, Diego de Silva. *Venus and Cupid* (Nat. Gal. Lond.)

1659

BRITISH ISLES

England	Theology	PEARSON, John. Exposition of the Creed

THE LOW COUNTRIES

| Holland | Literature | VONDEL, Joost van den. *Jephta* |
| | Painting | REMBRANDT. *Portrait of Jan Six* (Amsterdam) |

LATIN EUROPE

France	Literature	CORNEILLE, Pierre. *Oedipe*
		MOLIÈRE. *Les Précieuses ridicules* (first perf.; first pr. 1660)
	Music	CAMBERT, Robert. *La Pastorale en Musique* (*L'opéra d'Issy*)

1660

BRITISH ISLES

England	Literature	DRYDEN, John. *Astraea Redux*
	Philosophy	TAYLOR, Jeremy. *Ductor Dubitantium*
	Physics	BOYLE, Robert. *New Experiments*

THE LOW COUNTRIES

Holland	Painting	REMBRANDT. *Portrait of Himself* (*in old age*.) (Louvre)
		REMBRANDT. *Portrait of Himself* (*in old age*) (Nat. Gal. Lond.) (*circa*)
	Philosophy	SPINOZA, Baruch. *De Deo et Homine eiusque Felicitate*

CENTRAL EUROPE

| Germany | Literature | GRYPHIUS, Andreas. *Verlibtes Gespenste* |
| | | GRYPHIUS, Andreas. *Die gelibte Dornrose* |

LATIN EUROPE

France	Discoveries	Lake Superior and Lake Huron, by Megnard
	Literature	MOLIÈRE. *Sganarelle*
	Painting	MIGNARD, Pierre. *Portrait of Maria Mancini* (*circa*; Berlin)
Spain	Academies	Academy of Arts, Seville, fnd. by Murillo
	Literature	CALDERÓN DE LA BARCA, Pedro. *El José de las Mujeres*

1661

BRITISH ISLES

England	Physics	BOYLE, Robert. *Physiological Essays*
		BOYLE, Robert. *The Sceptical Chymist*
Scotland	Physics	GREGORY, James. Reflecting telescope inv.

THE LOW COUNTRIES

Holland Painting METSU, Gabriel. *Sportsman* (Hague)
OSTADE, Adriaen van. *The Alchymist* (Nat. Gal. Lond.)
REMBRANDT. *Hendrickje at the Window* (Berlin)
REMBRANDT. *Syndics of the Cloth Hall* (Amsterdam)

CENTRAL EUROPE

Germany Architecture ZUCCALI, Enrico. Theatine Church, Munich, bgn. (compl. 1675)
Libraries Electoral Library, Berlin, fnd.
Literature LOHENSTEIN, Daniel Caspar von. *Cleopatra*

LATIN EUROPE

France Architecture LE VAU. Palace at Versailles bgn. (compl. 1756)
Literature MOLIÈRE. *L'Ecole des Maris* (first perf.; first pr. 1660)
Italy Architecture BERNINI, Giovanni Lorenzo. Scala Regia in the Vatican blt.
Medicine MALPIGHI, Marcello. *De Pulmonibus*
Spain Painting VALDÉS LEAL, Juan de. *Immaculate Conception* (Nat. Gal. Lond.)

1662

BRITISH ISLES

England Church Act of Uniformity
History FULLER, Thomas. *History of the Worthies of England*
Physics BOYLE, Robert. Discovery of Boyle's Law
Societies Royal Society fnd.

THE LOW COUNTRIES

Holland Geography BLAEUV, Jan. *Geographia*
Painting METSU, Gabriel. *Game Dealer's Shop* (Dresden)

NORTHERN EUROPE

Denmark Medicine STENONIS; Nicolaus Stensen. *Observationes Anatomicae*

CENTRAL EUROPE

Austria Academies Academia Leopoldina, Vienna, fnd.

LATIN EUROPE

France	Architecture	LENÔTRE, André. Park of Versailles planned
	Literature	MOLIÈRE. *L'Ecole des Femmes* (first perf.; first pr. 1663)
	Philosophy	ARNAULD, Antoine. *L'Art de penser* (with Pierre Nicole)
		DESCARTES, René. *De Homine* (posth.)

1663

BRITISH ISLES

England	Architecture	WREN, Christopher. Pembroke College Library, Cambridge, bgn. (compl. 1664)
	Literature	BUTLER, Samuel. *Hudibras*, Pt. I
		SHAKESPEARE. The Third Folio (Chetwinde, London)
	Mathematics	NEWTON, Isaac. Discovery of the Binomial Theorem
	Theatre	Opening of Drury Lane Theatre
Scotland	Physics	GREGORY, James. *Optica Promota*

THE LOW COUNTRIES

Holland	Painting	REMBRANDT. *The Jewish Bride* (Amsterdam)
	Philosophy	SPINOZA, Baruch. *R. Des Cartes Principiorum Philosophiae pars I et II more geometrico demonstratae*

CENTRAL EUROPE

Germany	Literature	GRYPHIUS, Andreas. *Horribilicribrifax Teutsch*

LATIN EUROPE

France	Academies	Académie des Inscriptions fnd.
	Literature	CORNEILLE, Pierre. *Sophonisbe*
		QUINAULT, Philippe. *Astrate*
	Music	LULLY, Giovanni Battista. *Le Ballet des Arts*

HUNGARY

	History	BETHLEN, Jan. *Rerum Transsilvanicarum Libri IV*

1664

BRITISH ISLES

England	Architecture	WREN, Christopher. Designs Sheldonian Theatre, Oxford

England	Literature	BUTLER, Samuel. *Hudibras*, Pt. II
		ETHEREDGE, George. *The Comical Revenge or Love in a Tub*
		EVELYN, John. *Sylva*
		SHAKESPEARE. Reprint of the Third Folio (Chetwinde, London)
	Medicine	WILLIS, Thomas. *Cerebri Anatome Nervorumque Descriptio et Usus*

NORTHERN EUROPE

Denmark	Physics	WALGENSTEIN, Thomas. Inv. Magic Lantern

LATIN EUROPE

France	Colonization	French East India Company estab.
		French West India Company estab.
		French Company of the West estab.
	Literature	MOLIÈRE. *Le Tartufe* (first perf.; first pr. as *Le Tartuffe*, 1669)
		RACINE, Jean. *La Thébaïde*
Italy	Philology	Ed. Prin. of Petronius' *Cena Trimalchionis*
	Zoology	REDI, Francisco. *Osservazioni intorno alle Vipere*

1665

BRITISH ISLES

England	Chemistry	HOOKE, Robert. *Micrographia*
	Medicine	LOWER, Richard. First transfusion of blood from dog to dog.
	Poetics	DRYDEN, John. *Essay of Dramatic Poesy*
	Press	*London Gazette* fnd.
	Science	*Philosophical Transactions* iss.
	Theatre	Début of Nell Gwyn

THE LOW COUNTRIES

Holland	Painting	REMBRANDT. *Boaz and Ruth* (Amsterdam)
	Philosophy	GEULINCX, Arnold. *De Virtute et primis eius Proprietatibus* (ed. as *Ethica*, 1675)

CENTRAL EUROPE

Germany	Literature	HOFMANN VON HOFMANNSWALDAU, Christian. *Heldengedichte*
		LOHENSTEIN, Daniel Caspar von. *Epicharis*
		LOHENSTEIN, Daniel Caspar von. *Agrippina*
	Universities	Kiel fnd.

LATIN EUROPE

France   Literature   BRANTÔME, Pierre de Bourdeilles, Seigneur de. *Mémoires contenant les Vies des Dames galantes de son temps* (posth.)

LA FONTAINE, Jean de. *Contes et Nouvelles*

LA ROCHEFOUCAULD, François, Duc de. *Maximes*

MOLIÈRE. *Le Festin de Pierre* (first perf.; first pr. 1682)

RACINE, Jean. *Alexandre le Grand* (first perf.; first pr. 1666)

Mathematics   DESCARTES, René. *Ars Analytica Mathematum*

Periodicals   *Journal des Sçavans* iss.

1666

BRITISH ISLES

England   Literature   BUNYAN, John. *Grace Abounding*

Medicine   SYDENHAM, Thomas. *Methodus curandi Febres*

Physics   BOYLE, Robert. *Hydrostatical Paradoxes*

NORTHERN EUROPE

Denmark   Press   *Danske Mercurius* fnd.

Sweden   Universities   Lund fnd.

LATIN EUROPE

France   Academies   Académie Royale des Sciences, Paris, fnd.

Architecture   PERRAULT, Claude. East Front of Louvre, Paris, blt.

Crafts   Royal Gobelin Factory, Paris, fnd.

Literature   BOILEAU-DESPRÉAUX, Nicolas. *Satires*, Pt. I

MOLIÈRE. *Le Médecin malgré lui* (first perf.; first pr. 1667)

MOLIÈRE. *Le Misantrope*

Technics   Canal du Midi bgn.

1667

BRITISH ISLES

England   Literature   DRYDEN, John. *Annus Mirabilis*

DRYDEN, John. *The Indian Emperor*

MILTON, John. *Paradise Lost*

Medicine   NEEDHAM, Walter. *Disquisitio anatomica de formato Foetu*

LOWER, Richard, assisted by Christopher Wren. First transfusion in England of blood to man

Scotland   Botany   Botanical Garden, Edinburgh, fnd.

THE LOW COUNTRIES

Holland	Painting	HOBBEMA, Meindert. *Ruins of Brederode Castle* (Nat. Gal. Lond.)

NORTHERN EUROPE

Sweden	Universities	College of Antiquities, Upsala, fnd.

CENTRAL EUROPE

Germany	Literature	GERHARDT, Paul. *Geistliche Andachten*

LATIN EUROPE

France	Astronomy	Observatory of Paris estab.
	Literature	RACINE, Jean. *Andromaque* (first perf.; first pr. 1668)
	Medicine	DENIS, Jean-Baptiste. First transfusion of blood from lamb to man
	Painting	CLAUDE LORRAIN ; Claude Gelée. *Europa* (Buckingham Palace)
		CLAUDE LORRAIN; Claude Gelée. *The Ford* (Munich)
Italy	Music	CESTI, Marc Antonio. *Il Pomo d'Oro*

1668

BRITISH ISLES

England	Architecture	WREN, Christopher. Emmanuel College, Cambridge, bgn. (compl. 1677)
	Literature	ETHEREDGE, George. *She Wou'd, if She Cou'd*
	Medicine	MAYOW, John. *Tractatus de Respiratione et de Rachitide*
	Philosophy	GLANVILL, Joseph. *Plus ultra ; or, the Progress and Advancement of Knowledge*

THE LOW COUNTRIES

Holland	Painting	LELY, Peter. *Portrait of Simon Patrick* (Nat. Gal. Lond.)
		REMBRANDT. *The Flagellation* (Darmstadt)
		STEEN, Jan. *Twelfth Night* (Brussels)

CENTRAL EUROPE

Germany	Literature	GRIMMELSHAUSEN, Christoph von. *Der Abentheurliche Simplicissimus Teutsch*

LATIN EUROPE

France	Literature	LA FONTAINE, Jean de. *Fables Choisies*
		MOLIÈRE. *Amphitryon*

France	Literature	MOLIÈRE. *George Dandin* (first perf.; first pr. 1669)
		MOLIÈRE. *L'Avare* (first perf.; first pr. 1669)
		RACINE, Jean. *Les Plaideurs* (first perf.; first pr. 1669)
		SAINT-EVREMOND, Charles, Seigneur de. *Œuvres meslées*
	Medicine	MAURICEAU, François. *Traité des Maladies des Femmes grosses et de celles qui sont nouvellement accouchées*
Italy	Astronomy	CASSINI, Gian-Domenico. *Effemeridi dei Satelliti Gioviali*
	Press	*Giornale de' Litterati* iss.

SLAVONIC EUROPE

Poland	Architecture	Vilna, SS. Peter and Paul bgn. (compl. 1684)

1669

BRITISH ISLES

England	Literature	DRYDEN, John. *Tyrannic Love* (first acting; first pr. 1670)
		DRYDEN, John. *The wild Gallant*
	Mathematics	NEWTON, Isaac. *De analysi per Aequationes Numero Terminorum infinitas*
	Medicine	LOWER, Richard. *Tractatus de Corde*
	Theology	PENN, William. *No Cross, no Crown*

THE LOW COUNTRIES

Holland	Painting	VERMEER VAN DELFT, Jan. *The Geographer* (Frankfurt-on-Main)
	Physics	HUYGENS, Christian. *De Motu Corporum et Percussione*
	Zoology	SWAMMERDAM, Jan. *Bybel der Natuur*
		SWAMMERDAM, Jan. *Historia Insectorum generalis*

NORTHERN EUROPE

Denmark	Physics	STENONIS; Nicolaus Stensen. *De Solido intra Solidum naturaliter contento*

CENTRAL EUROPE

Germany	Chemistry	Brand discovers phosphorus
	Philosophy	LEIBNIZ, Gottfried Wilhelm. *Defensio Trinitatis....*
	Physics	BECHER, Johann Joachim. *Acta Laboratorii Chymici Monacensis seu Physica Subterranea* (germ of the phlogiston theory)

LATIN EUROPE

France

	Academies	Académie de Musique, Paris, fnd.
	Architecture	LENÔTRE, André. Great Terrace, Saint-Germain-en-Laye, bgn. (compl. 1670)
	Discoveries	Niagara Falls and Ohio River discovered by Robert Cavelier, Sieur de La Salle
	Literature	BOILEAU-DESPRÉAUX, Nicolas. *Epîtres*, Pt. I
		BOSSUET, Jacques-Bénigne. *Oraisons Funèbres* (-1687)
		Lettres Portugaises (attributed to Marianna Alcaforado)
		MOLIÈRE. *Monsieur de Pourceaugnac*
		RACINE, Jean. *Britannicus* (first perf.; first pr. 1670)
	Theatre	First French Opera House opnd. at Paris
Italy	Medicine	MALPIGHI, Marcello. *De Viscerum Structura*

1670

BRITISH ISLES

England

	History	MILTON, John. *History of Britain to the Conquest*
	Literature	BEHN, Mrs. Aphra. *The forced Marriage*
	Philosophy	GLANVILL, Joseph. *Scepsis scientifica; or, confessed Ignorance the Way to Science*

THE LOW COUNTRIES

Holland

	Painting	LELY, Peter. *Jane Kellaway as Diana* (Hampton Court)
		LELY, Peter. *Frans van Helmont* (compl. 1671; Nat. Gal. Lond.)
		VERMEER VAN DELFT, Jan. *The Pearl Necklace* (*circa*; Berlin)
	Philosophy	SPINOZA, Baruch. *Tractatus Theologico-Politicus*

CENTRAL EUROPE

Germany

	Literature	GRIMMELSHAUSEN, Christoph von. *Trutz Simplex*

LATIN EUROPE

France

	Literature	MOLIÈRE. *Le Bourgeois Gentilhomme* (first perf.; first pr. 1671)
		RACINE, Jean. *Bérénice* (first perf.; first pr. 1671)
	Philosophy	PASCAL, Blaise. *Pensées sur la Religion* (posth.)
	Theology	BOSSUET, Jacques-Bénigne. *Exposition de la Doctrine de l'Eglise Catholique*

| Italy | Zoology | REDI, Francisco. *Experimenta circa Generationem Insectorum* |
| Spain | Painting | MURILLO, Bartolomé Esteban. *Virgin of Seville* (Louvre) |

SLAVONIC EUROPE

| Czechoslovakia | Architecture | CARATTI, Francesco. Czernin Palace, Prague, bgn. (compl. 1682) |

1671

BRITISH ISLES

England	Architecture	WREN, Christopher. St. Lawrence Jewry, London, bgn. (compl. 1680)
		WREN, Christopher. St. Mary-le-Bow, London, bgn. (compl. 1680)
		WREN, Christopher. The Monument, London, blt.
	Literature	MILTON, John. *Paradise Regain'd*
		MILTON, John. *Samson Agonistes*
		BUCKINGHAM, George Villiers, Duke of. *The Rehearsal*
	Mathematics	NEWTON, Isaac. *Methodus Fluxionum*

CENTRAL EUROPE

| Germany | Literature | WEISE, Christian. *Die Drey Hauptverderber in Deutschland* |
| | Physics | LEIBNIZ, Gottfried Wilhelm. *Hypothesis Physica Nova* |

LATIN EUROPE

France	Academies	Académie d'Architecture, Paris, fnd.
	Colonization	French Senegal Company fnd.
	Geography	PICARD, Jean. *La Mesure de la Terre*
	Literature	MOLIÈRE. *Les Fourberies de Scapin*
	Music	CAMBERT, Robert. *Pomone* (Opera)
	Philosophy	NICOLE, Pierre. *Essais de Morale*, Pt. I
		QUESNEL, Pasquier. *Réflexions morales sur le Nouveau Testament*
Italy	Gardens	Gardens of Isola Bella, Lake Maggiore, compl. (bgn. 1632; design by Carlo Fontana and others)
	Universities	Urbino fnd.
	Zoology	REDI, Francisco. *Esperienze intorno a diverse cose naturali*
Spain	Painting	MURILLO, Bartolomé Esteban. Paintings in La Caridad, Seville (compl. 1674)

1672

BRITISH ISLES

England

Architecture	WREN, Christopher. St. Stephen Walbrook, London (compl. 1679)
Literature	DRYDEN, John. *The Conquest of Granada*
Medicine	WILLIS, John. *De Anima Brutorum*
Physics	NEWTON, Isaac. Inv. sextant

CENTRAL EUROPE

Germany

Jurisprudence	PUFENDORF, Samuel von. *De Jure Naturae et Gentium*
Physics	GUERICKE, Otto von. *Experimenta Nova Magdeburgica de vacuo Spatio*

LATIN EUROPE

France

Architecture	BRUANT, Liberal. Hôtel des Invalides, Paris, bgn.
Literature	CORNEILLE, Pierre. *Bérénice* (first perf.; first pr. 1671)
	MOLIÈRE. *Les Femmes Savantes*
	RACINE, Jean. *Bajazet*
Music	LULLY, Giovanni Battista. *Cadmus et Hermione.*
Press	*Mercure Galant* bgn. (after 1728 *Le Mercure de France*)

Spain

Painting	VALDÉS LEAL, Juan de. Frescoes in La Caridad, Seville (bgn. *c.* 1670)

1673

BRITISH ISLES

England

Botany	Chelsea Physick Gardens fnd.
Literature	DRYDEN, John. *Marriage à la Mode*
	LOCK, Matthew. *Psyche*
	TRAHERNE, Thomas. *Roman Forgeries*
Music	PURCELL, Henry. *Cadmus and Hermione*

THE LOW COUNTRIES

Holland

Physics	HUYGENS, Christian. *Horologium Oscillatorium*

CENTRAL EUROPE

Germany

Jurisprudence	PUFENDORF, Samuel von. *De Officio Hominis et Civis juxta legem naturalem*

LATIN EUROPE

France	Architecture	BLONDEL, François. Porte Saint-Denis, Paris, blt.
	Literature	MOLIÈRE. *Le Malade Imaginaire* (first perf.; first pr. 1674) RACINE, Jean. *Mithridate*
	Mathematics	LA HIRE, Philippe de. *Nouvelle Méthode en Géométrie*
	Painting	CLAUDE LORRAIN; Claude Gelée. *Aeneas at Delos* (Nat. Gal. Lond.)
	Theatre	First recorded mention of "Pierrot" in *La Suite du Festin de Pierre*

1674

BRITISH ISLES

England	Chemistry	MAYOW, John. *De Sal-nitro et Spiritu nitro-aereo*
	Literature	MILTON, John. *Paradise Lost*. Second edition

LATIN EUROPE

France	Architecture	BULLET, Pierre. Porte Saint-Martin, Paris, blt.
	Colonization	Pondicherry fnd.
	Literature	BOILEAU-DESPRÉAUX, Nicolas. *Le Lutrin* CORNEILLE, Pierre. *Suréna* RACINE, Jean. *Iphigénie en Aulide* (first perf.; first pr. 1675)
	Music	LULLY, Giovanni Battista. *Alceste*
	Philosophy	MALEBRANCHE, Nicolas. *De la Recherche de la Vérité*
	Poetics	BOILEAU - DESPRÉAUX, Nicolas. *L'Art Poétique.*

1675

BRITISH ISLES

England	Chemistry	BOYLE, Robert. *The Imperfection of the Chymist's Doctrine of Qualitie*
	Literature	DRYDEN, John. *Aureng Zebe* LEE, Nathaniel. *Nero* WYCHERLEY, William. *The Country Wife* (first pr.; acted in 1672 or 1673)

NORTHERN EUROPE

Denmark	Physics	ROEMER, Olaf. Discovery of velocity of light

CENTRAL EUROPE

Germany	Literature	SPENER, Philipp Jacob. *Pia Desideria*

LATIN EUROPE

France	Architecture	BLONDEL, François. *Cours d'Architecture*
		HARDOUIN-MANSART, Jules. Saint-Louis-des-Invalides (compl. 1710)
	Chemistry	LEMERY, Nicolas. *Cours de Chymie*
	Music	LULLY, Giovanni Battista. *Thésée*
Italy	Sculpture	BERNINI, Giovanni Lorenzo. *La Beata Albertone* (Rome)
Spain	Theology	MOLINOS, Miguel de. *Guía espiritual*

1676

BRITISH ISLES

England	Architecture	WREN, Christopher. St. Magnus, London Bridge, bgn. (compl. 1705)
	Astronomy	Greenwich Observatory opened (blt. by Christopher Wren)
	Literature	ETHEREDGE, Thomas. *The Man of the Mode*
		OTWAY, Thomas. *Don Carlos*

THE LOW COUNTRIES

Holland	Bacteriology	LEEUWENHOEK, Anthony van. Discovery of infusoria

LATIN EUROPE

Italy	Architecture	BENONI, Giuseppe. Dogana di Mare, Venice, bgn. (compl. 1682)

1677

BRITISH ISLES

England	Architecture	WREN, Christopher. Trinity College Library, Cambridge, bgn. (compl. 1692)
	Literature	LEE, Nathaniel. *The Rival Queens*
		WYCHERLEY, William. *The Plain Dealer* (first pr.; acted in 1674)

THE LOW COUNTRIES

Holland	Philosophy	SPINOZA, Baruch. *Ethica*

CENTRAL EUROPE

Austria	Universities	Innsbruck fnd.

LATIN EUROPE

France	Literature	LA FAYETTE, Marie-Madeleine de. *La Princesse de Clèves*
		RACINE, Jean. *Phèdre*
	Philosophy	DESCARTES, René. *Le Monde* (posth.)

[150]

| Italy | Academies | Accademia Fisico-Matematica, Rome, fnd. |
| Spain | Architecture | Zaragoza. Church of Nuestra Señora del Pilar bgn. (compl. 1681) |

1678

BRITISH ISLES

England   Literature   BUNYAN, John. *The Pilgrim's Progress* (Ponder, London)
DRYDEN, John. *All for Love*
DRYDEN, John, and LEE, Nathaniel. *Oedipus*
LEE, Nathaniel. *Mithridates, King of Ponthus*

              Universities   Quebec fnd.

CENTRAL EUROPE

Germany   Theatre   Hamburg. Opening of the first opera house in Germany

LATIN EUROPE

France   Architecture   LE BRUN, Charles. Hall of Mirrors, Versailles, bgn. (compl. 1684)

Spain   Painting   MURILLO, Bartolomé Esteban. *Immaculate Conception* (Louvre)

SLAVONIC EUROPE

Poland   Architecture   Warsaw. Vilanov Palace bgn. (compl. 1700)

1679

BRITISH ISLES

England   Astronomy   HALLEY, Edmund. *Catalogus Stellarum Australium*

              History   BURNET, Gilbert. *The History of the Reformation of the Church of England* (compl. 1715)
HOBBES, Thomas. *Behemoth*

              Literature   DRYDEN, John. *Troilus and Cressida*

CENTRAL EUROPE

Austria   Literature   ABRAHAM A SANTA CLARA; Ulrich Megerle. *Merck's Wien*

Germany   Literature   HOFMANN VON HOFMANNSWALDAU, Christian. *Deutsche Uebersetzungen und Gedichte*

LATIN EUROPE

France   Mathematics   FERMAT, Pierre de. *Varia Opera Mathematica*

Italy	Architecture	Palazzo Pesaro, Venice, bgn. (compl. 1710; plan by Longhena, Baldassare)
	Zoology	BORELLI, Giovanni Alfonso. *De Motu Animalium*
Portugal	Literature	VIEIRA, Antonio. *Sermões* (compl. 1748)

1680

BRITISH ISLES

England	Botany	MORISON, Robert. *Plantarum Historia universalis*
	Literature	BUNYAN, John. *The Life and Death of Mr. Badman*
		OTWAY, Thomas. *The Orphan*
	Politics	TEMPLE, Sir William. *Miscellanea*, Pt. I (Pt. II: 1690 ; Pt. III: 1701)

NORTHERN EUROPE

Sweden	Literature	ROSENHANE, Gustaf. *Venerid* (Swedish sonnets)

CENTRAL EUROPE

Germany	Literature	LOHENSTEIN, Daniel Caspar von. *Trauer- und Lustgedichte*
	Medicine	KIRCHER, Athanasius. *Physiologia Kircheriana*
	Theology	SPENER, Philipp Jacob. *Allgemeine Gottesgelehrsamkeit*

LATIN EUROPE

France	Architecture	Tuileries, Paris (compl. by Le Vau and D'Orbay; bgn. in 1564 by Philibert de l'Orme)
	Philosophy	MALEBRANCHE, Nicolas. *Traité de la Nature et de la Grâce*
	Theatre	Comédie Française fnd.
Italy	Architecture	Palazzo Rezzonico, Venice, compl. (plan by Baldassare Longhena)
	Medicine	RAMAZZINI, Bernardino. *De Morbis Artificum Diatriba* (first treatise on industrial diseases)
Spain	Painting	CARREÑO DE MIRANDA, Juan. *Portrait of Eugenia Martínez Vallejo* (Madrid)

SLAVONIC EUROPE

Czechoslovakia	Architecture	MARTINELLI, Domenico. Convent of Hradic (compl. 1730)

1681

BRITISH ISLES

England   Literature   DRYDEN, John. *Absalom and Achitophel* (Pt. I; Pt. II in 1682)
MARVELL, Andrew. *Miscellaneous Poems* (posth.)

LATIN EUROPE

France   Diplomatics   MABILLON, Jean. *De Re Diplomatica*
History   BOSSUET, Jacques-Bénigne. *Discours sur l'Histoire Universelle*

SLAVONIC EUROPE

Russia   Academies   Academy of Sciences, Moscow, fnd.

1682

BRITISH ISLES

England   Architecture   WREN, Christopher. Chelsea Hospital bgn. (compl. 1694)
Astronomy   HALLEY, Edmund. Disc. Halley's Comet
Botany   GREW, Nehemiah. *The Anatomy of Plants*
RAY, John. *Methodus Plantarum*
Colonization   Pennsylvania fnd. by William Penn
Literature   BUNYAN, John. *The Holy War*
DRYDEN, John. *Religio Laici*
OTWAY, Thomas. *Venice preserved*
DRYDEN, John, and LEE, Nathaniel. *The Duke of Guise*
Medicine   SYDENHAM, Thomas. *Dissertatio epistolaris ad Gulielmum Cole*
Physics   NEWTON, Isaac. Discovery of Laws of Gravitation
Science   BOYLE, Robert. *De ipsa Natura*
Scotland   Libraries   Advocates' Library, Edinburgh, fnd.

CENTRAL EUROPE

Germany   Literature   WEISE, Christian. *Masaniello*
Periodicals   *Acta Eruditorum Lipsiensium* bgn. (compl. 1745)

LATIN EUROPE

France   Colonization   Louisiana fnd. by Robert Cavelier, Sieur de La Salle
Philosophy   BAYLE, Pierre. *Pensées diverses à l'occasion de la Comète qui parut . . . Décembre* 1680

1683

BRITISH ISLES

England	Medicine	SYDENHAM, Thomas. *Tractatus de Podagra et Hydrope*
	Music	PURCELL, Henry. *Twelve Sonatas of Three Parts*
	Politics	PETTY, William. *Political Arithmetic*

THE LOW COUNTRIES

Holland	Bacteriology	Bacteria discovered by Leeuwenhoek

LATIN EUROPE

France	Literature	FONTENELLE, Bernard Le Bovier de. *Dialogues des Morts*
	Medicine	DUVERNEY, Guichard-Joseph. *Traité de l'Organe de l'Ouie* . . .

1684

BRITISH ISLES

England	Architecture	WREN, Christopher. St. Clement Danes, London, bgn.
	Literature	BUNYAN, John. *The Pilgrim's Progress*, Pt. II
	Medicine	BOYLE, Robert. *Memoirs for the Natural History of humane Blood*
Ireland	Societies	Dublin Philosophical Society fnd.

THE LOW COUNTRIES

Holland	Periodicals	Amsterdam, *Le Mercure Savant* fnd.

CENTRAL EUROPE

Germany	Mathematics	LEIBNIZ, Gottfried Wilhelm. *Nova Methodus pro Maximis et Minimis*

LATIN EUROPE

France	Periodicals	*Nouvelles de la République des Lettres* bgn. (ed. Bayle)
	Philosophy	MALEBRANCHE, Nicolas. *Traité de la Morale*
	Societies	Frères de la Doctrine Chrétienne fnd. by Jean-Baptiste de La Salle
Spain	History	SOLÍS, Antonio de. *Historia de la Conquista de México*

1685

BRITISH ISLES

England   Literature   SHAKESPEARE. *The Fourth Folio* (Herringman, Brewster and Bentley, London)

LATIN EUROPE

France   Architecture   HARDOUIN-MANSART, Jules. Orangerie, Versailles, bgn.

    Church   Revocation of the Edict of Nantes

    Mathematics   LA HIRE, Philippe. *Sectiones Conicae*

    Medicine   VIEUSSENS, Raymond de. *Neurographia universalis*

    Music   LULLY, Giovanni Battista. *Le Temple de la Paix*

Spain   Painting   COELLO, Claudio. *Sagrada Forma* (Adoration of the Host; Escorial) (*circa*)

SLAVONIC EUROPE

Russia   Academies   Slavo-Greco-Latin Academy, Moscow, fnd.

1686

BRITISH ISLES

England   Botany   RAY, John. *Historia Plantarum* (compl. 1704)

    Medicine   SYDENHAM, Thomas. *Schedula monitoria de novae Febris Ingressu*

    Meteorology   HALLEY, Edmund. First meteorological map

THE LOW COUNTRIES

Holland   Periodicals   *Bibliothèque Universelle* at Amsterdam bgn. (ed. Le Clerc)

CENTRAL EUROPE

Austria   Literature   ABRAHAM A SANTA CLARA; Ulrich Megerle. *Judas der Ertzschelm* (compl. 1695)

Germany   Mathematics   LEIBNIZ, Gottfried Wilhelm. *De Geometria recondita*

LATIN EUROPE

France   Literature   QUINAULT, PHILIPPE. *Armide*

    Music   LULLY, Giovanni Battista. *Armide et Renaud*

    Philosophy   FONTENELLE, Bernard Le Bovier de. *Entretiens sur la Pluralité des Mondes*

    Schools   Collège de Saint-Cyr fnd. by Madame de Maintenon

1687

BRITISH ISLES

England Literature DRYDEN, John. *The Hind and the Panther*
Mathematics NEWTON, Isaac. *Philosophiae Naturalis Principia Mathematica*
Painting KNELLER, Godfrey. *A Chinese Convert* (Kens. Palace)

CENTRAL EUROPE

Germany Philosophy TSCHIRNHAUS, Ehrenfried Walter von. *Medicina Mentis*

LATIN EUROPE

France Architecture HARDOUIN-MANSART, Jules. Grand Trianon, Versailles, blt.
Education FÉNELON, François de Salignac de la Mothe. *L'Education des Filles*
Gardens LENÔTRE, André. Gardens of Versailles compl.
Philosophy FONTENELLE, Bernard Le Bovier de. *Histoire des Oracles*
Physics AMONTONS, Guillaume. Inv. hygroscope
PAPIN, Denis. Inv. steam-cylinder

1688

BRITISH ISLES

England Colonization Bombay fnd.
Literature BEHN, Mrs. Aphra. *Oroonoko*
Politics HALIFAX, George Savile, Marquis of. *The Character of a Trimmer* (written in 1684)

THE LOW COUNTRIES

Holland Physics GEULINCX, Arnold. *Physica Vera*

LATIN EUROPE

France Aesthetics FONTENELLE, Bernard Le Bovier de. *Digression sur les Anciens et les Modernes*
Literature LA BRUYÈRE, Jean de. *Les Caractères de Théophraste, traduits du Grec*
Painting LE BRUN, Charles. *Adoration of the Shepherds* (Louvre)
Theology BOSSUET, Jacques-Bénigne. *Histoire des Variations des Eglises Protestantes*

SLAVONIC EUROPE

Poland Architecture BELLOTTI, Giuseppe, and TYLLMANS. Krasinski Palace, Warsaw, bgn. (compl. 1694)

[156]

1689

BRITISH ISLES

England	Church	Toleration Act
	Literature	LEE, Nathaniel. *The Princess of Cleve*
	Medicine	MORTON, Richard. *Phthisiologia seu Exercitatio de Phthisi*
	Music	PURCELL, Henry. *Dido and Aeneas*
	Philosophy	LOCKE, John. *A Letter concerning Toleration* (*Epistola de Tolerantia*)
	Politics	COLLIER, Jeremy. *The History of Passive Obedience* SELDEN, John. *Table-Talk* (posth.)

THE LOW COUNTRIES

Holland	Painting	HOBBEMA, Meindert. *The Avenue, Middelharnis, Holland* (Nat. Gal. Lond.)

CENTRAL EUROPE

Germany	Literature	LOHENSTEIN, Daniel Caspar von. *Arminius und Thusnelda*

LATIN EUROPE

France	Literature	RACINE, Jean. *Esther*
Spain	Literature	JUANA INÉS DE LA CRUZ. *Inundación castálida de la única poetisa, Musa décima*

1690

BRITISH ISLES

England	Colonization	Calcutta. English factory estab.
	Literature	DRYDEN, John. *Amphitryon* (music by Purcell) DRYDEN, John. *Don Sebastian* LEE, Nathaniel. *Massacre of Paris*
	Music	PURCELL, Henry. *Amphitryon* (text by Dryden) PURCELL, Henry. *Dioclesian*
	Philosophy	LOCKE, John. *An Essay concerning Humane Understanding*
	Politics	LOCKE, John. *Two Treatises of Government*
	Press	*Worcester Postman* bgn.

THE LOW COUNTRIES

Holland	Physics	HUYGENS, Christian. *Traité de la Lumière*

LATIN EUROPE

Italy	Academies	Accademia degli Arcadi, Rome, re-fnd.

1691

BRITISH ISLES

England Medicine HAVERS, Clopton. *Osteologia Nova*
Music PURCELL, Henry. *King Arthur*
Philology BENTLEY, Richard. *Epistola ad Joannem Millium*

THE LOW COUNTRIES

Flanders Architecture Brussels, Guild Houses blt.
Holland Philosophy GEULINCX, Arnold. *Metaphysica Vera*

LATIN EUROPE

France Literature RACINE, Jean. *Athalie*

1692

BRITISH ISLES

England Medicine SYDENHAM, Thomas. *Processus Integri in Morbis fere omnibus curandis*
Music PURCELL, Henry. *The Fairy Queen*
PURCELL, Henry. *The Libertine*
Theology BURNET, Thomas. *Archaeologia Philosophica*

LATIN EUROPE

France Aesthetics PERRAULT, Charles. *Parallèle des Anciens et des Modernes* (compl. 1696)

1693

BRITISH ISLES

England Education LOCKE, John. *Some Thoughts concerning Education*
Literature CONGREVE, William. *The Old Bachelor*
Zoology RAY, John. *Synopsis methodica Animalium quadrupedum et Serpentini Generis*

CENTRAL EUROPE

Austria Architecture HILDEBRANDT, Johann Lucas von. Vienna, Belvedere Palace planned (blt. 1714 and 1721-23)
Germany Jurisprudence LEIBNIZ, Gottfried Wilhelm. *Codex Juris Gentium Diplomaticus*
Universities Halle fnd.

LATIN EUROPE

Italy Music SCARLATTI, Alessandro. *Teodora*

1694

BRITISH ISLES

England	Biography	Fox, George. *Journal*
	Literature	Congreve, William. *The Double-Dealer*
		Dryden, John. *Love Triumphant*
	Music	Purcell, Henry. *Te Deum*
		Purcell, Henry. *Timon of Athens*

CENTRAL EUROPE

Germany	Philosophy	Leibniz, Gottfried Wilhelm. *De Primae Philosophiae Emendatione*

LATIN EUROPE

France	Aesthetics	Boileau-Despréaux, Nicolas. *Les Réflexions sur Longin* (compl. 1710)
	Philology	*Dictionnaire de l'Académie*
	Theatre	Bossuet, Jacques-Bénigne. *Maximes sur la Comédie*

1695

BRITISH ISLES

England	Literature	Congreve, William. *Love for Love*
	Music	Purcell, Henry. *The Tempest*
	Philosophy	Locke, John. *The Reasonableness of Christianity*
	Press	*The Lincoln, Rutland and Stamford Mercury* bgn.

THE LOW COUNTRIES

Holland	Bacteriology	Leeuwenhoek, Anthony van. *Arcana Naturae Detecta*

CENTRAL EUROPE

Austria	Architecture	Fischer von Erlach, Johann Bernhard. Palace at Schoenbrunn (compl. *c.* 1744)
Germany	Architecture	Nehring, Johann Arnold, and Schlueter, Johann Andreas. Arsenal (Zeughaus), Berlin (compl. 1707)
	Education	Francke, August Hermann. Estab. Orphan Asylum, Halle
	Philosophy	Leibniz, Gottfried Wilhelm. *Nouveau Système de la Nature*

LATIN EUROPE

France	Philology	Bayle, Pierre. *Dictionnaire Historique et Critique* (compl. 1697)
	Physics	La Hire, Philippe de. *Traité de Mécanique*

[159]

1696

BRITISH ISLES

England   Architecture   WREN, Christopher. Greenwich Hospital bgn. (compl. 1705)
       Colonization   Fort William (Calcutta) fnd.
       Theology   TOLAND, John. *Christianity not mysterious*

CENTRAL EUROPE

Austria   Architecture   FISCHER VON ERLACH, Johann Bernhard. Collegiate Church (Collegienkirche), Salzburg (compl. 1707)
Germany   Academies   Academy of Arts, Berlin, fnd.
       Literature   REUTER, Christian. *Schelmuffsky*

LATIN EUROPE

France   Architecture   HARDOUIN-MANSART, Jules. Palace Chapel, Versailles, bgn. (compl. 1710)
       Literature   REGNARD, Jean François. *Le Joueur*

1697

BRITISH ISLES

England   Literature   CONGREVE, William. *The Mourning Bride*
                     DRYDEN, John. *Alexander's Feast*
                     DRYDEN, John. *The Works of Virgil*
                     VANBRUGH, John. *The Provok'd Wife*
                     VANBRUGH, John. *The Relapse*
       Travels   DAMPIER, William. *A New Voyage round the World*

CENTRAL EUROPE

Germany   Chemistry   STAHL, Georg Ernst. *Zymotechnia Fundamentalis* (development of phlogiston theory)

LATIN EUROPE

France   Literature   PERRAULT, Charles. *Contes de ma Mère de l'Oye*
       Theology   FÉNELON, François de Salignac de la Mothe. *Explication des Maximes des Saints*

1698

BRITISH ISLES

England   Medicine   HARRIS, Walter. *De Morbis acutis Infantum*
       Physics   NEWTON, Isaac. Discovery of velocity of sound

[160]

LATIN EUROPE

France	Theology	BOSSUET, Jacques-Bénigne. *Relation sur le Quiétisme*

1699

BRITISH ISLES

England	Medicine	TYSON, Edward. *Orang-Outang, sive Homo Silvestris*
	Philology	BENTLEY, Richard. *A Dissertation upon the Epistles of Phalaris*
	Philosophy	SHAFTESBURY, Anthony Ashley, Earl of. *An Enquiry concerning Virtue*
	Societies	Society for Promoting Christian Knowledge fnd.
	Theatre	COLLIER, Jeremy. *A Short View of the Immorality and Profaneness of the English Stage*
Scotland	Press	*Edinburgh Gazette* fnd.

CENTRAL EUROPE

Germany	Architecture	GOETHE, Johann Friedrich Eosander, Freiherr von, and SCHLUETER, Andreas. S. Front of Palace, Berlin, bgn. (compl. 1706)

LATIN EUROPE

France	Architecture	HARDOUIN-MANSART, Jules. Place Vendôme, Paris, planned
	Literature	FÉNELON, François de Salignac de la Mothe. *Les Aventures de Télémaque*

1700

BRITISH ISLES

England	Literature	CONGREVE, William. *The Way of the World*
		DRYDEN, John. *Fables, ancient and modern*

CENTRAL EUROPE

Germany	Academies	Academy of Sciences, Berlin, fnd.
	Sculpture	SCHLUETER, Andreas. Statue of Elector Frederick William of Brandenburg (Berlin)

LATIN EUROPE

France	Literature	REGNARD, Jean-François. *Le Retour Imprévu*
Italy	Music	CORELLI, Arcangelo. *XII Suonate a violino e violone o cembalo*

[161]

1701

BRITISH ISLES

England	Politics	DEFOE, Daniel. *The True-born English-man*
	Societies	Society for the Propagation of the Gospel in Foreign Parts fnd.
	Universities	Yale University at New Haven (Conn.) fnd.

CENTRAL EUROPE

Germany Jurisprudence THOMASIUS, Christian. *De Crimine Magiae*

LATIN EUROPE

France	Colonization	La Ville d'Etroit (Detroit, Mich.) fnd.
	Painting	RIGAUD, Hyacinthe. *Portrait of King Louis XIV* (Louvre)
	Periodicals	*Journal de Trévoux* bgn. (compl. 1767)

SLAVONIC EUROPE

Czechoslovakia Architecture FISCHER VON ERLACH, Johann Bernhard. Clam-Gallas Palace, Prague, bgn. (compl. 1712)

1702

BRITISH ISLES

England	Architecture	HAWKSMOOR, Nicholas, and VANBRUGH, John. Howard Castle bgn. (compl. 1714)
	History	CLARENDON, Edward Hyde, Earl of. *The History of the Rebellion and Civil Wars in England* (posth., bgn. 1641)
	Literature	STEELE, Richard. *The Funeral or Grief à la Mode*
		VANBRUGH, John. *The False Friend*
	Politics	DEFOE, Daniel. *The Shortest Way with the Dissenters*
	Press	*Daily Courant* fnd. (first daily newspaper in Great Britain)

CENTRAL EUROPE

Austria	Architecture	FISCHER VON ERLACH, Johann Bernhard. Peterskirche, Vienna, bgn. (compl. 1713)
		PRANDAUER, Jakob. Church at Melk bgn. (compl. 1726)
Germany	Universities	Breslau fnd.

LATIN EUROPE

Italy	Architecture	FONTANA, Carlo. Church of SS. Apostoli, Rome, bgn. (compl. 1724)

1703

BRITISH ISLES

England   Literature   STEELE, Richard. *The Lying Lover*
            Travels   DAMPIER, William. *A Voyage to New Holland in* ... 1699

LATIN EUROPE

Italy   Warfare   MONTECUCCOLI, Raimondo, Prince. *Memorie sull'arte della Guerra*

SLAVONIC EUROPE

Russia   Colonization   St. Petersburg (Leningrad) fnd.
            Press   *Vyedomosti* (News) fnd. (first Russian newspaper)

1704

BRITISH ISLES

England   Literature   SWIFT, Jonathan. *A Tale of a Tub*
            Physics   NEWTON, Isaac. *Opticks*
            Philosophy   TOLAND, John. *Letters to Serena*
            Press   *The Review* bgn. (weekly, compl. 1713); ed. Daniel Defoe
                      The Boston News Letter bgn. (first Anglo-American newspaper)

CENTRAL EUROPE

Germany   Philosophy   LEIBNIZ, Gottfried Wilhelm. *Nouveaux Essais sur l'Entendement Humain* (first pr. 1765)

Switzerland   Architecture   Convent at Maria Einsiedeln bgn. (compl. 1718)

LATIN EUROPE

France   Literature   REGNARD, Jean-François. *Les Folies amoureuses*

SLAVONIC EUROPE

Russia   Architecture   Admiralty at St. Petersburg (Leningrad) bgn.

1705

BRITISH ISLES

England   Astronomy   HALLEY, Edmund. *Synopsis of the Astronomy of Comets*
            Literature   STEELE, Richard. *The Tender Husband*

England	Music	HANDEL, George Frideric. *Almira*
	Philosophy	SHAFTESBURY, Anthony Ashley, Earl of. *The Sociable Enthusiast*
	Physics	NEWCOMEN, Thomas. Inv. atmospheric engine
	Theatre	London. His Majesty's Theatre opened

CENTRAL EUROPE

Austria	Architecture	FISCHER VON ERLACH, Johann Bernhard. Schwarzenberg Palace, Vienna, bgn. (compl. 1714)
Germany	Astronomy	Berlin Observatory estab.

LATIN EUROPE

France	Literature	CRÉBILLON, père, Prosper-Jolyot de. *Idoménée*

1706

GREAT BRITAIN

England	Literature	FARQUHAR, George. *The Recruiting Officer*

LATIN EUROPE

Italy	Poetics	MURATORI, Antonio. *Della perfetta Poesia*

1707

GREAT BRITAIN

	Literature	FARQUHAR, George. *The Beaux Stratagem*
	Mathematics	NEWTON, Isaac. *Universal Arithmetic* (publ. William Whiston)
	Music	HANDEL, George Frideric. *Rodrigo*

CENTRAL EUROPE

Germany	Jurisprudence	LEIBNIZ, Gottfried Wilhelm. *Methodi novae discendae docendaeque Jurisprudentiae*
	Music	BACH, Johann Sebastian. *"Ratswahl"* Cantata (*"Gott ist mein Koenig"*)

LATIN EUROPE

France	Literature	CRÉBILLON, père, Prosper-Jolyot de. *Atrée et Thyeste*
		LE SAGE, Alain-René. *Le Diable Boiteux*
	Physics	PAPIN, Denis. *Ars nova ad Aquam Ignis adminiculo efficacissime elevandam*
		PAPIN, Denis, constr. first steamboat
	Theology	BOURDALOUE, Louis. *Avent et Carême*
Italy	Music	SCARLATTI, Alessandro. *Mitridate Eupatore*

1708

THE LOW COUNTRIES

Holland   Bacteriology   LEEUWENHOEK, Anthony van. *Arcana Naturae ope ... Microscopiorum detecta ...*

Medicine   BOERHAAVE, Herman. *Institutiones Medicae*

CENTRAL EUROPE

Germany   Medicine   STAHL, Georg Ernst. *Theoria Medica Vera*

LATIN EUROPE

France   Archaeology   MONTFAUCON, Bernard de. *Palaeographia Graeca*

Literature   REGNARD, Jean-François. *Le Légataire Universel*

Theatre   Début of Adrienne Lecouvreur

1709

GREAT BRITAIN

Literature   PHILIPS, Ambrose. *Pastorals*
            POPE, Alexander. *Pastorals*

Physics   BERKELEY, George. *Essays towards a New Theory of Vision*

Press   *The Tatler* bgn. (ed. Steele)

THE LOW COUNTRIES

Holland   Medicine   BOERHAAVE, Herman. *Aphorismi*

CENTRAL EUROPE

Germany   Porcelain   BOETTGER, Johann Gottfried. Inv. Porcelain

LATIN EUROPE

France   Church   Destruction of Port-Royal-des-Champs (end of Jansenism)

Literature   CRÉBILLON, père, Prosper-Jolyot de. *Electre*
            LE SAGE, Alain-René. *Turcaret*

Theology   BOURDALOUE, Louis. *Mystères*

Italy   Music   CRISTOFORI, Bartolommeo. Inv. the piano-forte

Portugal   Aeronautics   GUSMÃO, Bartholomeu Lourenço. Makes first balloon ascent, Lisbon

[165]

1710

GREAT BRITAIN

Architecture	WREN, Christopher. Compl. St. Paul's, London
Colonization	English South Sea Company fnd.
Music	HANDEL, George Frideric. *Rinaldo*
Philosophy	BERKELEY, George. *Treatise concerning the Principles of Human Knowledge*

CENTRAL EUROPE

Germany

Philosophy	LEIBNIZ, Gottfried Wilhelm. *Essai de Théodicée*
Porcelain	Meissen. Porcelain factory fnd.

SLAVONIC EUROPE

Russia

Architecture	St. Petersburg (Leningrad) Summer Palace bgn. (compl. 1712)
Colonization	Kronstadt fnd.

1711

GREAT BRITAIN

Literature	POPE, Alexander. *Essay on Criticism*
Philosophy	SHAFTESBURY, Anthony Ashley, Earl of. *Characteristicks*
Press	*The Spectator* bgn. (ed. by Addison and Steele)

CENTRAL EUROPE

Germany

Architecture	WELSCH, Maximilian von. Palace, Biebrich, bgn. (compl. 1721)
	POEPPELMANN, Matthäus Daniel. Zwinger, Dresden, bgn. (compl. 1722)
	NEUMANN, Johann Balthasar. Neumuenster Church, Wuerzburg, bgn. (compl. 1719)
	DIENTZENHOFER, Johann, and WELSCH, Maximilian von. Palace at Pommersfelden bgn. (compl. 1718)

LATIN EUROPE

France

Literature	CRÉBILLON, père, Prosper-Jolyot de. *Rhadamiste et Zénobie*

Italy

Archaeology	Excavations at Herculaneum bgn.

[166]

1712

GREAT BRITAIN

Astronomy	FLAMSTEED, John. *Historia Coelestis*
Literature	POPE, Alexander. *The Rape of the Lock*
Politics	ARBUTHNOT, John. *The History of John Bull*

CENTRAL EUROPE

Germany

Architecture	DIENTZENHOFER, Johann. Cathedral, Fulda, bgn.
Philosophy	WOLFF, Christian, Freiherr von. *Vernuenftige Gedanken von den Kraeften des menschlichen Verstandes*

LATIN EUROPE

France

Literature	FÉNELON, François de Salignac de la Mothe. *Dialogues des Morts*
	ROUSSEAU, Jean-Baptiste. *Œuvres*

Italy

Music	CORELLI, Arcangelo. *Concerti Grossi*

1713

GREAT BRITAIN

Architecture	HAWKSMOOR, Nicholas. Oxford. Queen's College bgn. (compl. 1719)
Literature	ADDISON, Joseph. *Cato*
Music	HANDEL, George Frideric. *"Utrecht" Te Deum*
Philosophy	BERKELEY, George. *Three Dialogues*

CENTRAL EUROPE

Switzerland

Mathematics	BERNOULLI, Jacob. *Ars Conjectandi*

LATIN EUROPE

France

Music	COUPERIN, François. *Pièces de Clavecin, Livre I*
Politics	SAINT-PIERRE, Charles-Irénée Castel de. *Projet de Paix Perpétuelle*
Printing	DIDOT, François, estab. as master-printer at Paris
Theology	FÉNELON, François de Salignac de la Mothe. *Traité de l'Existence de Dieu*. Part I

Italy

Literature	MAFFEI, Francisco-Scipione. *Merope*

ROMAN CATHOLIC CHURCH

BULL: *Unigenitus*

1714

GREAT BRITAIN

Architecture GIBBS, James. St. Mary-le-Strand, London, bgn. (compl. 1723)

Literature ARBUTHNOT, John, POPE, Alexander, and SWIFT, Jonathan. *Memoirs of Martinus Scriblerus*

GAY, John. *The Shepherd's Week*

Philosophy MANDEVILLE, Bernard de. *The Fable of the Bees ; or, private Vices publick Benefits*

Universities Worcester College, Oxford, fnd.

CENTRAL EUROPE

Germany Periodicals *Der Vernuenftler* bgn. (first German periodical)

Philosophy LEIBNIZ, Gottfried Wilhelm. *La Monadologie* (first pr. 1720)

LATIN EUROPE

Spain Academies Spanish Academy (Academia Española) fnd.

1715

GREAT BRITAIN

Architecture VANBRUGH, John. Blenheim Palace compl.

Literature POPE, Alexander. *The Iliad of Homer* (compl. 1720)

Music HANDEL, George Frideric. *Water Music* (first compl. perf. 1717)

Periodicals *The Freeholder* bgn. (ed. by Addison)

LATIN EUROPE

France Literature LE SAGE, Alain-René. *Histoire de Gil Blas de Santillane*

1716

GREAT BRITAIN

Education SHAFTESBURY, Anthony Ashley, Earl of. *Letters to a Student*

CENTRAL EUROPE

Austria Architecture FISCHER VON ERLACH, Johann Bernhard Karlskirche, Vienna, bgn. (compl. 1737)

Germany Chemistry KUNCKEL, Johann. *Laboratorium Chymicum*

Music TELEMANN, Georg Philipp. *Passionsmusik*

[168]

LATIN EUROPE

France	Music	COUPERIN, François. *L'Art de toucher le Clavecin*
	Painting	WATTEAU, Antoine. *Music Lesson* (Wallace Coll.)
Italy	Press	*Diario di Roma* bgn.

1717

GREAT BRITAIN

	Literature	CIBBER, Colley. *The Non-Juror*
	Universities	Downing College, Cambridge, fnd. (charter in 1800)

LATIN EUROPE

France	Colonization	John Law's Mississippi Company fnd.
	History	RETZ, Jean-François de Gondi, Cardinal de. *Mémoires* (posth.)
	Painting	WATTEAU, Antoine. *L'Embarquement pour Cythère* (Louvre)
Italy	Architecture	JUVARA, Filippo. La Superga, near Turin, bgn. (compl. 1731)

SLAVONIC EUROPE

Russia	Libraries	Imperial Library, St. Petersburg (Leningrad), fnd.

1718

CENTRAL EUROPE

Austria	Porcelain	Vienna. Porcelain factory fnd.
Germany	Medicine	HOFFMANN, Friedrich. *Medicina Rationalis Systematica* (compl. 1740)
	Porcelain	Ansbach. Porcelain factory fnd.

LATIN EUROPE

France	Colonization	New Orleans fnd.
	Literature	VOLTAIRE. *Œdipe* (first perf.; first pr. 1719)
	Painting	WATTEAU, Antoine. *Jugement de Paris* (Louvre)
	Rhetoric	FÉNELON, François de Salignac de la Mothe. *Dialogues sur l'Eloquence* (written 1681-86)
Italy	Architecture	JUVARA, Filippo. Palazzo Madama, Turin, bgn. (compl. 1720)

1719

GREAT BRITAIN

	Literature	DEFOE, Daniel. *The Life and strange surprising Adventures of Robinson Crusoe*

[169]

NORTHERN EUROPE

Denmark   Literature   HOLBERG, Ludvig. *Peder Paars* (compl. 1720)

CENTRAL EUROPE

Germany   Architecture   DIENTZENHOFER, Johann. Church of Banz bgn.

              Philosophy   LEIBNIZ, Gottfried Wilhelm. *Principes de la Nature et de la Grâce*

LATIN EUROPE

France   Archaeology   MARIVAUX, Pierre-Carlet de Chamblain de. *L'Antiquité expliquée*

              Painting   LANCRET, Nicolas. *Une Conversation galante* (Wall. Coll. Lond.)

                              WATTEAU, Antoine. *Gilles* (Louvre)

1720

GREAT BRITAIN

Libraries   Cambridge University Library fnd.

Literature   DEFOE, Daniel. *Adventures of Captain Singleton*

Mathematics   MACLAURIN, Colin. *De Linearum Geometricarum Proprietatibus*

                      MACLAURIN, Colin. *Geometria Organica*

Music   HANDEL, George Frideric. *Suite de Pièces pour le Clavecin*

Theatre   Old Haymarket Theatre opened

CENTRAL EUROPE

Germany   Architecture   WELSCH, Maximilian von, and NEUMANN, Johann Balthasar. Palace at Bruchsal bgn. (compl. *c.* 1755)

                      FREIMONT, Clément, and d'HAUBERAT, Guillaume. Palace, Mannheim (compl. 1729 and 1749-60)

              Porcelain   Bayreuth. Porcelain factory fnd.

LATIN EUROPE

France   Painting   WATTEAU, Antoine. *Bal sous la Colonnade* (*circa* ; Dulwich)

                      WATTEAU, Antoine. *Enseigne de M. Gersaint* (Berlin)

Italy   Philosophy   VICO, Giovanni Battista. *De uno universi Juris Principio*

[170]

1721

GREAT BRITAIN

Architecture GIBBS, James. St. Martin-in-the-Fields, London, bgn.

Music HANDEL, George Frideric. *Acis and Galatea*

THE LOW COUNTRIES

Holland Medicine PALFIJN, Jan. First exhibition of obstetric forceps (in the French Academy of Surgery)

CENTRAL EUROPE

Austria Architecture HILDEBRANDT, Johann Lukas von. Mirabell Palace, Salzburg, bgn. (compl. 1727)

Germany Literature BROCKES, Berthold Heinrich. *Irdisches Vergnuegen in Gott*

Music BACH, Johann Sebastian. *Concerts avec plusieurs Instruments* (The Brandenburg Concertos, bgn. *c.* 1716)

Switzerland Aesthetics BODMER, Johann Jakob, and BREITINGER, Johann Jakob. *Discourse der Mahlern*

Architecture BEER, Franz, and MOOSBRUGGER, Kaspar. Church of Maria Einsiedeln Monastery bgn. (compl. 1725)

LATIN EUROPE

France Politics MONTESQUIEU, Charles de. *Lettres Persanes*

Italy Literature METASTASIO. *Gli Orti Esperidi*

Music SCARLATTI, Alessandro. *Griselda*

Spain Universities Caracas (Venezuela) fnd.

EASTERN ORTHODOX CHURCH

Establishment of the Holy Governing Synod

1722

GREAT BRITAIN

Architecture GIBBS, James. Cambridge Senate House bgn. (compl. 1730)

Literature DEFOE, Daniel. *A Journal of the Plague Year*

DEFOE, Daniel. *Moll Flanders*

STEELE, Richard. *The Conscious Lovers* (first perf.; first pr. 1756)

[171]

NORTHERN EUROPE

Denmark Literature HOLBERG, Ludvig. *De politiske Kandestøber*
HOLBERG, Ludvig. *Jeppe paa Bjerget*
HOLBERG, Ludvig. *Jean de France*

CENTRAL EUROPE

Germany Architecture NEUMANN, Johann Balthasar. Bishop's Palace, Wuerzburg, bgn. (compl. 1744)
Music BACH, Johann Sebastian. *Clavierbuechlein fuer Anna Magdalena Bach*
BACH, Johann Sebastian. *Das wohltemperierte Clavier*, Pt. I (The "Forty-eight")
Press *Vossische Zeitung* bgn.

LATIN EUROPE

France Music RAMEAU, Jean-Philippe. *Traité de l'Harmonie*
Universities Dijon fnd.

1723

GREAT BRITAIN

Politics SWIFT, Jonathan. *Letters by M. B. Drapier at Dublin*

CENTRAL EUROPE

Germany Music BACH, Johann Sebastian. *Magnificat*

LATIN EUROPE

France Literature LA MOTTE, Antoine-Houdart de. *Inès de Castro*
VOLTAIRE. *La Henriade* (clandestine Rouen ed. under the title *La Ligue*)
Italy History MURATORI, Antonio. *Rerum Italicarum Scriptores* (compl. 1751)

1724

GREAT BRITAIN

History BURNET, Gilbert. *The History of my Own Time* (posth.; compl. 1735)
Literature DEFOE, Daniel. *Memoirs of a Cavalier*

NORTHERN EUROPE

Denmark   Literature   HOLBERG, Ludvig. *Ulysses von Ithacia*

CENTRAL EUROPE

Germany   Literature   GUENTHER, Johann Christian. *Gedichte* (posth.)

                Music   BACH, Johann Sebastian. *The St. John Passion*

                                   TELEMANN, Georg Philipp. *Die ungleiche Heyrath*

                Physics   FAHRENHEIT, Gabriel Dominik. Thermometer scale inv.

LATIN EUROPE

France   Music   RAMEAU, Jean-Philippe. *Pièces de Clavecin*

Italy   Astronomy   Bologna Observatory estab.

                Literature   METASTASIO. *Didone abbandonata.*

1725

GREAT BRITAIN

                Literature   POPE, Alexander. *The Odyssey of Homer* (compl. 1726)

                                   SHAKESPEARE. *The Works of Shakespear* ... ed. by Pope

                                   YOUNG, Edward. *The Universal Passion* (compl. 1727)

CENTRAL EUROPE

Germany   Architecture   NEUMANN, Johann Balthasar. Palace at Bruehl (compl. 1728)

                Music   FUX, Johann Joseph. *Gradus ad Parnassum*

LATIN EUROPE

France   Literature   MONTESQUIEU, Charles de. *Le Temple de Gnide*

                                   SÉVIGNÉ, Marie, Marquise de. *Lettres* (posth.; compl. 1734)

                Music   Concerts Spirituels estab. at Paris

Italy   Philosophy   VICO, Giovanni Battista. *Principii di una Scienza Nuova*

SLAVONIC EUROPE

Russia   Astronomy   St. Petersburg (Leningrad) Observatory estab.

1726

GREAT BRITAIN

Literature   SWIFT, Jonathan. *Travels into several remote Nations of the World. In Four Parts. By Lemuel Gulliver*
THOMSON, James. *The Seasons* (compl. 1730)
Medicine   HALES, Stephen. First measurement of blood-pressure

CENTRAL EUROPE

Germany   Architecture   BAEHR, Georg. Frauenkirche, Dresden, bgn. (compl. 1742)

LATIN EUROPE

Spain   Philology   *Diccionario de la Lengua Castellana* (*Diccionario de Autoridades*; compl. 1739)
Press   *Gaceta de Madrid* fnd.

1727

GREAT BRITAIN

Literature   GAY, John. *Fables*
POPE, Alexander, and SWIFT, Jonathan. *Memoirs of a Parish Clerk*

CENTRAL EUROPE

Germany   Music   BACH, Johann Sebastian. *Trauermusik*

LATIN EUROPE

Italy   Universities   Camerino fnd.
Spain   Architecture   CAYÓN, Torquato. Palace and Gardens of La Granja bgn. (compl. 1743)
Literature   FEIJÓO, Benito Jerónimo. *Teatro crítico universal* (compl. 1739)

1728

GREAT BRITAIN

Literature   POPE, Alexander. *The Dunciad* (compl. 1742)
Music   PEPUSCH, John Christopher. *The Beggar's Opera* (text by John Gay)

NORTHERN EUROPE

Denmark   Discoveries   Behring Strait discovered by Vitus Behring

CENTRAL EUROPE

Germany   Literature   *Faustbuch des Christlich Meinenden*
              Rhetoric   GOTTSCHED, Johann Christoph. *Redekunst*

LATIN EUROPE

France   Medicine   FAUCHARD, Pierre. *Le Chirurgien Dentiste ou Traité des Dents*
              Painting   COYPEL, Nicolas. *Judgment of Paris* (Stockholm)
Italy   Literature CELLINI, Benvenuto. *Vita di Benvenuto Cellini* (posth.; written between 1558 and 1566)
Spain   Universities Habana (Cuba) fnd.

SLAVONIC EUROPE

Russia   Academies   St. Petersburg (Leningrad) Academy of Sciences fnd.

1729

GREAT BRITAIN

Literature   GAY, John. *Polly*
Physics   BRADLEY, James. Aberration of light discovered
Theology   LAW, William. *A serious Call to a devout and Holy Life*

CENTRAL EUROPE

Germany   Music   BACH, Johann Sebastian. *The St. Matthew Passion*
Switzerland Literature HALLER, Albrecht von. *Die Alpen*

LATIN EUROPE

Italy   Architecture   FUGA, Ferdinando. Rome, Palazzo Corsini (della Consulta) recons. (compl. 1732)
                            JUVARA, Filippo. Palace at Stupinigi bgn. (compl. 1773)

1730

GREAT BRITAIN

Literature.   FIELDING, Henry. *The Tragedy of Tragedies, or the Life and Death of Tom Thumb the Great*
               LILLO, George. *The London Merchant*

NORTHERN EUROPE

Sweden   Astronomy   Observatory at Upsala fnd.

CENTRAL EUROPE

Germany	Architecture	Schwaebisch-Hall Town Hall bgn. (compl. 1735)
	Music	HASSE, Johann Adolph. *Artaserse*
	Poetics	GOTTSCHED, Johann Christoph. *Critische Dichtkunst*

LATIN EUROPE

France	Literature	VOLTAIRE. *Brutus*
	Physics	RÉAUMUR, René-Antoine-Ferchault de. Inv. thermometer scale
Italy	Music	VIVALDI, Antonio. *Twelve Violin Concerti (circa)*

1731

GREAT BRITAIN

Painting	HOGARTH, William. *A Harlot's Progress* (engravings)
Press	*The Gentleman's Magazine* bgn.
Societies	The Philosophical Society of Edinburgh fnd.

NORTHERN EUROPE

Denmark	Literature	HOLBERG, Ludvig. *Erasmus Montanus*

CENTRAL EUROPE

Germany	Architecture	NEUMANN, Johann Balthasar. Palace at Werneck bgn. (compl. 1747)
	Literature	SCHNABEL, Johann Gottfried. *Die Insel Felsenburg* (compl. 1743)
	Music	BACH, Johann Sebastian. *Clavieruebung*, Pt. I
		MATTHESON, Johann. *Grosse Generalbassschule*

LATIN EUROPE

France	Literature	MARIVAUX, Pierre-Carlet de Chamblain de. *La Vie de Marianne* (compl. 1745)
		PRÉVOST D'EXILES, Antoine-François. *Manon Lescaut* (in " Mémoires d'un Homme de Qualité ")
		VOLTAIRE. *Histoire de Charles XII*

1732

GREAT BRITAIN

Colonization	Georgia fnd.
Music	HANDEL, George Frideric. *Esther*
Philosophy	BERKELEY, George. *Alciphron*
Theatre	New Covent Garden Theatre opnd.
	Début of Susannah Maria Cibber, *née* Arne

THE LOW COUNTRIES

Holland   Chemistry   BOERHAAVE, Herman. *Elementa Chemiae*

NORTHERN EUROPE

Sweden   Periodicals   *Svenska Argus* ed. by Olof Dalin (compl. 1733)

CENTRAL EUROPE

Germany   Literature   GOTTSCHED, Johann Christoph. *Sterbender Cato*

LATIN EUROPE

France   Literature   DESTOUCHES, Philippe. *Le Glorieux*
                              VOLTAIRE. *Zaïre*
Italy   Physics   ALGAROTTI, Francesco, Conte. *Newtonianismo per le Dame*

1733

GREAT BRITAIN

    Music   HANDEL, George Frideric. *Athalia*
                  HANDEL, George Frideric. *Deborah*
    Philosophy   POPE, Alexander. *Essay on Man*

CENTRAL EUROPE

Germany   Architecture   ASAM, Cosmas Damian and Egid Quirin. Church of St. John Nepomucene, Munich, bgn. (compl. 1746)
           Music   BACH, Johann Sebastian. *Mass in B minor* (compl. 1738)

LATIN EUROPE

France   Literature   LA CHAUSSÉE, Pierre-Claude Nivelle de. *Fausse Antipathie* (first " Comédie larmoyante ")
                  VOLTAIRE. *La Mort de César*
           Painting   CHARDIN, Jean-Baptiste-Siméon. *Lady sealing a Letter* (Potsdam)
           Politics   VOLTAIRE. *Letters concerning the English Nation* (English edition of the " Lettres Philosophiques " excluding " Sur les pensées de M. Pascal.")
           Literature   METASTASIO. *Olimpiade*
           Music   PERGOLESI, Giovanni Battista. *La Serva Padrona*
                  SCARLATTI, Giuseppe Domenico. *Pièces pour le Clavecin*

1734

GREAT BRITAIN

Printing	CASLON, William. First specimen-sheet
Societies	Society of Dilettanti fnd.

NORTHERN EUROPE

Sweden   Science   SWEDENBORG, Emanuel. *Opera Philosophica et Mineralia*

CENTRAL EUROPE

Germany

Music	BACH, Johann Sebastian. *Christmas Oratorio*
Universities	Goettingen fnd.

LATIN EUROPE

France

History	MONTESQUIEU, Charles de. *Considérations sur les Causes de la Grandeur des Romains et de leur Décadence*
Literature	GRESSET, Jean-Baptiste Louis. *Vert-Vert* VOLTAIRE. *Adelaïde du Guesclin*
Painting	BOUCHER, François. *Rinaldo et Armide* (Louvre)
Philosophy	VOLTAIRE. *Lettres philosophiques* (Rouen edition) VOLTAIRE. *Lettres écrites de Londres sur les Anglois et autres sujets* ("Lettres philosophiques" including "Sur les pensées de M. Pascal." London edition)

Italy

Literature	METASTASIO. *La Clemenza di Tito*
Museums	Museo Capitolino, Rome, fnd.
Painting	LONGHI, Pietro. *Fall of the Giants* (Palazzo Sagredo, Venice)

1735

GREAT BRITAIN

Painting	HOGARTH, William. *A Rake's Progress* (Soane Mus., London, and engravings)
Theology	WESLEY, John. *The Christian's Pattern* (transl. of Thomas à Kempis, *Imitatio Christi*)

NORTHERN EUROPE

Denmark	Astronomy	ROEMER, Olaf. *Basis Astronomiae*
Sweden	Science	LINNAEUS, Carl. *Systema Naturae*

CENTRAL EUROPE

Germany   Music   BACH, Johann Sebastian.   *Clavieruebung,*
                               Pt. II

LATIN EUROPE

France   Literature   FAVART, Charles-Simon. *Les deux Jumelles*
                 Music   RAMEAU, Jean-Philippe. *Les Indes Galantes*
                 Universities Rennes fnd.
Italy   Architecture FUGA, Ferdinando.   Rome, Fontana di
                               Trevi bgn. (compl. 1762)

1736

GREAT BRITAIN

Music   HANDEL, George Frideric.   *Alexander's
              Feast*

NORTHERN EUROPE

Sweden   Botany   LINNAEUS, Carl. *Fundamenta Botanica*

CENTRAL EUROPE

Germany   Architecture NEUMANN, Johann Balthasar.   Schoenborn
                               Chapel, Wuerzburg, bgn.
                 Music   BACH, Johann Sebastian. *Easter Oratorio*
Switzerland Medicine   HALLER, Albrecht von. *Dissertatio de Vasis
                               Cordis propriis*

LATIN EUROPE

France   Discoveries   CONDAMINE, Charles-Marie de la.   Traverse
                               of South America
                 Literature   VOLTAIRE. *Alzire*
                 Medicine   PETIT, Jean-Louis. First opening of mastoid
                               for abscess in middle ear
                 Painting   LA TOUR, Maurice. *Voltaire* (Louvre)
Italy   Music   PERGOLESI, Giovanni Battista. *Stabat Mater*
                 Porcelain   Porcelain factory, Capo di Monte, fnd.

1737

GREAT BRITAIN

Libraries   GIBBS, James.   Oxford, Radcliffe Library
              bgn. (compl. 1747)

NORTHERN EUROPE

Sweden   Botany   LINNAEUS, Carl. *Genera Plantarum*

[179]

CENTRAL EUROPE

Germany   Libraries   Goettingen Library opnd.

LATIN EUROPE

France   Geography   ANVILLE, Jean-Baptiste-Bourguignon d'. *Atlas Général* (compl. 1780)

    Philosophy   ARGENS, Jean-Baptiste de Boyer, Marquis d'. *Philosophie du bon sens*

Italy   Music   VIVALDI, Antonio. *Twelve Trios*

    Theatre   Naples, San Carlo Theatre opnd.

Spain   Philology   MAYANS Y SISCAR, Gregorio. *Orígenes de la Lengua Castellana*

    Poetics   LUZÁN, Ignacio de. *Poética*

1738

GREAT BRITAIN

History   BOLINGBROKE, Henry St. John, Viscount. *Letters on the Study and the Use of History*

Music   HANDEL, George Frideric. *Israel in Egypt*

    HANDEL, George Frideric. *Saul*

CENTRAL EUROPE

Germany   Architecture   CHIAVERI, Gaetano. Dresden, Hofkirche bgn. (compl. 1755)

    Philosophy   WOLFF, Christian, Freiherr von. *Philosophia practica universalis* (compl. 1739)

Switzerland   Physics   BERNOULLI, Daniel. *Hydrodynamica*

LATIN EUROPE

France   Painting   BOUCHER, François. *The Breakfast* (Louvre)

    Porcelain   Porcelain factory at Vincennes fnd. (transferred to Sèvres in 1756)

Italy   History   MURATORI, Antonio. *Antiquitates Italicae Medii Aevi* (compl. 1743)

    Music   JOMMELLI, Niccolò. *Odoardo*

1739

GREAT BRITAIN

Music   HANDEL, George Frideric. *Twelve Concerti Grossi*, op. 6

Painting   HOGARTH, William. *Portrait of Captain Coram* (Foundling Hospital, London)

Theology   WESLEY, John. *Journal*, Pt. I

    WHITEFIELD, George. *Sermons on various Subjects*

    Wesleyan Methodist Society fnd.

CENTRAL EUROPE

Germany Music MATTHESON, Johann. *Der vollkommene Capellmeister*
Periodicals Issue of *Goettingische Anzeigen von Gelehrten Sachen*

LATIN EUROPE

France Painting CHARDIN, Jean-Baptiste-Siméon. *La Pourvoyeuse* (Louvre)
LANCRET, Nicolas. *Fête Champêtre* (Berlin)
Philosophy ARGENS, Jean-Baptiste de Boyer, Marquis d' *Lettres Chinoises*
Italy Painting TIEPOLO, Giovanni Battista. *Institution of the Rosary* (Venice)

1740

GREAT BRITAIN

Literature RICHARDSON, Samuel. *Pamela*
Music ARNE, Thomas Augustine. *Alfred* (contain. " *Rule Britannia* ")
Philosophy HUME, David. *A Treatise of Human Nature*
Porcelain Porcelain factory, Chelsea, fnd.
Universities Hertford College, Oxford, fnd.

NORTHERN EUROPE

Sweden Zoology SWEDENBORG, Emanuel. *Oeconomia Regni Animalis* (compl. 1741)

CENTRAL EUROPE

Germany Politics FRIEDRICH II, King of Prussia (Frederick the Great). *Antimachiavell*
Theatre Début of Konrad Ekhof
Switzerland Aesthetics BODMER, Johann Jakob. *Kritische Abhandlung von dem Wunderbaren in der Poesie*
Poetics BREITINGER, Johann Jakob. *Kritische Dichtkunst*

LATIN EUROPE

France Medicine ASTRUC, Jean. *De Morbis venereis Libri novem*
Italy Literature METASTASIO. *Attilio Regolo*

1741

GREAT BRITAIN

Music HANDEL, George Frideric. *Samson*
Printing Robert Foulis's press est. at Glasgow
Theatre GARRICK, David. Début as Richard III

NORTHERN EUROPE

Denmark	Literature	HOLBERG, Ludvig. *Nicolai Klimii Iter Subterraneum*
Sweden	Academies	Swedish Academy of Sciences, Stockholm, fnd.

CENTRAL EUROPE

Austria	Theatre	Vienna. Burgtheater opnd.
Germany	Music	GLUCK, Christoph Willibald. *Artaserse*

LATIN EUROPE

France	Literature	VOLTAIRE. *Mahomet*
	Painting	NATTIER, Jean-Marc. *Mlle de Beaujolais* (Chantilly)
	Philosophy	ARGENS, Jean-Baptiste Le Boyer, Marquis d'. *Lettres Cabbalistiques*
Italy	Music	JOMMELLI, Niccolò. *Merope*

1742

GREAT BRITAIN

Literature	COLLINS, William. *Persian Eclogues* (publ. as *Oriental Eclogues* in 1759)
	FIELDING, Henry. *The History of the Adventures of Joseph Andrews*
	YOUNG, Edward. *Night Thoughts on Life, Death and Immortality*
Mathematics	MACLAURIN, Colin. *A Treatise of Fluxions*
Music	HANDEL, George Frideric. *The Messiah* (first perf.)

NORTHERN EUROPE

Denmark	Physics	CELSIUS, Anders. Inv. thermometer scale
	Societies	Danish Royal Society fnd.

CENTRAL EUROPE

Germany	Music	Leipzig, first " Gewandhaus " concert
	Universities	Erlangen fnd.

LATIN EUROPE

France	Literature	CRÉBILLON, fils, Claude-Prosper-Jolyot de. *Le Sopha*
	Painting	BOUCHER, François. *Diana leaving the bath* (Louvre)

SLAVONIC EUROPE

Russia	Architecture	RASTRELLI, Bartolomeo. St. Petersburg (Leningrad) Anchikov Palace bgn. (compl. 1753)

1743

GREAT BRITAIN

Literature FIELDING, Henry. *Miscellanies* (cont. *History of the Life of the late Mr. Jonathan Wild the Great*)

Music HANDEL, George Frideric. *" Dettingen " Te Deum*

CENTRAL EUROPE

Germany Architecture NEUMANN, Johann Balthasar. Church at Vierzehnheiligen (compl. 1772)

Switzerland Medicine HALLER, Albrecht von. *Icones Anatomicae* (compl. 1782)

LATIN EUROPE

France Literature VOLTAIRE. *Mérope*

 Physics ALEMBERT, Jean Le Rond d'. *Traité de Dynamique*

Spain Universities Santiago de Chile fnd.

SLAVONIC EUROPE

Russia Architecture RASTRELLI, Bartolomeo. Palace at Tsarskoie Selo bgn. (compl. 1756)

1744

GREAT BRITAIN

Painting HOGARTH, William. *Marriage à la Mode* (engravings)

Philosophy BERKELEY, George. *Siris*

CENTRAL EUROPE

Germany Architecture Bamberg. Town Hall bgn. (compl. 1750)

 Music BACH, Johann Sebastian. *Das wohltemperierte Clavier*, Pt. II

 Periodicals *Bremer Beitraege* bgn.

Switzerland Astronomy EULER, Leonhard. *Theoria Motuum Planetarum*

 Mathematics EULER, Leonhard. *Methodus inveniendi Lineas curvas maximi minimive Proprietate gaudentes* (Calculus of Variations)

LATIN EUROPE

France Physics ALEMBERT, Jean Le Rond d'. *Traité de l'Equilibre*

Italy History MURATORI, Antonio. *Annali d' Italia* (compl. 1749)

[183]

SLAVONIC EUROPE

Russia	Architecture	RASTRELLI, Bartolomeo. Kiev. St. Andrew's Cathedral bgn. (compl. 1753)
		RASTRELLI, Bartolomeo. Smolny Monastery, near St. Petersburg, bgn. (compl. 1751)
	Porcelain	Porcelain factory, St. Petersburg (Leningrad), fnd.

1745

GREAT BRITAIN

	Painting	HOGARTH, William. *Portrait of Himself* (Nat. Gal. Lond.)

NORTHERN EUROPE

Sweden	Botany	LINNAEUS, Carl. *Flora Svecica*
	Theology	SWEDENBORG, Emanuel. *De Cultura et Amore Dei*

CENTRAL EUROPE

Germany	Architecture	KNOBELSDORFF, Georg Wenceslaus von. Palace (Stadtschloss), Potsdam, bgn. (compl. 1751)
		KNOBELSDORFF, Georg Wenceslaus von. " Sanssouci " near Potsdam bgn. (compl. 1747)
	Physics	KLEIST, Ewald Juergen von. Inv. of Leyden jar

LATIN EUROPE

France	Painting	LIOTARD, Jean-Etienne. *The Chocolate Girl* (Dresden)
	Philosophy	LA METTRIE, Julien-Offrey de. *Histoire Naturelle de l'Ame*
Italy	Music	SCARLATTI, Giuseppe Domenico. *Esercizi per Gravicembalo*

1746

GREAT BRITAIN

	Chemistry	ROEBUCK, John. First use of lead chambers in manufacturing sulphuric acid, at Prestonpans
	Music	HANDEL, George Frideric. *Judas Maccabaeus*

CENTRAL EUROPE

Germany	Literature	GELLERT, Christian Fuerchtegott. *Fabeln und Erzaehlungen* bgn. (compl. 1748)
	Porcelain	Porcelain factory, Fuerstenberg, fnd.

LATIN EUROPE

France Painting LIOTARD, Jean-Etienne. *The Reading Girl* (Amsterdam)

Philosophy CONDILLAC, Etienne-Bonnot de. *Essai sur l'Origine des Connaissances Humaines*
DIDEROT, Denis. *Les Pensées Philosophiques*
VAUVENARGUES, Luc de Clapiers, Marquis de. *Réflexions et Maximes*

Italy Architecture MARCHIONNE, Carlo. Rome. Villa Albani bgn. (compl. 1760)

SLAVONIC EUROPE

Russia Architecture RASTRELLI, Bartolomeo. Peterhof Palace, near St. Petersburg, bgn. (compl. 1747)

1747

GREAT BRITAIN

Literature COLLINS, William. *Odes*
Painting HOGARTH, William. *Industry and Idleness* (engravings)
Universities United College, St. Andrews, fnd.

NORTHERN EUROPE

Sweden History DALIN, Olof. *Svea Rikets historia* (History of Sweden; compl. 1762)

CENTRAL EUROPE

Germany Music BACH, Johann Sebastian. *Das Musikalische Opfer*
Schools Berlin. Oekonomisch-mathematische Realschule fnd.

LATIN EUROPE

France Literature GRESSET, Jean Baptiste Louis. *Le Méchant*
Spain History FLÓREZ, Enrique. *España Sagrada*

1748

GREAT BRITAIN

Astronomy BRADLEY, James. Discovery of the nutation of the earth's axis
Literature RICHARDSON, Samuel. *Clarissa*
SMOLLETT, Tobias. *The Adventures of Roderick Random*
Mathematics MACLAURIN, Colin. *Algebra*
Philosophy HUME, David. *An Inquiry concerning Human Understanding*

[185]

CENTRAL EUROPE

Austria	Astronomy	Kremsmuenster. Observatory estab.
Germany	Literature	KLOPSTOCK, Friedrich Gottlieb. *Messias*, Pt. I
Switzerland	Mathematics	EULER, Leonhard. *Introductio in Analysin Infinitorum*

LATIN EUROPE

France	Jurisprudence	MONTESQUIEU, Charles de. *De l'Esprit des Lois*
	Literature	DIDEROT, Denis. *Les Bijoux indiscrets*
		VOLTAIRE. *Semiramis*
		VOLTAIRE. *Zadig*
	Philosophy	LA METTRIE, Julien-Offrey de. *L'Homme Machine*
Italy	Literature	GOLDONI, Carlo. *La Putta onorata*
	Music	JOMMELLI, Niccolò. *Didone*
	Theology	LIGUORI, Alfonso Maria de'. *Theologia Moralis*
Spain	Travels	ULLOA, Antonio de. *Relación de un Viaje a la América Meridional*

1749

GREAT BRITAIN

	Astronomy	HALLEY, Edmund. *Tabulae Astronomicae* (posth.)
	Libraries	Radcliffe Library, Oxford, opnd.
	Literature	COLLINS, William. *Elegy on Thomson*
		FIELDING, Henry. *The History of Tom Jones, a Foundling*
		JOHNSON, Samuel. *Irene*
	Politics	BOLINGBROKE, Henry St. John, Viscount. *The Idea of a Patriot King*

NORTHERN EUROPE

Denmark	Press	*Berlingske Tidende* fnd.
Sweden	Philosophy	SWEDENBORG, Emanuel. *Arcana Coelestia*

CENTRAL EUROPE

Germany	Literature	KLEIST, Ewald von. *Der Fruehling*
	Music	BACH, Carl Philipp Emanuel. *Magnificat*
		BACH, Johann Sebastian. *Die Kunst der Fuge*

LATIN EUROPE

France	Literature	VOLTAIRE. *Nanine*
	Medicine	SENAC, Jean-Baptiste. *Traité de la Structure du Cœur*

France Natural BUFFON, George-Louis Leclerc, Comte de.
     History   *Théorie de la Terre*
           BUFFON, George-Louis Leclerc, Comte de.
           Histoire Naturelle (compl. 1788)
     Philosophy CONDILLAC, Etienne-Bonnot de. *Traité des*
           Systèmes
           DIDEROT, Denis. *Lettres sur les Aveugles à*
           l'Usance de ceux qui voient

1750

GREAT BRITAIN

     Chemistry WATSON, William. Describes platinum
     Painting HOGARTH, William. *The March to Finchley*
           (engravings)
     Periodicals *The Rambler* bgn. (compl. 1752; ed. Samuel
           Johnson)
     Politics HALIFAX, George Savile, Marquis of.
           Moral and Miscellaneous Thoughts and
           Reflexions (posth.)

NORTHERN EUROPE

Sweden Astronomy Stockholm Observatory estab.

CENTRAL EUROPE

Germany Philosophy WOLFF, Christian, Freiherr von. *Philosophia*
           Moralis
     Porcelain WEGELY, Wilhelm Caspar. Porcelain fac-
           tory, Berlin, fnd.

LATIN EUROPE

France Literature VOLTAIRE. *Oreste*
     Painting LA TOUR, Maurice. *Self-Portrait* (Amiens)
     Philosophy MAUPERTUIS, Pierre-Louis-Moreau de. *Essai*
           sur la Philosophie Morale
Italy   Painting PIRANESI, Giovanni Battista. *Carceri* (en-
           gravings)

1751

GREAT BRITAIN

     Literature FIELDING, Henry. *Amelia*
           GRAY, Thomas. *An Elegy wrote in a*
           Country Churchyard
           SMOLLETT, Tobias. *The Adventures of*
           Peregrine Pickle
     Music   HANDEL, George Frideric. *Jephtha*
     Philosophy HUME, David. *Inquiry concerning the*
           Principles of Morals

NORTHERN EUROPE

Sweden   Botany   LINNAEUS, Carl. *Philosophia Botanica*

LATIN EUROPE

France   History   VOLTAIRE. *Siècle de Louis XIV*
    Philosophy   DIDEROT, Denis, and ALEMBERT, Jean Le Rond d'. *Dictionnaire Encyclopédique* (compl. 1772)
Italy   Literature   METASTASIO. *Il Re Pastore*
    Music   JOMMELLI, Niccolò. *Iphigenie in Aulide*

SLAVONIC EUROPE

Czechoslovakia   Astronomy   Prague. Observatory fnd.

1752

GREAT BRITAIN

Chronology   Adoption of the Gregorian Calendar
Medicine   PRINGLE, John. *Observations on the Diseases of the Army*
    SMELLIE, William. *A Treatise on the Theory and Practice of Midwifery*
Politics   HUME, David. *Political Discourses*

NORTHERN EUROPE

Denmark   Literature   HOLBERG, Ludvig. *Don Ranudo de Colibrados*

CENTRAL EUROPE

Germany   Music   QUANTZ, Johann Joachim. *Méthode pour apprendre à jouer de la Flûte traversière*
    Societies   Gesellschaft der Wissenschaften, Goettingen, fnd.
Switzerland   Mathematics   EULER, Leonhard. *Principes de la Trigonométrie Sphérique*
    Music   ROUSSEAU, Jean-Jacques. *Le Devin du Village*

LATIN EUROPE

France   Literature   VOLTAIRE. *Le Micromégas*
    Schools   Ecole Militaire estab.
Italy   Architecture   VANVITELLI, Luigi. Royal Palace, Caserta, bgn. (compl. 1774)

SLAVONIC EUROPE

Russia   Architecture   RASTRELLI, Bartolomeo. St. Petersburg, Stroganov Palace bgn. (compl. 1754)

1753

GREAT BRITAIN

Aesthetics	HOGARTH, William. *The Analysis of Beauty*
Literature	RICHARDSON, Samuel. *The History of Sir Charles Grandison*
Museums	Foundation Grant for British Museum by Parliament
Painting	GAINSBOROUGH, Thomas. *Great Cornard Wood* (Nat. Gal. Lond.)

NORTHERN EUROPE

Sweden Botany LINNAEUS, Carl. *Species Plantarum*

CENTRAL EUROPE

Germany Music BACH, Carl Philipp Emanuel. *Versuch ueber die wahre Art das Clavier zu spielen*, Pt. I (Pt. II, 1762)
MARPURG, Friedrich Wilhelm. *Abhandlung von der Fuge*

Switzerland Astronomy EULER, Leonhard. *Theoria Motus Lunae*
Politics ROUSSEAU, Jean-Jacques. *Discours sur l'Origine et les Fondements de l'Inégalité parmi les Hommes*

LATIN EUROPE

France Philosophy VOLTAIRE. *Sur les Mœurs*
Italy Literature GOLDONI, Carlo. *La Locandiera*
Painting TIEPOLO, Giovanni Battista. Frescoes in the Bishop's Palace, Wuerzburg, (bgn. 1751)

1754

GREAT BRITAIN

Crafts	CHIPPENDALE, Thomas. *The Gentleman and Cabinet-Maker's Director*
History	HUME, David. *History of England*, Pt. I (compl. 1757)

NORTHERN EUROPE

Denmark Academies Danish Academy of Arts, Copenhagen, fnd.

CENTRAL EUROPE

Switzerland Literature GESSNER, Salomon. *Daphnis*

LATIN EUROPE

France Philosophy CONDILLAC, Etienne-Bonnot de. *Traité des Sensations*

[189]

SLAVONIC EUROPE

Russia Architecture RASTRELLI, Bartolomeo. St. Petersburg (Leningrad). Winter Palace bgn. (compl. 1762)

1755

GREAT BRITAIN

Chemistry BLACK, Joseph. *Experiments upon Magnesia Alba, Quicklime, and some other Alcaline Substances* (first desc. of carbon dioxide)

Dictionaries JOHNSON, Samuel. *A Dictionary of the English Language*

Literature YOUNG, Edward. *The Centaur not fabulous*

Philosophy HUTCHESON, Francis. *A System of Moral Philosophy*

Universities Philadelphia fnd.

CENTRAL EUROPE

Germany Astronomy KANT, Immanuel. *Allgemeine Naturgeschichte und Theorie des Himmels*

Literature LESSING, Gotthold Ephraim. *Miss Sara Sampson*

Music HASSE, Johann Adolph. *Ezio*

Switzerland Mathematics EULER, Leonhard. *Institutiones Calculi Differentialis*

Psychology BONNET, Charles. *Essai de Psychologie*

LATIN EUROPE

France Astronomy BAILLY, Jean Sylvain. *Histoire de l'Astronomie* bgn. (compl. 1787)

Literature VOLTAIRE. *L'Orphelin de la Chine*
VOLTAIRE. *La Pucelle d'Orléans* (first authorized ed.)

Painting BOUCHER, François. *Portrait of Mme de Pompadour* (Nat. Gal. Edinburgh)
LA TOUR, Maurice-Quentin de. *Portrait of Mme de Pompadour* (Louvre)

SLAVONIC EUROPE

Russia Universities Moscow fnd.

1756

GREAT BRITAIN

Politics BURKE, Edmund. *A Vindication of Natural Society*

[190]

THE LOW COUNTRIES

Belgium	Periodicals	*Journal Encyclopédique*, Liège, fnd.

CENTRAL EUROPE

Austria	Astronomy	Vienna Observatory fnd.
Germany	Porcelain	Porcelain factory, Frankenthal (Palatinate), fnd.
Switzerland	Literature	GESSNER, Salomon. *Idyllen*

LATIN EUROPE

France	Philosophy	HOLBACH, Paul-Henri Thiry, Baron d'. *Le Christianisme dévoilé*
	Politics	MIRABEAU, Victor-Riquetti, Marquis de. *L'Ami des Hommes, ou Traité de la Population*
Italy	Painting	PIRANESI, Giovanni Battista. *Le Antichità Romane* (engravings)
Portugal	Societies	Lisbon. Arcadia Ulysiponense fnd.

SLAVONIC EUROPE

Russia	Theatre	First permanent theatre in Russia fnd. by Empress Elizabeth Petrovna

1757

GREAT BRITAIN

	Philosophy	HUME, David. *Four Dissertations* (incl. *The Natural History of Religion*)
	Printing	The " Baskerville Virgil " : *Publii Virgilii Maronis Bucolica, Georgica, et Aeneis*, pr. John Baskerville
	Technics	Eddystone Lighthouse bgn. (compl. 1759)

CENTRAL EUROPE

Germany	Literature	GELLERT, Christian Fuerchtegott. *Geistliche Oden und Lieder*
Switzerland	Medicine	HALLER, Albrecht von. *Elementa Physiologiae . . .* (compl. 1765)
	Philology	BODMER, Johann Jakob. *Chriemhildens Rache und die Klage*

LATIN EUROPE

France	Architecture	SOUFFLOT, Jacques-Louis. Panthéon, Paris, bgn. (compl. 1780)
	Philosophy	DIDEROT, Denis. *Pensées sur l'Interprétation de la Nature*

[191]

1758

GREAT BRITAIN

Literature	WALPOLE, Horace. *A Catalogue of the Royal and Noble Authors of England*
Painting	HOGARTH, William. *Hogarth painting the Comic Muse* (Nat. Port. Gal. Lond.)

THE LOW COUNTRIES

Holland — Medicine — VAN SWIETEN, Geerard. *Ratio medendi* (compl. 1779)

NORTHERN EUROPE

Sweden — Theology — SWEDENBORG, Emanuel. *De Coelo . . . et de Inferno*
SWEDENBORG, Emanuel. *De Novo Hierosolyma*

CENTRAL EUROPE

Germany

Literature	GLEIM, Johann Wilhelm Ludwig. *Kriegs- und Siegeslieder der Preussen von einem Preussischen Grenadier*
Porcelain	Porcelain factory, Ludwigsburg (Wuerttemberg), estab.
	Porcelain factory at Nymphenburg, near Munich, fnd.

LATIN EUROPE

France

Economics	QUESNAY, François. *Tableau Economique*
Philosophy	HELVÉTIUS, Claude-Adrien. *De l'Esprit*

Spain — Literature — ISLA, José Francisco de. *Fray Gerundio*

1759

GREAT BRITAIN

History	ROBERTSON, William. *History of Scotland during the Reigns of Queen Mary and James VI*
Literature	JOHNSON, Samuel. *Rasselas*
	STERNE, Laurence. *The Life and Opinions of Tristram Shandy*, Pts. I and II
	YOUNG, Edward. *Conjectures on Original Composition*
Museums	British Museum opnd.
Philosophy	SMITH, Adam. *The Theory of Moral Sentiments*

CENTRAL EUROPE

Austria	Music	HAYDN, Joseph. *Symphony* No. 1
Germany	Academies	Akademie der Wissenschaften, Munich, fnd.
	Biology	WOLFF, Caspar Friedrich. *Theoria Generationis*
	Literature	LESSING, Gotthold Ephraim. *Fabeln*
	Periodicals	*Briefe, die neueste Litteratur betreffend* (comp. 1766; ed. Lessing, Mendelssohn and Nicolai)
	Philosophy	HAMANN, Johann Georg. *Sokratische Denkwuerdigkeiten*

LATIN EUROPE

France	Literature	VOLTAIRE. *Candide*
	Philosophy	ALEMBERT, Jean Le Rond d'. *Eléments de Philosophie*
Spain	Porcelain	Porcelain factory, Buen Retiro (*circa*)

SLAVONIC EUROPE

Jugoslavia	Philosophy	BOSCOVICH, Ruggiero Giuseppe. *Philosophiae Naturalis Theoria reducta ad unicam Legem Virium in Natura existentium*

1760

GREAT BRITAIN

	Literature	MACPHERSON, James. *Fragments of Ancient Poetry, collected in the Highlands*
	Painting	REYNOLDS, Joshua. *Portrait of Nelly O'Brien* (Wall. Coll. Lond.)
		WILSON, Richard. *Niobe* (Nat. Gal. Lond.)

NORTHERN EUROPE

Norway	Societies	Norwegian Royal Society of Sciences fnd.

CENTRAL EUROPE

Germany	Literature	FRIEDRICH II, King of Prussia; Frederick the Great. *Poésies diverses*
	Music	BACH, Carl Philipp Emanuel. *Sonaten fuer Clavier* (compl. 1763)

LATIN EUROPE

France	Literature	DIDEROT, Denis. *Jacques le Fataliste* (publ. 1797)
		DIDEROT, Denis. *Le Neveu de Rameau* (publ. 1805)
		DIDEROT, Denis. *La Religieuse* (publ. 1797)
		VOLTAIRE. *Tancrède*
Italy	Painting	TIEPOLO, Giovanni Battista. *Madonna della Verità* (Venice)

[193]

1761

GREAT BRITAIN

Architecture	ADAM, Robert. Syon House bgn. (compl. 1762)
	ADAM, Robert. Kedleston Hall, Derbyshire, bgn. (compl. 1765)
Literature	STERNE, Laurence. *The Life and Opinions of Tristram Shandy*, Pts. III and IV

CENTRAL EUROPE

Austria	Medicine	AUENBRUGGER, Leopold. *Inventum Novum ex Percussione Thoracis Humani* ...
Germany	Music	GLUCK, Christoph Willibald. *Don Juan*
Switzerland	Literature	ROUSSEAU, Jean-Jacques. *Julie; ou, La Nouvelle Héloïse*

LATIN EUROPE

France	Painting	GREUZE, Jean-Baptiste. *L'Accordée du Village* (Louvre)
	Literature	GOLDONI, Carlo. *I Rusteghi*
		GOZZI, Carlo. *Il Corvo*
Italy	Medicine	MORGAGNI, Giovanni Battista. *De Sedibus et Causis Morborum* ...

1762

GREAT BRITAIN

Literature	MACPHERSON, James. *Fingal*
	WALPOLE, Horace. *Anecdotes of Painting* (compl. 1771)

CENTRAL EUROPE

Germany	Archaeology	WINCKELMANN, Johann Joachim. *Anmerkungen ueber die Baukunst der Alten*
	Music	GLUCK, Christoph Willibald. *Orfeo ed Euridice* (first version)
Switzerland	Education	ROUSSEAU, Jean-Jacques. *Emile; ou, de l'Education*
	Politics	ROUSSEAU, Jean-Jacques. *Du Contrat Social; ou, Principes du Droit Politique*

LATIN EUROPE

France	Architecture	GABRIEL, Ange-Jacques. Petit Trianon, Versailles, bgn. (compl. 1764)
	Libraries	Paris. Bibliothèque de l'Université de France opnd.
	Veterinary Medicine	BOURGELAT, Claude. First European Veterinary School, Lyons, fnd.
Italy	Literature	GOZZI, Carlo. *Turandotte*

1763

GREAT BRITAIN

Literature MACPHERSON, James. *Temora*
Physics EDGEWORTH, Richard Lovell. First modern Optic Telegraph constr. between London and Newmarket.

CENTRAL EUROPE

Germany Architecture BUERING, Johann Gottfried, and MANGER, Heinrich Ludwig. Neues Palais, Potsdam, bgn. (compl. 1766)
Literature WIELAND, Christoph Martin. *Shakespeares Theatralische Werke* bgn. (compl. 1766)
Music BACH, Johann Christian. *Six Concerts pour le Clavecin, deux Violons et un Violoncelle*
Philosophy KANT, Immanuel. *Der einzig moegliche Beweisgrund zu einer Demonstration des Daseyns Gottes*

LATIN EUROPE

France Philosophy VOLTAIRE. *Traité sur la Tolérance*
Italy Archaeology Pompeii excavations bgn.
Literature PARINI, Giuseppe. *Il Mattino*

1764

GREAT BRITAIN

Architecture ADAM, Robert. Kenwood Lodge, Hampstead Heath, blt.
Literature WALPOLE, Horace. *The Castle of Otranto*
Philosophy REID, Thomas. *An Inquiry into the Human Mind, on the Principles of Common Sense*
Physics WATT, James. Inv. first steam-engine
Universities Providence, Rhode Island, fnd.

CENTRAL EUROPE

Austria Music HAYDN, Joseph. *String Quartet*, op. 1 (comp. 1755)
MOZART, Wolfgang Amadeus. *Sonates pour le Clavecin, Œuvre Première*
Germany Music GLUCK, Christoph Willibald. *La Rencontre Imprévue*
Philosophy KANT, Immanuel. *Beobachtungen ueber das Gefuehl des Schoenen und Erhabenen*
Switzerland Natural History BONNET, Charles. *Contemplation de la Nature* bgn. (compl. 1765)

[195]

LATIN EUROPE

France   Colonization   St. Louis, Missouri, fnd.

                Philosophy   VOLTAIRE. *Dictionnaire Philosophique*

Italy   Jurisprudence BECCARIA, Cesare, Marchese. *Dei Delitti e delle Pene*

                Societies   Milan. Società del Caffè fnd.

                Universities Cagliari (Sardinia) fnd.

1765

GREAT BRITAIN

Jurisprudence BLACKSTONE, William. *Commentaries on the Laws of England* bgn. (compl. 1769)

Literature   PERCY, Thomas. *Reliques of Ancient English Poetry*

CENTRAL EUROPE

Switzerland   Physics   EULER, Leonhard. *Theoria Motus Corporum Solidorum seu Rigidorum*

LATIN EUROPE

France   Architecture GABRIEL, Ange-Jacques. Paris. Plan of the Place de la Concorde

            Literature   MARMONTEL, Jean-François. *Contes Moraux*

            Mathematics CONDORCET, Marie-Jean de Caritat, Marquis de. *Du Calcul Intégral*

Italy   Literature   PARINI, Giuseppe. *Il Mezzogiorno*

SLAVONIC EUROPE

Poland   Theatre   Warsaw National Theatre opnd.

1766

GREAT BRITAIN

Chemistry   CAVENDISH, Henry. *Three Papers containing Experiments with factitious Airs* (disc. of hydrogen)

Literature   GOLDSMITH, Oliver. *The Vicar of Wakefield*

CENTRAL EUROPE

Germany   Aesthetics   LESSING, Gotthold Ephraim. *Laokoon*

            Literature   WIELAND, Christoph Martin. *Agathon*

            Philosophy   KANT, Immanuel. *Traeume eines Geistersehers*

LATIN EUROPE

France Aesthetics DIDEROT, Denis. *Essai sur la Peinture*
Painting FRAGONARD, Jean-Honoré. *The Swing*
(Wall. Coll. Lond.)

1767

GREAT BRITAIN

Literature STERNE, Laurence. *The Life and Opinions of Tristram Shandy*, Part IX and end

CENTRAL EUROPE

Germany Archaeology WINCKELMANN, Johann Joachim. *Anmerkungen ueber die Geschichte der Kunst des Altertums*
Literature LESSING, Gotthold Ephraim. *Hamburgische Dramaturgie*
LESSING, Gotthold Ephraim. *Minna von Barnhelm*
Music GLUCK, Christoph Willibald. *Alceste*
Philosophy MENDELSSOHN, Moses. *Phaedon, oder ueber die Unsterblichkeit der Seele*

LATIN EUROPE

France Literature BEAUMARCHAIS, Pierre-Augustin Caron de. *Eugénie*
VOLTAIRE. *L'Ingénu*
Societies Société des Economistes fnd.

1768

GREAT BRITAIN

Academies Royal Academy of Arts fnd.
Education PRIESTLEY, Joseph. *An Essay on the First Principles of Government* . . .
Encyclopaedia *Encyclopaedia Britannica* publ.
Libraries First circulating library in England
Literature STERNE, Laurence. *A Sentimental Journey through France and Italy. By Mr. Yorick*
WALPOLE, Horace. *The Mysterious Mother*
Porcelain Porcelain factory, Plymouth, fnd.
Travels Cook's first voyage bgn. (compl. 1771)

NORTHERN EUROPE

Sweden Philosophy SWEDENBORG, Emanuel. *Delitiae Sapientiae*

[197]

CENTRAL EUROPE

Austria	Music	MOZART, Wolfgang Amadeus. *Bastien und Bastienne*
Germany	Education	BASEDOW, Johann Bernhard. *Vorstellung an Menschenfreunde*
	Literature	WIELAND, Christoph Martin. *Musarion oder die Philosophie der Grazien*

LATIN EUROPE

France	Economics	QUESNAY, François. *La Physiocratie*
	Theology	HOLBACH, Paul-Henri Thiry, Baron d'. *Théologie Portative*
Italy	Printing	Giovanni Battista Bodoni's press at Parma estab. (First " Bodoni ": *I Voti. Canto per la felicemente restituta Salute di sua Eccellenza il Signor D. Guglielmo Du Tillot, Marchese di Felino* . . .)

1769

GREAT BRITAIN

Architecture	ADAM, Robert, John, and James. Adelphi, London, bgn.
History	ROBERTSON, William. *History of the Reign of the Emperor Charles V*
Physics	WATT, James. Steam engine patented
Politics	FRANCIS, Sir Philip. *Letters of Junius* bgn. (compl. 1772)
Press	*The Morning Chronicle* bgn.

NORTHERN EUROPE

Denmark	Literature	EWALD, Johann. *Adam og Eva*

CENTRAL EUROPE

Austria	Jurisprudence	*Constitutio Criminalis Theresiana*
Germany	Literature	HERDER, Johann Gottfried. *Kritische Waelder*
	Music	BACH, Carl Philipp Emanuel. *Passions-Cantate*
		BACH, Carl Philipp Emanuel. *Die Israeliten in der Wueste*
Switzerland	Natural History	BONNET, Charles. *Palingénésie philosophique* bgn. (compl. 1770)

LATIN EUROPE

France	Economics	TURGOT, Anne-Robert-Jacques. *Réflexions sur la Formation et la Distribution des Richesses*
	Literature	VOLTAIRE. *Les Guèbres*
Italy	Museums	Museo Pio-Clementiano, Rome, fnd.
	Philology	FORCELLINI, Egidio. *Totius Latinitatis Lexicon*

1770

GREAT BRITAIN

Discoveries	BRUCE, James. Re-discovery of the Sources of the Blue Nile
Literature	GOLDSMITH, Oliver. *The Deserted Village*
Painting	GAINSBOROUGH, Thomas. *The Blue Boy* (Huntington Coll., California)
Porcelain	Porcelain factory, Bristol, fnd.

NORTHERN EUROPE

Denmark   Literature   EWALD, Johann. *Rolf Krage*

CENTRAL EUROPE

Switzerland   Mathematics   EULER, Leonhard. *Institutiones Calculi Integralis* (bgn. 1768)

LATIN EUROPE

France   Literature   BEAUMARCHAIS, Pierre-Augustin Caron de. *Les deux Amis*

DORAT, Claude-Joseph. *Les Baisers*

Natural History   HOLBACH, Paul-Henri Thiry, Baron d'. *Système de la Nature*

Philosophy   VOLTAIRE. *Questions sur l'Encyclopédie* bgn. (compl. 1772)

Italy   Economics   GALIANI, Ferdinando. *Dialogues sur le Commerce des Blés*

Medicine   COTUGNO, Domenico. First demonstration of albumen in the urine

1771

GREAT BRITAIN

Aesthetics	REYNOLDS, Joshua. *Discourses*
Discoveries	HEARNE, Samuel. Discovery of the Great Slave Lake
Literature	SMOLLETT, Tobias. *The Expedition of Humphrey Clinker*

NORTHERN EUROPE

Sweden   Theology   SWEDENBORG, Emanuel. *Vera Christiana Religio*

CENTRAL EUROPE

Germany   Literature   KLOPSTOCK, Friedrich Gottlieb. *Oden*

WIELAND, Christoph Martin. *Der neue Amadis*

[199]

LATIN EUROPE

France

	Painting	FRAGONARD, Jean-Honoré. *Souvenirs (circa;* Wallace Coll.)
	Sculpture	HOUDON, Jean-Antoine. *Bust of Diderot*
	Technics	CUGNOT, Nicolas-Joseph. Inv. of steam-automobile
	Travels	BOUGAINVILLE, Louis-Antoine de. *Voyage autour du Monde . . .*

1772

GREAT BRITAIN

Botany	*The Botanical Magazine* bgn.
Physics	PRIESTLEY, Joseph. *History of Discoveries relating to Light . . .*
Press	*Morning Post* bgn.
Travels	Cook's second voyage bgn. (compl. 1775)

NORTHERN EUROPE

Norway   Societies   Copenhagen. Norske Selskab (Norwegian Society) fnd.

CENTRAL EUROPE

Austria   Music   HAYDN, Joseph. *The " Farewell " Symphony*
Germany   Literature   LESSING, Gotthold Ephraim. *Emilia Galotti*

LATIN EUROPE

France

	Literature	CHODERLOS DE LACLOS, Pierre-Ambroise-François. *Les Liaisons dangereuses*
	Politics	MIRABEAU, Honoré de Riquetti, Comte de. *Essai sur le Despotisme*

HUNGARY

Literature   BESSENYEI, György. *Agis tragédiája* (The Tragedy of Agis)

1773

GREAT BRITAIN

Literature	GOLDSMITH, Oliver. *She Stoops to Conquer*
Painting	REYNOLDS, Joshua. *The Strawberry Girl* (Wall. Coll. Lond.)
	REYNOLDS, Joshua. *The Graces decorating Hymen* (Wall. Coll. Lond.)
Technics	First iron bridge, near Coalbrookdale, bgn. (compl. 1779)

NORTHERN EUROPE

Denmark   Literature   EWALD, Johann. *Pebersvendene*
Sweden   Theatre   Stockholm National Theatre fnd.

CENTRAL EUROPE

Germany   Aesthetics   HERDER, Johann Gottfried. *Von Deutscher Art und Kunst*
   Literature   BUERGER, Gottfried August. *Lenore*
     GOETHE, Johann Wolfgang. *Goetz von Berlichingen*
   Periodicals   *Der Teutsche Mercur* bgn. (ed. by Wieland; compl. 1810)

SLAVONIC EUROPE

Czechoslovakia   Societies   Societas Scientiarum Bohemica fnd.

ROMAN CATHOLIC CHURCH

BULL: *Dominus et Redemptor* (Suppression of the Society of Jesus)

1774

GREAT BRITAIN

Chemistry   PRIESTLEY, Joseph. Discovery of ammonia gas and oxygen
Education   CHESTERFIELD, Philip Dormer Stanhope, Earl of. *Letters written to his son, Philip Stanhope*
Medicine   HUNTER, William. *Anatomia humani Uteri gravidi*
Politics   BURKE, Edmund. *A Speech on American Taxation*

NORTHERN EUROPE

Sweden   Chemistry   SCHEELE, Karl Wilhelm. Discovery of chlorine

CENTRAL EUROPE

Austria   Music   HAYDN, Joseph. "*L'Impériale*" Symphony
     MOZART, Wolfgang Amadeus. *La finta Giardiniera*
Germany   Education   BASEDOW, Johann Bernhard. *Elementarwerk* bgn. (compl. 1793)
   Literature   GOETHE, Johann Wolfgang. *Clavigo*
     GOETHE, Johann Wolfgang. *Die Leiden des jungen Werthers*
     LENZ, Jacob Michael Reinhold. *Der Hofmeister*

| Germany | Music | GLUCK, Christoph Willibald. *Iphigénie en Aulide* |
| | Schools | BASEDOW, Johann Bernhard. Dessau Philanthropinum fnd. |

LATIN EUROPE

| France | Chemistry | LAVOISIER, Antoine-Laurent. *Opuscules Physiques et Chymiques* (theory of combustion) |
| Italy | Music | JOMMELLI, Niccolò. *Miserere* |

1775

GREAT BRITAIN

	Chemistry	PRIESTLEY, Joseph. *Experiments and Observations on different Kinds of Air* bgn. (compl. 1777)
	Literature	JOHNSON, Samuel. *A Journey to the Western Islands of Scotland*
		SHERIDAN, Richard Brinsley. *The Rivals*
	Painting	GAINSBOROUGH, Thomas. *The Watering Place* (Nat. Gal. Lond.)
		REYNOLDS, Joshua. *Miss Bowles* (" *Love me, love my dog* ") (Wall. Coll. Lond.)
	Theatre	Début of Sarah Siddons

NORTHERN EUROPE

| Denmark | Porcelain | First Copenhagen porcelain factory estab. |

CENTRAL EUROPE

Austria	Music	MOZART, Wolfgang Amadeus. *Il Re Pastore*
Germany	Literature	CLAUDIUS, Matthias. *Asmus omnia Secum portans oder saemmtliche Werke des Wandsbecker Boten* bgn. (compl. 1812)
	Schools	Hohe Karlsschule, near Stuttgart, fnd.
Switzerland	Physiognomics	LAVATER, Johann Kaspar. *Physiognomische Fragmente* bgn. (compl. 1778)

LATIN EUROPE

France	Economics	NECKER, Jacques. *Sur la Législation et le Commerce des Grains*
	Literature	BEAUMARCHAIS, Pierre-Augustin-Caron de. *Le Barbier de Seville*
Italy	Literature	ALFIERI, Vittorio. *Filippo II*
		ALFIERI, Vittorio. *Polinice*
	Physics	VOLTA, Alessandro. Inv. of electrophorus

1776

GREAT BRITAIN

Architecture	CHAMBERS, William. Somerset House, London, bgn. (compl. 1786)
Botany	WITHERING, William. *A Botanical Arrangement of all the Vegetables naturally growing in Great Britain*
Economics	SMITH, Adam. *An Inquiry into the Nature and Causes of the Wealth of Nations*
History	GIBBON, Edward. *History of the Decline and Fall of the Roman Empire*, Vol. I
Politics	PAINE, Thomas. *Common Sense*
Theatre	Début of John Philip Kemble
Travels	Cook's third voyage bgn. (compl. 1779)

CENTRAL EUROPE

Austria	Music	MOZART, Wolfgang Amadeus. *"Haffner" Serenade in D*
Germany	Literature	GOETHE, Johann Wolfgang. *Stella*
		KLINGER, Friedrich Maximilian. *Sturm und Drang* (first pr.; first perf. 1777)
		LEISEWITZ, Johann Anton. *Julius von Tarent*
		LENZ, Jacob Michael Reinhold. *Die Soldaten*
		WAGNER, Heinrich Leopold. *Die Kindermoerderin*
		WIELAND, Christoph Martin. *Die Abderiten*

LATIN EUROPE

France	Literature	CAZOTTE, Jacques. *Le Diable amoureux*
		RÉTIF DE LA BRETONNE, Nicolas-Edme. *Le Paysan perverti*
Italy	Literature	ALFIERI, Vittorio. *Antigone*

SLAVONIC EUROPE

Yugoslavia	Universities	Zagreb fnd.

1777

GREAT BRITAIN

History	ROBERTSON, William. *The History of America*
Literature	CHATTERTON, Thomas. *Poems supposed to have been written at Bristol by Thomas Rowley and others in the 15th Century* (posth.)
	SHERIDAN, Richard Brinsley. *The School for Scandal* (first perf.; pr. 1778)

| Medicine | CULLEN, William. *First Lines of the Practice of Physic* |
| Technics | Grand Trunk Canal opnd. |

NORTHERN EUROPE

Sweden — Chemistry — SCHEELE, Karl Wilhelm. *Chemische Abhandlungen von der Luft und dem Feuer* (written in German)

CENTRAL EUROPE

Germany	Music	BACH, Carl Philipp Emanuel. *Die Auferstehung und Himmelfahrt Christi*
		GLUCK, Christoph Willibald. *Armide*
	Theatre	Début of August Wilhelm Iffland

LATIN EUROPE

France	Painting	GREUZE, Jean-Baptiste. *La Cruche cassée* (Louvre)
		MOREAU, le Jeune, Jean-Michel. *Monument du Costume* (engravings)
Italy	Politics	ALFIERI, Vittorio. *Della Tirannide*

1778

GREAT BRITAIN

| Literature | BURNEY, Fanny; Mme. Frances D'Arblay. *Evelina* |
| Painting | GAINSBOROUGH, Thomas. *Portrait of the Duchess of Devonshire* (Earl Spencer's Coll.) |

CENTRAL EUROPE

Austria	Music	MOZART, Wolfgang Amadeus. *Symphony in D* (" Paris ")
Germany	Literature	BUERGER, Gottfried August. *Gedichte*
		HERDER, Johann Gottfried. *Volkslieder* bgn. (compl. 1779)

LATIN EUROPE

France	Botany	JUSSIEU, Bernard de. *Genera Plantarum* bgn. (compl. 1789)
		LAMARCK, Jean-Baptiste-Antoine de Monnel, Chevalier de. *Flore Française*
	Natural History	BUFFON, George-Louis Leclerc, Comte de. *Les Epoques de la Nature*
	Sculpture	HOUDON, Jean-Antoine. *Voltaire assis*
Italy	Music	PICCINNI, Nicola. *Roland*
	Theatre	Scala Theatre, Milan, opnd.

1779

GREAT BRITAIN

Literature	SHERIDAN, Richard Brinsley. *The Critic*
Painting	REYNOLDS, Joshua. *Portrait of Admiral Keppel* (Nat. Gal. Lond.)

NORTHERN EUROPE

Denmark

Literature	EWALD, Johann. *Fiskerne*
Porcelain	Copenhagen. Royal porcelain factory fnd.

CENTRAL EUROPE

Germany

Literature	LESSING, Gotthold Ephraim. *Nathan der Weise*
Medicine	FRANK, Johann Peter. *System einer vollstaendigen medicinischen Polizei* bgn. (compl. 1819)
Music	BACH, Johann Christian. *Amadis de Gaule* GLUCK, Christoph Willibald. *Iphigénie en Tauride*

LATIN EUROPE

France
Portugal
Spain

Sculpture	HOUDON, Jean-Antoine. Bust of Molière
Academies	Royal Academy of Sciences, Lisbon, fnd.
Literature	IRIARTE, Tomás de. *La Musica* SÁNCHEZ, Tomás Antonio. Ed. Prin. *Poema del Cid*

SLAVONIC EUROPE

Poland

Literature	KRASICKI, Ignacy. *Bajki i Przypowieści* (Fables and Parables)

1780

GREAT BRITAIN

Jurisprudence	BENTHAM, Jeremy. *An Introduction to the Principles of Morals and Legislation*
Painting	GAINSBOROUGH, Thomas. *Portrait of Mrs. Robinson as Perdita* (Nat. Gal. Lond.)
Technics	Birmingham. First metal pens made by Harrison

CENTRAL EUROPE

Germany

Aesthetics	FRIEDRICH II, King of Prussia; Frederick the Great. *De la Littérature Allemande*
Literature	WIELAND, Christoph Martin. *Oberon*
Philosophy	LESSING, Gotthold Ephraim. *Die Erziehung des Menschengeschlechts*
Universities	Münster fnd.

LATIN EUROPE

Italy

Biology	SPALLANZANI, Lazaro. *Dissertazioni di Fisica animale e vegetale*
Jurisprudence	FILANGIERI, Gaetano. *La Scienza della Legislazione* bgn. (compl. 1785)
Literature	ALFIERI, Vittorio. *Maria Stuarda*

1781

GREAT BRITAIN

Biographies	JOHNSON, Samuel. *The Lives of the most eminent English Poets*
Chemistry	CAVENDISH, Henry. Demonstration of the compound Nature of Water
History	GIBBON, Edward. *History of the Decline and Fall of the Roman Empire*, Vols. II and III
Painting	ROMNEY, George. *Mrs. Robinson (Perdita)* (Wallace Coll.)

CENTRAL EUROPE

Austria
Germany

Music	MOZART, Wolfgang Amadeus. *Idomeneo*
Astronomy	HERSCHEL, Friedrich Wilhelm. Discovery of the planet Uranus.
Literature	SCHILLER, Friedrich. *Die Raeuber*
	VOSS, Johann Heinrich. *Odyssee*
Music	Leipzig, Gewandhaus opnd.
Philosophy	KANT, Immanuel. *Critik der reinen Vernunft*

Switzerland

Education	PESTALOZZI, Johann Heinrich. *Lienhard und Gertrud*

LATIN EUROPE

France
Italy

Sculpture	HOUDON, Jean-Antoine. *Bust of Voltaire*
Music	PICCINNI, Nicola. *Iphigénie en Tauride*

1782

GREAT BRITAIN

Academies	Dublin. Royal Irish Academy fnd.
Literature	BURNEY, Fanny; Mme. Frances D'Arblay. *Cecilia*
	COWPER, William. *Table-Talk*

CENTRAL EUROPE

Austria

Music	MOZART, Wolfgang Amadeus. *Die Entfuehrung aus dem Serail* (Il Seraglio)
	MOZART, Wolfgang Amadeus. *Symphony in D (" Haffner ")*

Germany	Literature	MUSAEUS, Karl August. *Volksmaerchen der Deutschen*
Switzerland	Literature	ROUSSEAU, Jean-Jacques. *Confessions*

LATIN EUROPE

France	History	MERCIER, Sébastien. *Tableau de Paris* bgn. (compl. 1788)
	Painting	FRAGONARD, Jean-Honoré. *Fête à Rambouillet* (Nat. Gal. Lond.) (*circa*)
	Sculpture	FALCONET, Etienne-Maurice. Monument of Peter the Great (Leningrad)
	Theatre	Paris. Théâtre Français fnd.
Italy	Literature	ALFIERI, Vittorio. *Merope*
	Music	PAISIELLO, Giovanni. *Il Barbiere di Seviglia*
	Painting	GUARDI, Francesco. *The Concert* (Munich)

1783

GREAT BRITAIN

	Literature	CRABBE, George. *The Village*
	Societies	Royal Society of Edinburgh fnd.

NORTHERN EUROPE

Sweden	Literature-	BELLMAN, Carl Michael. *Bacchi tempel*

CENTRAL EUROPE

Austria	Music	MOZART, Wolfgang Amadeus. *Mass in C minor*
Germany	Literature	HOELTY, Ludwig Heinrich Christoph. *Gedichte* (posth.)
		SCHILLER, Friedrich. *Die Verschwoerung des Fiesco*
	Music	BEETHOVEN, Ludwig van. *Drei Sonaten fuer Clavier*
	Philosophy	KANT, Immanuel. *Prolegomena zu einer jeden kuenftigen Metaphysik* . . .
		MENDELSSOHN, Moses. *Jerusalem, oder ueber religioese Macht und Judentum*

LATIN EUROPE

France	Aeronautics	MONTGOLFIER, Jacques-Etienne. First balloon constr.
		LENORMAND, Sébastien. First parachute constr.
	Sculpture	HOUDON, Jean-Antoine. *Diane chasseresse*
Italy	Physics	VOLTA, Alessandro. Inv. of condenser
Spain	History	MASDEU, Juan Francisco de. *Historia crítica de España y de la Cultura española* bgn. (compl. 1805)

1784

GREAT BRITAIN

Astronomy	HERSCHEL, Sir William; previously Friedrich Wilhelm. *Account of some observations tending to investigate the construction of the heavens*
Chemistry	CAVENDISH, Henry. *Experiments on Air* bgn. (compl. 1785)
Painting	GAINSBOROUGH, Thomas. *Portrait of Mrs. Siddons* (Nat. Gal. Lond.)
Physics.	WATT, James. First modern steam-heating

THE LOW COUNTRIES

Belgium Music GRÉTRY, André-Ernest-Modeste. *La Caravane du Caire*
GRÉTRY, André-Ernest-Modeste. *Richard Cœur de Lion*

CENTRAL EUROPE

Germany History HERDER, Johann Gottfried. *Ideen zu einer Philosophie der Geschichte*
KANT, Immanuel. *Idee zu einer allgemeinen Geschichte in weltbürgerlicher Absicht*
Literature SCHILLER, Friedrich. *Kabale und Liebe*

LATIN EUROPE

France Literature BEAUMARCHAIS, Pierre-Augustin Caron de. *La folle Journée; ou, Le Mariage de Figaro*
Painting DAVID, Jacques-Louis. *Le Serment des Horaces* (Louvre)
Italy Music PAISIELLO, Giovanni. *Il Re Teodoro*
SALIERI, Antonio. *Les Danaides*

SLAVONIC EUROPE

Poland Universities Lwow fnd.

1785

GREAT BRITAIN

Botany	WITHERING, William. *An Account of the Foxglove and some of its medical Uses*
Education	Sunday Schools Union fnd.
Geology	HUTTON, James. *A Theory of the Earth* (paper read; first pr. as a book 1795)
Literature	COWPER, William. *The Task*
Painting	REYNOLDS, Joshua. *Venus* ("The Snake in the Grass"; Nat. Gal. Lond.)

Philosophy	REID, Thomas. *Essays on the intellectual Powers of Man*
Technics	CARTWRIGHT, Edmund. Inv. of power-loom
Theology	PALEY, William. *Principles of moral and political Philosophy*

CENTRAL EUROPE

Austria Music MOZART, Wolfgang Amadeus. *Piano Concerto in D minor*

MOZART, Wolfgang Amadeus. *Six String Quartets*, dedicated to Haydn

Germany Literature IFFLAND, August Wilhelm. *Die Jaeger*

MORITZ, Karl Philipp. *Anton Reiser* bgn. (compl. 1790)

Periodicals *Allgemeine Literaturzeitung* bgn.

Philosophy KANT, Immanuel. *Grundlegung zur Metaphysik der Sitten*

LATIN EUROPE

France Theatre Début of François-Joseph Talma

1786

GREAT BRITAIN

Literature BURNS, Robert. *Poems, chiefly in the Scottish dialect*

Painting HOPPNER, John. *Portrait of a Lady* (Wall. Coll. Lond.)

REYNOLDS, Joshua. *Lady Ann Bingham* (Althorpe, England)

THE LOW COUNTRIES

Holland Literature BILDERDIJK, Willem. *Elias*

NORTHERN EUROPE

Sweden Academies Swedish Academy fnd.

CENTRAL EUROPE

Austria Music DITTERS VON DITTERSDORF, Karl. *Doctor und Apotheker*

HAYDN, Joseph. *Six " Paris " Symphonies*

MOZART, Wolfgang Amadeus. *Le Nozze di Figaro* (The Marriage of Figaro)

MOZART, Wolfgang Amadeus. *Der Schauspieldirektor* (The Impresario).

LATIN EUROPE

Italy	Politics	ALFIERI, Vittorio. *Del Principe e delle Lettere*
Spain	Literature	CRUZ, Ramón de la. *Teatro o Colección de los Sainetes*

1787

GREAT BRITAIN

Economics	BENTHAM, Jeremy. *Defence of Usury*
Libraries	King's Inn Library, Dublin, fnd.
Painting	REYNOLDS, Joshua. *Angels' Heads* (Wall. Coll. Lond.)

CENTRAL EUROPE

Austria	Music	MOZART, Wolfgang Amadeus. *Eine kleine Nachtmusik*
		MOZART, Wolfgang Amadeus. *Il Dissoluto punito ossia il Don Giovanni*
Germany	Literature	GOETHE, Johann Wolfgang. *Iphigenie*
		HEINSE, Wilhelm. *Ardinghello und die glueckseligen Inseln*
		SCHILLER, Friedrich. *Don Carlos*

LATIN EUROPE

France	Literature	BEAUMARCHAIS, Pierre-Augustin Caron de. *Tarare*
		LOUVET DE COUVRAY, Jean-Baptiste. *Une année de la vie du Chevalier de Faublas*
		SAINT-PIERRE, Jacques-Henri Bernardin de. *Paul et Virginie*
	Painting	VIGÉE-LEBRUN, Elisabeth-Louise. *Portrait of herself with her daughter* (Louvre)
Italy	Literature	MONTI, Vincenzo. *Versi*
	Music	SALIERI, Antonio. *Tarare*
Spain	Politics	CAMPOMANES, Pedro Rodríguez. *Cartas político-económicas* bgn. (compl. 1790)
	Universities	Quito (Ecuador) fnd.

1788

GREAT BRITAIN

History	GIBBON, Edward. *History of the Decline and Fall of the Roman Empire* (last three vols.)
Painting	REYNOLDS, Joshua. *The Age of Innocence* (Nat. Gal. Lond.)

Philosophy	REID, Thomas. *Essays on the Active Powers of Man*
Press	*The Times* bgn.

CENTRAL EUROPE

Austria   Music   HAYDN, Joseph. *" Oxford" Symphony*
MOZART, Wolfgang Amadeus. *Symphony in C (" Jupiter ")*

Germany   History   FRIEDRICH II, King of Prussia; Frederick the Great. *Œuvres Posthumes* (cont. *Histoire de mon Temps*)

Literature   GOETHE, Johann Wolfgang. *Egmont*

Philosophy   KANT, Immanuel. *Critik der praktischen Vernunft*

LATIN EUROPE

France   Education   BARTHÉLÉMY, Jean Jacques. *Voyage du jeune Anacharsis en Grèce*

Physics   LAGRANGE, Joseph-Louis, Comte de. *Mécanique analytique*

Politics   SIEYÈS, Emmanuel-Joseph. *Qu'est-ce que le Tiers-état ?*
MIRABEAU, Honoré de Riquetti, Comte de. *De la Monarchie Prussienne sous Frédéric le Grand*

Italy   Biography   CASANOVA, Giacomo. *Histoire de ma Fuite* (written in French)

Typography   BODONI, Giovanni Battista. *Manuale Tipografico* (partial ed.; compl. ed. 1818)

1789

GREAT BRITAIN

Jurisprudence   BENTHAM, Jeremy. *International Law*

Literature   BLAKE, William. *Songs of Innocence*

Natural History   WHITE, Gilbert. *The Natural History and Antiquities of Selborne*

Painting   ROMNEY, George. *Portrait of Mrs. Mark Currie* (Nat. Gal. Lond.)

Travels   MACKENZIE, Alexander. First Canadian journey

THE LOW COUNTRIES

Belgium   Music   GRÉTRY, André-Ernest-Modeste. *Raoul Barbe-Bleue*

CENTRAL EUROPE

Germany   Literature   GOETHE, Johann Wolfgang. *Torquato Tasso*
KOTZEBUE, August. *Menschenhass und Reue*

LATIN EUROPE

France

Chemistry	LAVOISIER, Antoine-Laurent. *Traité élémentaire de Chimie*
Politics	SIEYÈS, Emmanuel-Joseph. *Déclaration des Droits de l'Homme*
Press	*Journal des Débats* bgn. *Le Moniteur* bgn.

1790

GREAT BRITAIN

Literature	BLAKE, William. *Marriage of Heaven and Hell* RADCLIFFE, Mrs. Anne. *The Sicilian Romance*
Politics	BURKE, Edmund. *Reflections on the Revolution in France*
Travels	BRUCE, James. *Travels to discover the Source of the Nile in* ... 1768-1773

NORTHERN EUROPE

Sweden | Literature | BELLMAN, Carl Michael. *Fredmans Epistlar*

CENTRAL EUROPE

Austria
Germany

Music	MOZART, Wolfgang Amadeus. *Così fan tutte*
Architecture	LANGHANS, Karl Gotthard. Berlin, Brandenburger Tor
Biology	GOETHE, Johann Wolfgang. *Versuch die Metamorphose der Pflanze zu erklaeren*
Literature	GOETHE, Johann Wolfgang. *Faust. Ein Fragment*
Philosophy	KANT, Immanuel. *Critik der Urteilskraft*

HUNGARY

Literature	GVADÁNYI, Joszef, Count. *Peleskei nótariús*

1791

GREAT BRITAIN

Biographies	BOSWELL, James. *The Life of Samuel Johnson, LL.D.*
Politics	PAINE, Thomas. *Rights of Man* bgn. (compl. 1792) WOLLSTONECRAFT, Mary. *A Vindication of the Rights of Woman*
Sociology	BENTHAM, Jeremy. *The Panopticon or the Inspection House*

NORTHERN EUROPE

Sweden	Literature	BELLMAN, Carl Michael. *Fredmans Sånger*

CENTRAL EUROPE

Austria	Music	HAYDN, Joseph. *London Symphony No. 3*, ("*The Surprise*"; Symphonie mit dem Paukenschlag)
		MOZART, Wolfgang Amadeus. *Ave Verum Corpus*
		MOZART, Wolfgang Amadeus. *Die Zauberfloete* (The Magic Flute)
		MOZART, Wolfgang Amadeus. *La Clemenza di Tito*
		MOZART, Wolfgang Amadeus. *Requiem*

LATIN EUROPE

France	Literature	SAINT-PIERRE, Jacques-Henri Bernardin de. *La Chaumière Indienne*
		VOLNEY, Constantin-François, Comte de. *Les Ruines*
Italy	Music	CHERUBINI, Luigi. *Lodoïska*
	Physics	GALVANI, Aloisio. *De Viribus Electricitatis in Motu musculari commentarius*

1792

GREAT BRITAIN

Societies	Baptist Missionary Society fnd.
Technics	MURDOCH, William. First gas light used in Boulton and Watt's factory, Soho

CENTRAL EUROPE

Germany	Philosophy	FICHTE, Johann Gottlieb. *Versuch einer Kritik aller Offenbarung*

LATIN EUROPE

France	Literature	FLORIAN, Jean-Pierre-Claris de. *Fables*
	Music	ROUGET DE LISLE, Claude-Joseph. *La Marseillaise*
	Politics	MIRABEAU, Honoré de Riquetti, Comte de. *Lettres écrites du Donjon de Vincennes* (posth.)
Italy	Music	CIMAROSA, Domenico. *Il Matrimonio segreto*
Spain	Literature	FERNÁNDEZ DE MORATÍN, Leandro. *La Comedia nueva*

SLAVONIC EUROPE

Russia	Colonization	Odessa fnd.

[213]

1793

GREAT BRITAIN

Medicine   BAILLIE, Matthew. *The morbid Anatomy of some of the most important Parts of the human Body*

Painting   FLAXMAN, John. Illustrations to Homer's *Iliad* and *Odyssey* bgn. (compl. 1795)

STUBBS, George. *Two Royal Saddle Horses and Anderson, their Groom* (Windsor)

Travels   MACKENZIE, Alexander. Second Canadian journey

CENTRAL EUROPE

Germany   Literature   VOSS, Johann Heinrich. *Ilias*

Philosophy   HERDER, Johann Gottfried. *Briefe zur Befoerderung der Humanitaet* bgn. (compl. 1797)

KANT, Immanuel. *Die Religion innerhalb der Grenzen der blossen Vernunft*

LATIN EUROPE

France   Museums   Paris. Museum Central des Arts (Louvre Museum) fnd.

Physics   First public Optic Telegraph (between Paris and Lille) estab.

Italy   Literature   MONTI, Vincenzo. *La Bassvilliana*

Music   PAGANINI, Niccolò. First concert

Sculpture   CANOVA, Antonio. *Cupid and Psyche*

Spain   Literature   CADALSO, José. *Cartas marruecas*

1794

GREAT BRITAIN

Biology   DARWIN, Erasmus. *Zoonomia, or, the Laws of Organic Life*, bgn. (compl. 1796)

Literature   BLAKE, William. *Songs of Experience*

BLAKE, William. *The Book of Urizen*

RADCLIFFE, Mrs. Anne. *The Mysteries of Udolpho*

Medicine   HUNTER, John. *On the Blood, Inflammation and Gunshot Wounds*

Politics   PAINE, Thomas. *The Age of Reason* bgn. (compl. 1795)

CENTRAL EUROPE

Austria   Music   HAYDN, Joseph. *London Symphony No. 11* ("*The Clock*")

HAYDN, Joseph. *London Symphony No. 12* ("*Military*")

Germany	Jurisprudence	*Allgemeines Landrecht fuer die Preussischen Staaten*
	Literature	GOETHE, Johann Wolfgang. *Reinecke Fuchs*
	Philosophy	FICHTE, Johann Gottlieb. *Grundlage der gesamten Wissenschaftslehre*

LATIN EUROPE

France	Literature	MAISTRE, Xavier de. *Voyage autour de ma Chambre*
	Mathematics	LEGENDRE, Adrien-Marie. *Eléments de Géométrie*
	Politics	CONDORCET, Marie-Jean de Caritat, Marquis de. *Esquisse d'un Tableau historique des Progrès de l'Esprit humain*
	Universities	Paris. Ecole Polytechnique fnd.

1795

GREAT BRITAIN

	Architecture	SOANE, Sir John. Bank of England, London, bgn. (compl. 1827)
	Literature	BLAKE, William. *The Book of Los*
		BLAKE, William. *Nebuchadnezzar (circa)*
		BLAKE, William. *Newton*
		BURNEY, Fanny ; Mme Frances D'Arblay. *Camilla.*
		SOUTHEY, Robert. *Poems*

CENTRAL EUROPE

Germany	Literature	GOETHE, Johann Wolfgang. *Wilhelm Meisters Lehrjahre*
		JEAN PAUL ; Jean Paul Friedrich Richter. *Hesperus*
		VOSS, Johann Heinrich. *Luise*
	Philology	WOLF, Friedrich August. *Prolegomena zu Homer*
	Philosophy	KANT, Immanuel. *Zum ewigen Frieden. Ein philosophischer Entwurf*

LATIN EUROPE

France	Academies	Paris. Conservatoire de Musique fnd.
		Paris. Institut National fnd.
Spain	Painting	GOYA Y LUCIENTES, Francisco de. *Portrait of the Duchess of Alba* (Palacio de Liria, Madrid)
	Politics	JOVELLANOS, Gaspar Melchor de. *Informe sobre la Ley agraria*

1796

GREAT BRITAIN

Literature	COLERIDGE, Samuel Taylor. *Poems on various Subjects*
	SOUTHEY, Robert. *Joan of Arc*
Medicine	JENNER, Edward. Performs first small-pox vaccination

CENTRAL EUROPE

Germany

Music	BEETHOVEN, Ludwig van. *Adelaide* (song)
Philosophy	FICHTE, Johann Gottlieb. *Grundlage des Naturrechts nach den Principien der Wissenschaftslehre*
Technics	SENEFELDER, Alois. Inv. of lithography

LATIN EUROPE

France

Astronomy	LAPLACE, Pierre-Simon, Marquis de. *Exposition du Système du Monde*
Literature	RÉTIF DE LA BRETONNE, Nicolas-Edme. *Monsieur Nicolas, ou le Cœur humain dévoilé*

Portugal

Libraries	National Library, Lisbon, fnd.

Spain

Painting	GOYA Y LUCIENTES, Francisco de. *Caprichos* (etchings; compl. *c.* 1803)

1797

GREAT BRITAIN

Painting	TURNER, William. *Moonlight, Millbank* (Nat. Gal. Lond.)

CENTRAL EUROPE

Austria

Music	HAYDN, Joseph. "*Gott erhalte Franz den Kaiser*" (Austrian National Anthem)

Germany

Aesthetics	WACKENRODER, Wilhelm, and TIECK, Ludwig. *Herzensergiessungen eines kunstliebenden Klosterbruders*
Astronomy	OLBERS, Heinrich Wilhelm Matthias. *Ueber die leichteste und bequemste Methode die Bahn eines Cometen zu berechnen*
Literature	HOELDERLIN, Friedrich. *Hyperion*
	SCHLEGEL, August Wilhelm, and TIECK, Ludwig. Transl. of Shakespeare's Works bgn. (compl. 1810)
	TIECK, Ludwig. *Der gestiefelte Kater*
Medicine	HUFELAND, Christoph Wilhelm. *Makrobiotik: Die Kunst, das menschliche Leben zu verlängern*

Germany	Philosophy	SCHELLING, Friedrich Wilhelm Joseph. *Ideen zu einer Philosophie der Natur*
		SCHELLING, Friedrich Wilhelm Joseph. *Neue Deduction des Naturrechts*

LATIN EUROPE

France	Literature	DIDEROT, Denis. *Jacques le Fataliste* (posth.)
		DIDEROT, Denis. *La Réligieuse* (posth.)
	Mathematics	LAGRANGE, Joseph-Louis, Comte de. *Théorie des Fonctions analytiques*
Italy	Theatre	Début of Angelica Catalani

1798

GREAT BRITAIN

Economics	MALTHUS, Thomas Robert. *An Essay on the Principle of Population*
Literature	LANDOR, Walter Savage. *Gebir*
	WORDSWORTH, William, and COLERIDGE, Samuel Taylor. *Lyrical Ballads*
Medicine	JENNER, Edward. *Inquiry into the Causes and Effects of the Variolae Vaccinae*
	WILLAN, Robert. *The Description and Treatment of Cutaneous Diseases* bgn. (compl. 1808)

CENTRAL EUROPE

Austria	Music	HAYDN, Joseph. *The Creation*
Germany	Literature	GOETHE, Johann Wolfgang. *Hermann und Dorothea*
	Philosophy	KANT, Immanuel. *Anthropologie in pragmatischer Hinsicht*
		SCHELLING, Friedrich Wilhelm Joseph. *Von der Weltseele*
	Press	*Cotta's Allgemeine Zeitung* bgn.

LATIN EUROPE

France	Mathematics	LEGENDRE, Adrien-Marie. *Essai sur la Théorie des Nombres*
		MONGE, Gaspard. *Géométrie déscriptive*
Italy	Literature	FOSCOLO, Ugo. *Ultime Lettere di Jacopo Ortis*

1799

GREAT BRITAIN

Literature	CAMPBELL, Thomas. *The Pleasures of Hope*
Travels	PARK, Mungo. *Travels in the Interior districts of Africa*

CENTRAL EUROPE

Germany	Literature	SCHILLER, Friedrich. *Wallenstein*
		SCHLEGEL, Friedrich. *Lucinde*
	Music	BEETHOVEN, Ludwig van. *Sonata in C minor* (" *Pathétique* ")
	Philosophy	SCHELLING, Friedrich Wilhelm Joseph. *Erster Entwurf eines Systems der Natur-philosophie*
	Theology	SCHLEIERMACHER, Friedrich Ernst Daniel. *Ueber die Religion. Reden an die Gebildeten unter ihren Veraechtern*
Switzerland	Schools	Burgdorf. Pestalozzi's school estab.

LATIN EUROPE

France	Astronomy	LAPLACE, Pierre-Simon, Marquis de. *Traité de Mécanique Céleste* bgn. (compl. 1825)
	Literature	PARNY, Evariste, Vicomte de. *La Guerre des Dieux*

1800

GREAT BRITAIN

Colonization	Ottawa. First permanent settlement
Literature	MOORE, Thomas. *Anacreon*
Physics	NICHOLSON, William, and CARLISLE, Anthony, discovery of electrolysis

CENTRAL EUROPE

Germany	Literature	JEAN PAUL; Jean Paul Friedrich Richter. *Titan* bgn. (compl. 1803)
		NOVALIS; Friedrich von Hardenberg. *Hymnen an die Nacht*
		SCHILLER, Friedrich. *Maria Stuart*
	Music	BEETHOVEN, Ludwig van. *Symphony No. 1 in C major*
	Philosophy	FICHTE, Johann Gottlieb. *Die Bestimmung des Menschen*
		SCHELLING, Friedrich Wilhelm Joseph. *System des transcendentalen Idealismus*
	Politics	FICHTE, Johann Gottlieb. *Der geschlossene Handelsstaat*
	Theology	SCHLEIERMACHER, Friedrich Ernst Daniel. *Monologen*

LATIN EUROPE

France	Literature	CHATEAUBRIAND, René, Vicomte de. *Atala*
		STAËL, Anne-Louise-Germaine de. *De la Littérature*

France	Music	BOIELDIEU, François-Adrien. *Le Calife de Bagdad*
	Painting	DAVID, Jacques-Louis. *Portrait of Mme Récamier* (Louvre)
Italy	Music	CHERUBINI, Luigi. *Les deux Journées*
Spain	Painting	GOYA Y LUCIENTES, Francisco de. *Portrait of the Family of King Charles IV* (Prado, Madrid)

1801

GREAT BRITAIN

| Press | *The Observer* iss. |

CENTRAL EUROPE

Austria	Music	HAYDN, Joseph. *The Seasons*
Germany	Literature	SCHILLER, Friedrich. *Die Jungfrau von Orleans*
	Mathematics	GAUSS, Karl Friedrich. *Disquisitiones Arithmeticae*
	Music	BEETHOVEN, Ludwig van. *Six String Quartets*, op. 18
Switzerland	Education	PESTALOZZI, Johann Heinrich. *Wie Gertrud ihre Kinder lehrt*

LATIN EUROPE

France	Medicine	BICHAT, Marie-François-Xavier. *Anatomie Générale*
	Painting	DAVID, Jacques-Louis. *Napoléon au Grand Saint-Bernard* (Louvre)
Italy	Astronomy	Discovery of the planet Ceres by Giuseppe Piazzi

1802

GREAT BRITAIN

Chemistry	DALTON, John. *Experimental Essays in the Constitution of Gases*
Literature	SCOTT, Walter. *Minstrelsy of the Scottish Border*, Vols. I and II (Vol. III, 1803)
Periodicals	*The Edinburgh Review* iss.
	William Cobbett's *Weekly Political Register* iss. (ended 1835)
Technics	WEDGWOOD, Thomas. Acc. of a method of copying painting upon glass (origin of photography)
Theology	PALEY, William. *Natural Theology*

CENTRAL EUROPE

Germany	Literature	NOVALIS; Friedrich von Hardenberg. *Schriften* (posth.)
	Music	BEETHOVEN, Ludwig van. *Symphony No. 2 in D major*
		BEETHOVEN, Ludwig van. *Sonata quasi una Fantasia*, op. 27, no. 2 (The "Moonlight ")

LATIN EUROPE

France	Literature	STAËL, Anne-Louise-Germaine de. *Delphine*
	Theology	CHATEAUBRIAND, René, Vicomte de. *Génie du Christianisme*
Italy	Literature	CASTI, Giovanni Battista. *Gli Animali Parlanti*
Spain	Painting	GOYA Y LUCIENTES, Francisco de. *La maja desnuda* (*circa*; Prado, Madrid)
		GOYA Y LUCIENTES, Francisco de. *La maja vestida* (*circa* ; Prado, Madrid)

SLAVONIC EUROPE

Russia	Universities	Dorpat (Tartu), fnd.

1803

GREAT BRITAIN

	Education	LANCASTER, Joseph. *Improvements in Education as it respects the industrious Classes*
	Technics	First iron rail used, Wallbottle Mine nr. Newcastle-upon-Tyne

CENTRAL EUROPE

Germany	Literature	SCHILLER, Friedrich. *Die Braut von Messina*
	Music	BEETHOVEN, Ludwig van. *Sonata in E major* (*The Kreutzer*)

LATIN EUROPE

France	Chemistry	BERTHOLLET, Claude-Louis. *Essai de Statique Chimique*
	Jurisprudence	Code Napoléon
Italy	Biography	ALFIERI, Vittorio. *Vita*

1804

GREAT BRITAIN

	Literature	BLAKE, William. *Jerusalem*
		BLAKE, William. *Milton*
	Societies	British and Foreign Bible Society fnd.

CENTRAL EUROPE

Germany Literature HOELDERLIN, Friedrich. *Antigone* (trans. Sophocles)

HOELDERLIN, Friedrich. *Oedipus Rex* (trans. Sophocles)

SCHILLER, Friedrich. *Wilhelm Tell*

Music BEETHOVEN, Ludwig van. *Symphony No. 3 in E flat major (Eroica)*

Periodicals *Jenaische Allgemeine Literaturzeitung* iss.

SLAVONIC EUROPE

Russia Universities Kazan fnd.

Kharkov fnd.

1805

GREAT BRITAIN

Literature SCOTT, Walter. *The Lay of the last Minstrel*

SOUTHEY, Robert. *Madoc . . . and other Poems*

Painting TURNER, William. *Shipwreck* (Nat. Gal. Lond.)

NORTHERN EUROPE

Denmark Literature OEHLENSCHLÄGER, Adam Gottlob. *Aladdin's Lampe*

OEHLENSCHLÄGER, Adam Gottlob. *Hakon Jarl*

CENTRAL EUROPE

Germany Literature HERDER, Johann Gottfried. *Der Cid*

Nachtwachen von Bonaventura (ascr. to Friedrich Gottlob Wetzel)

Music BEETHOVEN, Ludwig van. *Fidelio*

BEETHOVEN, Ludwig van. *Leonore Overture No. 2*

Painting RUNGE, Philipp Otto. *The Morning* (Hamburg)

Switzerland Education Pestalozzi's School, Yverdun, fnd.

LATIN EUROPE

France Botany CANDOLLE, Augustin de. *Flore Française*

Literature CHATEAUBRIAND, René, Vicomte de. *René*

Painting INGRES, Jean-Dominique. *Portrait of Mme Rivière* (Louvre)

Italy Music PAGANINI, Niccolò. First professional tour in Italy

Sculpture CANOVA, Antonio. Paolina Borghese as Venus (Villa Borghese, Rome)

Spain	Literature	FERNÁNDEZ DE MORATÍN, Leandro. *El Sí de las Niñas*
	Painting	GOYA Y LUCIENTES, Francisco de. *Portrait of Doña Isabel Cobos de Porcel* (*circa* ; Nat. Gal. Lond.)

1806

GREAT BRITAIN

	Chemistry	DAVY, Humphry. *On some Chemical Agencies of Electricity*

NORTHERN EUROPE

Norway	Philosophy	STEFFENS, Henrik. *Grundzuege der philosophischen Naturwissenschaft*

CENTRAL EUROPE

Germany	Literature	ARNIM, Achim von, and BRENTANO, Clemens. *Des Knaben Wunderhorn*
	Music	BEETHOVEN, Ludwig van. *Leonore Overture No. 3*
		BEETHOVEN, Ludwig van. *Symphony No. 4 in B flat major*
		BEETHOVEN, Ludwig van. *Violin Concerto, op. 61*
	Pedagogy	HERBART, Johann Friedrich. *Allgemeine Paedagogik*
	Philology	ADELUNG, Johann Christoph. *Mithridates* bgn. (compl. 1817)

LATIN EUROPE

Italy	Museums	Brera Museum, Milan, opnd.

1807

GREAT BRITAIN

	Chemistry	DAVY, Humphry. *On some new Phenomena of Chemical Changes produced by Electricity*
		DAVY, Humphry. *On . . . the general Nature of Alkaline Bodies*
	Literature	BYRON, George Gordon, Lord. *Hours of Idleness*
		CRABBE, George. *The Parish Register*
		MOORE, Thomas. *Irish Melodies* bgn. (compl. 1834)
		WORDSWORTH, William. *Poems in two Volumes*

[222]

CENTRAL EUROPE

Germany	Archaeology	WOLF, Friedrich August. *Darstellung der Altertumswissenschaft*
	Literature	JEAN PAUL; Jean Paul Friedrich Richter. *Levana*
	Music	BEETHOVEN, Ludwig van. *Coriolanus Overture*
		BEETHOVEN, Ludwig van. *Sonata in F minor (" Appassionata ")*
		BEETHOVEN, Ludwig van. *Three String Quartets*, op. 59 (first perf.; first pr. 1808)
	Plant-Geography	HUMBOLDT, Alexander von. *Ideen zu einer Geographie der Pflanze*
	Philosophy	HEGEL, Georg Wilhelm Friedrich. *Phaenomenologie des Geistes*
Switzerland	History	SISMONDI, Jean-Charles-Léonard-Simonde de. *Histoire des Républiques Italiennes au Moyen âge* bgn. (compl. 1817)

LATIN EUROPE

France	Literature	STAËL, Anne-Louise-Germaine de. *Corinne*
	Music	MÉHUL, Etienne-Nicolas. *Joseph*
	Politics	SAINT-SIMON, Claude-Henri, Comte de. *Introduction aux Travaux Scientifiques du xixe Siècle*
Italy	Literature	FOSCOLO, Ugo. *I Sepolcri*
	Music	SPONTINI, Gasparo Luigi Pacifico. *La Vestale*
Spain	Literature	QUINTANA, Manuel José. *Vidas de Españoles célebres* bgn. (compl. 1833)

1808

GREAT BRITAIN

	Chemistry	DALTON, John. *A New System of Chemical Philosophy* bgn. (compl. 1827)
	Literature	SCOTT, Walter. *Marmion*
	Periodicals	*Quarterly Review* iss.

NORTHERN EUROPE

Sweden	Chemistry	BERZELIUS, Jöns Jakob. *Laerebok i Kemien* bgn. (compl. 1818)

CENTRAL EUROPE

Germany	Geography	HUMBOLDT, Alexander von. *Ansichten der Natur*
	History	EICHHORN, Karl Friedrich. *Deutsche Staats- und Rechtsgeschichte* bgn. (compl. 1823)

Germany	Literature	ARNIM, Achim von. *Troesteinsamkeit*
		GOETHE, Johann Wolfgang. *Faust. Der Tragoedie erster Teil*
		KLEIST, Heinrich von. *Penthesilea*
	Music	BEETHOVEN, Ludwig van. *Symphony No. 5 in C minor*
		BEETHOVEN, Ludwig van. *Symphony No. 6 in F major (Pastoral)*
	Painting	FRIEDRICH, Kaspar David. *Das Kreuz auf dem Felsen* (Nat. Gal. Berlin)
	Philology	SCHLEGEL, Friedrich. *Ueber Sprache und Weisheit der Inder*
	Philosophy	HERBART, Johann Friedrich. *Hauptpunkte der Logik*
	Politics	FICHTE, Johann Gottlieb. *Reden an die Deutsche Nation*

LATIN EUROPE

France	Literature	CHATEAUBRIAND, René, Vicomte de. *Les Aventures du dernier Abencérage*
	Painting	DAVID, Jacques-Louis. *Le Sacre de Napoléon* (Louvre)
		INGRES, Jean-Dominique. *La Grande Baigneuse* (Louvre)
	Universities	Lyons fnd.
Spain	Painting	GOYA Y LUCIENTES, Francisco de. *El Dos de Mayo* (Prado, Madrid)
		GOYA Y LUCIENTES, Francisco de. *Execution of Citizens of Madrid* (Prado, Madrid)

1809

GREAT BRITAIN

	Literature	BYRON, George Gordon, Lord. *English Bards and Scotch Reviewers*

CENTRAL EUROPE

Germany	Astronomy	GAUSS, Karl Friedrich. *Theoria Motus Corporum Coelestium*
	Encyclopaedia	*Brockhaus' Conversations Lexicon* iss. (compl. 1811)
	Literature	GOETHE, Johann Wolfgang. *Die Wahlverwandtschaften*
		JEAN PAUL; Jean Paul Friedrich Richter. *Des Feldpredigers Schmelzle Reise nach Flaetz*
	Medicine	GALL, Franz Joseph. *Anatomie et Physiologie du Système nerveux . . .*
	Music	BEETHOVEN, Ludwig van. *Piano Concerto in E flat major*
		WEIGL, Joseph. *Die Schweizerfamilie*

LATIN EUROPE

France   Literature   CHATEAUBRIAND, René, Vicomte de. *Les Martyrs*

            Zoology   LAMARCK, Jean-Baptiste-Antoine de Monnel. *Philosophie Zoologique*

Italy   Music   SPONTINI, Gasparo. *Fernando Cortez*

SLAVONIC EUROPE

Russia   Literature   KRYLOV, Alexander. *Fables* bgn. (compl. 1811)

1810

GREAT BRITAIN

Literature   CRABBE, George. *The Borough*
SCOTT, Walter. *The Lady of the Lake*
SHELLEY, Percy Bysshe and Elisabeth. *Original poetry by Victor and Cazire*

CENTRAL EUROPE

Germany   Literature   KLEIST, Heinrich von. *Das Kaethchen von Heilbronn*
KLEIST, Heinrich von. *Michael Kohlhaas*

            Medicine   HAHNEMANN, Samuel Christian Friedrich. *Organon der rationellen Heilkunde*

            Music   BEETHOVEN, Ludwig van. *Egmont Overture*

            Physics   GOETHE, Johann Wolfgang. *Farbenlehre*

            Universities   Berlin fnd.

LATIN EUROPE

France   Jurisprudence   Code Pénal

            Literature   STAËL, Anne-Louise-Germaine de. *De l'Allemagne*

            Music   ISOUARD, Nicolas. *Cendrillon*

Spain   Painting   GOYA Y LUCIENTES, Francisco de. *Los Desastres de la Guerra* bgn. (engravings; compl. 1813)

            Politics   JOVELLANOS, Gaspar Melchor de. *Memoria en la Defensa de la Junta Central*

1811

GREAT BRITAIN

Literature   AUSTEN, Jane. *Sense and Sensibility*
Painting   LAWRENCE, Thomas. *Portrait of Benjamin West* (Nat. Gal. Lond.)

NORTHERN EUROPE

Denmark   Literature   OEHLENSCHLÄGER, Adam. *Correggio*
           Sculpture   THORWALDSEN, Bertel. *Alexander the Great*
Norway   Universities   Christiania (Oslo) fnd.

CENTRAL EUROPE

Germany   History   NIEBUHR, Berthold Georg. *Roemische Geschichte*
           FOUQUÉ, Friedrich Heinrich, Freiherr de la Motte. *Undine*
           Literature   GOETHE, Johann Wolfgang. *Aus meinem Leben*, Pt. I
           HEBEL, Johann Peter. *Schatzkaestlein des Rheinischen Hausfreunds*
           KLEIST, Heinrich von. *Der zerbrochene Krug*

LATIN EUROPE

France   Chemistry   GAY-LUSSAC, Joseph-Louis, and THENARD, Louis-Jacques. *Recherches Physiques et Chimiques*
           Physics   POISSON, Siméon-Denis. *Traité de Mécanique*, Pt. I (Pt. II, 1833)
Italy   Chemistry   AVOGADRO, Amadeo, Conte di Quaregna. *Essai d'une Manière de déterminer les Masses relatives des Molécules élémentaires des Corps* . . . (Avogadro's Hypothesis)

1812

GREAT BRITAIN

Chemistry   DAVY, Humphry. *Elements of Chemical Philosophy*
Literature   BYRON, George Gordon, Lord. *Childe Harold's Pilgrimage*, Pt. 1

CENTRAL EUROPE

Germany   Literature   GOETHE, Johann Wolfgang. *Gedichte*
           GRIMM, Jakob and Wilhelm. *Kinder- und Hausmaerchen*
           TIECK, Ludwig. *Phantasus*
           Music   BEETHOVEN, Ludwig van. *Symphony No. 7 in A major*
           BEETHOVEN, Ludwig van. *Symphony No. 8 in F major*

LATIN EUROPE

France   Medicine   LEGALLOIS, Julien-Jules-César. *Expériences sur le Principe de la Vie*
           Music   BOIELDIEU, François-Adrien. *Jean de Paris*
Italy   Universities   Genoa fnd.

1813

GREAT BRITAIN

Economics	OWEN, Robert. *A New View of Society*
Literature	AUSTEN, Jane. *Pride and Prejudice*
	BYRON, George Gordon, Lord. *The Bride of Abydos*
	BYRON, George Gordon, Lord. *The Giaour*
	SCOTT, Walter. *Rokeby*
	SHELLEY, Percy Bysshe. *Queen Mab*
Painting	TURNER, William. *Frosty Morning* (Nat. Gal. Lond.)
Societies	Royal Philharmonic Society fnd.

CENTRAL EUROPE

Germany

Medicine	MESMER, Franz Anton. *Allgemeine Erlaeuterungen ueber den Magnetismus*
Music	BEETHOVEN, Ludwig van. *Die Schlacht bei Vittoria* (The " Battle Symphony ")
Politics	ARNDT, Ernst Moritz. *Der Rhein, Deutschlands Strom, nicht Deutschlands Grenze*

LATIN EUROPE

France	Chemistry	THENARD, Louis-Jacques. *Traité de Chimie Elémentaire* bgn. (compl. 1816)
Italy	Literature	MANZONI, Alessandro. *Inni Sacri*
	Music	ROSSINI, Gioachino. *Tancredi*
Spain	Politics	MARTÍNEZ MARINA, Francisco. *Teoría de las Cortes*

1814

GREAT BRITAIN

Literature	AUSTEN, Jane. *Mansfield Park*
	BYRON, George Gordon, Lord. *Lara*
	BYRON, George Gordon, Lord. *The Corsair*
	SCOTT, Walter. *Waverley*
	WORDSWORTH, William. *The Excursion*
Societies	The British and Foreign School Society fnd.
Technics	STEPHENSON, George. First steam locomotive engine constr.
	First public gas-lighting, London
Theatre	Début of Edmund Kean

NORTHERN EUROPE

Denmark	Literature	OEHLENSCHLÄGER, Adam. *Helge*

[227]

CENTRAL EUROPE

Austria   Music   SCHUBERT, Franz. *Gretchen am Spinnrad* (song)

Germany   Literature   CHAMISSO, Adalbert von. *Peter Schlemihl's wundersame Geschichte*
HOFFMANN, Ernst Theodor Amadeus. *Phantasiestuecke in Callot's Manier*
KOERNER, Theodor. *Leier und Schwert* (posth.)

1815

GREAT BRITAIN

Literature   BYRON, George Gordon, Lord. *Hebrew Melodies*
SCOTT, Walter. *Guy Mannering*
SCOTT, Walter. *The Lord of the Isles*
Painting   TURNER, William. *Dido building Carthage* (Nat. Gal. Lond.)

CENTRAL EUROPE

Austria   Music   SCHUBERT, Franz. *Erlkoenig* (song)
SCHUBERT, Franz. *Heidenroeslein* (song)

Germany   Jurisprudence   SAVIGNY, Friedrich Karl. *Geschichte des Roemischen Rechts im Mittelalter*, Pt. I
SAVIGNY, Friedrich Karl. *Vom Beruf unserer Zeit fuer Gesetzgebung und Rechtswissenschaft*
Literature   EICHENDORFF, Joseph, Freiherr von. *Ahnung und Gegenwart*
HOFFMANN, Ernst Theodor Amadeus. *Elixiere des Teufels*
UHLAND, Ludwig. *Gedichte*

LATIN EUROPE

France   Literature   BÉRANGER, Pierre-Jean de. *Chansons*
Medicine   LAENNEC, René-Théophile-Hyacinthe. Mediate auscultation discovered
Zoology   LAMARCK, Jean-Baptiste-Antoine de Monnel. *De l'Histoire Naturelle des Animaux sans Vertèbres*
Spain   Painting   GOYA Y LUCIENTES, Francisco de. *Tauromaquia* (engravings)

1816

GREAT BRITAIN

Literature   AUSTEN, Jane. *Emma*
BYRON, George Gordon, Lord. *The Prisoner of Chillon*

THE ANNALS 1816-1817

Literature	BYRON, George Gordon, Lord. *The Siege of Corinth*
	HUNT, James Henry Leigh. *The Story of Rimini*
	SCOTT, Walter. *The Antiquary*
	SHELLEY, Percy Bysshe. *Alastor*
	SHELLEY, Percy Bysshe. *The Revolt of Islam*
Technics	DAVY, Humphry. Safety lamp inv.

THE LOW COUNTRIES

Belgium   Universities   Ghent fnd.

CENTRAL EUROPE

Austria	Music	SCHUBERT, Franz. *Symphony No. 5 in B flat*
Germany	Music	BEETHOVEN, Ludwig van. *An die ferne Geliebte* (song)

LATIN EUROPE

France	Literature	CONSTANT, Benjamin. *Adolphe*
Italy	Music	ROSSINI, Gioachino. *Il Barbiere di Seviglia*
Spain	Literature	FERNÁNDEZ DE LIZARDÍ, José Joaquín. *El periquillo Sarniento*
	Painting	GOYA Y LUCIENTES, Francisco de. *Portrait of the Duke of Osuna* (Bayonne)

1817

GREAT BRITAIN

Economics	RICARDO, David. *Principles of Political Economy and Taxation*
Literature	BYRON, George Gordon, Lord. *Manfred*
	COLERIDGE, Samuel Taylor. *Biographia Literaria*
	CRABBE, George. *Tales of the Hall* (compl. 1818)
	KEATS, John. *Poems*
	MOORE, Thomas. *Lalla Rookh*
	SCOTT, Walter. *Old Mortality*
Painting	CONSTABLE, John. *Cottage in a Cornfield* (Vict. and Alb. Mus.)
	CONSTABLE, John. *Flatford Mill* (Nat. Gal. Lond.)
Periodicals	*Blackwood's Magazine* iss.

THE LOW COUNTRIES

Belgium   Universities   Liège fnd.
                                    Louvain refnd.

CENTRAL EUROPE

Austria	Literature	GRILLPARZER, Franz. *Die Ahnfrau*
Germany	Archaeology	BOECKH, August. *Die Staatshaushaltung der Athener*
	Geography	RITTER, Karl. *Die Erdkunde im Verhaeltnis zur Natur und zur Geschichte des Menschen*
	Literature	BRENTANO, Clemens. *Geschichte vom braven Kasperl und dem schoenen Annerl*
		HOFFMANN, Ernst Theodor Amadeus. *Nachtstuecke*
	Philosophy	HEGEL, Georg Friedrich Wilhelm. *Encyclopaedie der philosophischen Wissenschaften im Grundrisse*

LATIN EUROPE

France	History of Art	STENDHAL; Henri Beyle. *Histoire de la Peinture en Italie*
	Zoology	CUVIER, George-Chrétien. *Le Règne Animal*
Italy	Music	ROSSINI, Gioachino. *La Gazza Ladra*
Spain	History	LLORENTE, Juan Antonio. *Histoire critique de l'Inquisition d'Espagne* bgn. (compl. 1818)

SLAVONIC EUROPE

Russia	Architecture	St. Isaac's Cathedral, St. Petersburg (Leningrad), bgn. (compl. 1851)

1818

GREAT BRITAIN

History	EVELYN, John. *Diary* first pub. (written 1641-1706 ; compl. 1819 ; posth.)
Literature	AUSTEN, Jane. *Northanger Abbey* (posth.)
	AUSTEN, Jane. *Persuasion* (posth.)
	HAZLITT, William. *Lectures on the English Poets*
	KEATS, John. *Endymion*
	KEATS, John. *Isabella*
	SCOTT, Walter. *Rob Roy*
	SCOTT, Walter. *The Heart of Midlothian*
Theatre	The Royal Coburg Theatre, London (" Old Vic."), opnd.

CENTRAL EUROPE

Austria	Music	SCHUBERT, Franz. *Symphony No. 6 in C major*
Germany	Architecture	SCHINKEL, Karl Friedrich. Royal Theatre (Schauspielhaus), Berlin, bgn. (compl. 1821)

Germany	Astronomy	BESSEL, Friedrich Wilhelm. *Fundamenta Astronomiae*
	Music	WEBER, Karl Maria von. *Jubelouvertuere*
	Philosophy	SCHOPENHAUER, Arthur. *Die Welt als Wille und Vorstellung*
	Universities	Bonn fnd.

LATIN EUROPE

France	Literature	DELAVIGNE, Casimir. *Les Messéniennes*
	Medicine	GEOFFROY SAINT-HILAIRE, Etienne. *Philosophie Anatomique* bgn. (compl. 1823)
	Music	BOIELDIEU, François-Adrien. *Le petit Chaperon Rouge*
Italy	Music	ROSSINI, Gioachino. *Mosè in Egitto*
Spain	Museums	Prado Museum, Madrid, fnd.

SLAVONIC EUROPE

Czechoslovakia	Philology	DOBROVSKY, Joseph. *Geschichte der boehmischen Sprache*
Russia	History	KARAMSIN, Nicolai Michailovich. *History of the Russian State* bgn. (compl. 1824)
Yugoslavia	Philology	KARAJICH, Vuk Stefanovich. *Lexicon Serbico-Germanico-Latinum (Srpski Ryechnik)*

1819

GREAT BRITAIN

Literature	BYRON, George Gordon, Lord. *Don Juan* bgn. (compl. 1824)
	BYRON, George Gordon, Lord. *Mazeppa*
	CAMPBELL, Thomas. *Specimens of the British Poets*
	SCOTT, Walter. *The Bride of Lammermoor*
	SHELLEY, Percy Bysshe. *The Cenci*
	WORDSWORTH, William. *Peter Bell*
Technics	Menai Strait Suspension Bridge bgn. (compl. 1821)

NORTHERN EUROPE

Denmark	Press	*Morgenbladet* iss.
Sweden	Chemistry	BERZELIUS, Jöns Jakob. Electrochemical Theory disc.
	Mineralogy	BERZELIUS, Jöns Jakob. *Nouveau Système de Minéralogie*

CENTRAL EUROPE

Austria	Literature	GRILLPARZER, Franz. *Sappho*
	Music	SCHUBERT, Franz. *Forellenquintett*

[231]

Germany	Literature	GOETHE, Johann Wolfgang. *West-oestlicher Divan*
		HOFFMANN, Ernst Theodor Amadeus. *Maerchen der Serapionsbrueder*
	Philology	GRIMM, Jakob. *Deutsche Grammatik*

LATIN EUROPE

France	Literature	CHÉNIER, André. *Poésies* (posth.)
		DESBORDES-VALMORE, Marceline. *Elégies, Marie et Romances*
	Painting	GÉRICAULT, Jean-Louis. *Le Radeau de la Méduse* (Louvre)
	Politics	SAINT-SIMON, Claude-Henri, Comte de. *La Politique*
Italy	Music	SPONTINI, Gasparo. *Olympia*
Spain	Painting	GOYA Y LUCIENTES, Francisco de. *Portrait of Doña Antonia Zárate* (Louvre)
	Politics	BOLÍVAR, Simón. *Discurso pronunciado ante el Congreso de Angostura*

HUNGARY

	Literature	KISFALUDY, Károly. *A Tatárok Magyarorszagon* (The Tartars in Hungary)

1820

GREAT BRITAIN

	Economics	MALTHUS, Thomas Robert. *Principles of Political Economy*
	Literature	BYRON, George Gordon, Lord. *Marino Faliero*
		KEATS, John. *Lamia*
		KEATS, John. *Odes*
		SCOTT, Walter. *Ivanhoe*
		SCOTT, Walter. *The Monastery*
		SCOTT, Walter. *The Abbot*
		SHELLEY, Percy Bysshe. *Oedipus Tyrannus*
		SHELLEY, Percy Bysshe. *Prometheus Unbound*
	Painting	CONSTABLE, John. *Harwich Lighthouse* (Tate Gal. Lond.)

THE LOW COUNTRIES

Holland	Literature	BILDERDIJK, Willem. *De Ondergang der eerste Wereld*

NORTHERN EUROPE

Denmark	Physics	OERSTED, Hans Christian. Magnetic field discovered
	Sculpture	THORWALDSEN, Bertel. *The Lion of Lucerne* (Lucerne)

CENTRAL EUROPE

Germany	Literature	HOFFMANN, Ernst Theodor Amadeus. *Lebensansichten des Katers Murr*

LATIN EUROPE

France	Literature	LAMARTINE, Alphonse de. *Méditations Poétiques*
Italy	Literature	MANZONI, Alessandro. *Conte di Carmagnola*

SLAVONIC EUROPE

Russia	Literature	PUSHKIN, Alexander. *Ruslan and Lyudmila*

1821

GREAT BRITAIN

Literature	BYRON, George Gordon, Lord. *Cain*
	BYRON, George Gordon, Lord. *Sardanapalus*
	BYRON, George Gordon, Lord. *The Two Foscari*
	HAZLITT, William. *Table-Talk* (compl. 1822)
	SCOTT, Walter. *Kenilworth*
	SHELLEY, Percy Bysshe. *Epipsychidion*
	SHELLEY, Percy Bysshe. *Adonais*
Painting	CONSTABLE, John. *The Hay Wain* (Nat. Gal. Lond.)
Physics	FARADAY, Michael. Electro-magnetic rotation disc.
Press	*Manchester Guardian* iss.

CENTRAL EUROPE

Austria	Music	SCHUBERT, Franz. *Alfonso und Estrella* (first perf. by Liszt 1854)
Germany	Literature	GOETHE, Johann Wolfgang. *Wilhelm Meisters Wanderjahre*
		HOFFMANN, Ernst Theodor Amadeus. *Prinzessin Brambilla*
		KLEIST, Heinrich von. *Die Hermannschlacht* (posth.)
		KLEIST, Heinrich von. *Prinz Friedrich von Homburg* (posth.)
	Music	WEBER, Karl Maria von. *Der Freischuetz*
		WEBER, Karl Maria von. *Preciosa*
	Philosophy	HEGEL, Georg Friedrich Wilhelm. *Grundlinien der Philosophie des Rechts*
	Theatre	Début of Wilhelmine Schroeder-Devrient
		Début of Henriette Sontag
	Theology	SCHLEIERMACHER, Friedrich Ernst Daniel. *Der christliche Glaube nach den Grundsaetzen der evangelischen Kirche* bgn. (compl. 1822)

LATIN EUROPE

France Academies Ecole Nationale des Chartes, Paris, fnd.
      Literature   MAISTRE, Joseph de. *Soirées de Saint-Pétersbourg*

SLAVONIC EUROPE

Czechoslovakia Literature   KOLLÁR, Jan. *Básně* (poems)
Russia   Literature   PUSHKIN, Alexander. *The Robber Brothers*

HUNGARY

      Literature   KATONA, Joszef. *Bánk bán*

1822

GREAT BRITAIN

      Academies Royal Academy of Music fnd. (chartered 1830)
      Literature   BEDDOES, Thomas Lovell. *The Bride's Tragedy*
            DE QUINCEY, Thomas. *Confessions of an English Opium-Eater*
            SCOTT, Walter. *The Pirate*
            SCOTT, Walter. *The Fortunes of Nigel*
            SHELLEY, Percy Bysshe. *Hellas*
            WORDSWORTH, William. *Memorials of a Tour on the Continent*
      Technics   BABBAGE, Charles. Calculating machine inv.

CENTRAL EUROPE

Austria   Literature   GRILLPARZER, Franz. *Das goldne Vliess*
      Music   SCHUBERT, Franz. *Symphony No. 8 in B minor (The "Unfinished")*
            SCHUBERT, Franz. *Fantasia in C minor ("The Wanderer")*
Germany Architecture SCHINKEL, Karl Friedrich. Altes Museum, Berlin, bgn. (compl. 1828)
      Literature   HEINE, Heinrich. *Gedichte*
            HOFFMANN, Ernst Theodor Amadeus. *Meister Floh*
      Philosophy BAADER, Franz von. *Fermenta Cognitionis*

LATIN EUROPE

France   History   LAS CASES, Emanuel, Marquis de. *Mémorial de Sainte-Hélène*
      Literature   HUGO, Victor. *Odes*
            STENDHAL; Henri Beyle. *De l'Amour*
            VIGNY, Alfred de. *Poèmes*

France	Painting	DELACROIX, Ferdinand. *La Barque de Dante* (Louvre)
	Physics	FOURIER, Jean-Baptiste-Joseph. *Théorie Analytique de la Chaleur*
Italy	Literature	MANZONI, Alessandro. *Adelchi*
		MANZONI, Alessandro. *Il Cinque Maggio*
	Theatre	Début of Giuditta Pasta

SLAVONIC EUROPE

Russia	Literature	PUSHKIN, Alexander. *The Prisoner of the Caucasus*

1823

GREAT BRITAIN

Literature	LAMB, Charles. *Essays of Elia*
	SCOTT, Walter. *Quentin Durward*
	SCOTT, Walter. *Peveril of the Peak*

CENTRAL EUROPE

Austria	Music	SCHUBERT, Franz. *Die schoene Muellerin* (songs)
		SCHUBERT, Franz. *Rosamunde*
Germany	Literature	ECKERMANN, Johann Peter. *Gespraeche mit Goethe*, Pt. I
		RUECKERT, Friedrich. *Liebesfruehling*
	Mathematics	GAUSS, Karl Friedrich. *Theoria Combinationis Observationum Erroribus minimis obnoxiae*
	Music	BEETHOVEN, Ludwig van. *Missa Solemnis*
		WEBER, Karl Maria von. *Euryanthe*
	Painting	FRIEDRICH, Kaspar David. *Sunrise at the Beach* (Nat. Gal. Berlin)
	Philology	SCHLEGEL, August Wilhelm. *Indische Bibliothek* bgn. (compl. 1830)

LATIN EUROPE

France	Biography	STENDHAL; Henri Beyle. *Vie de Rossini*
	History	THIERS, Adolphe. *Histoire de la Révolution Française*
	Literature	LAMARTINE, Alphonse de. *Nouvelles Méditations Poétiques*
	Politics	SAINT-SIMON, Claude-Henri, Comte de. *Catéchisme des Industriels* bgn. (compl. 1824)

SLAVONIC EUROPE

Russia	Literature	GRIBOYEDOV, Alexander. *Góre ot Umá* (Woe from Wit; first pr.; first perf. 1829)

[235]

Yugoslavia Folklore KARAJICH, Vuk Stefanovich. *Srpske Narodne Pyesme* (Serbian Songs of the Common People; compl. 1833)

1824

GREAT BRITAIN

Education OWEN, Robert Dale. *An Outline of the System of Education at New Lanark*
Literature LANDOR, Walter Savage. *Imaginary Conversations* bgn. (compl. 1862)
SCOTT, Walter. *St. Ronan's Well*
SCOTT, Walter. *Redgauntlet*
Museums National Gallery, London, fnd.
Technics ASPDIN, Joseph. Portland cement first prod.

NORTHERN EUROPE

Norway Philosophy STEFFENS, Henrik. *Anthropologie*
Sweden Literature ATTERBOM, Per Daniel Amadeus. *Lycksalighetens Oe* bgn. (Isle of Happiness; compl. 1827)

CENTRAL EUROPE

Austria Music SCHUBERT, Franz. *Divertissement à la Hongroise*
SCHUBERT, Franz. *String Quartet in D minor* bgn. (*Death and the Maiden*; compl. 1826)
Germany History RANKE, Leopold. *Geschichte der Romanischen und Germanischen Voelker von 1494-1534*, Vol. I
Music BEETHOVEN, Ludwig van. *Symphony No. 9 in D minor* (*The Choral*)
MENDELSSOHN-BARTHOLDY, Felix. *Symphony No. 1 in C minor*

LATIN EUROPE

France History MIGNET, François-Auguste-Marie. *Histoire de la Révolution Française*
Painting DELACROIX, Ferdinand. *Les Massacres de Scio* (Louvre)
Philology CHAMPOLLION, Jean-François. *Précis du Système Hiéroglyphique*
Physics CARNOT, Nicolas-Léonard-Sadi. *Réflexions sur la Puissance motrice du Feu*
Press *Le Globe* iss.
Italy Literature LEOPARDI, Giacomo. *Canzoni e Versi*
Spain Literature BELLO, Andrés. *Silva a la agricultura de la zona tórrida* bgn. (compl. 1826)

SLAVONIC EUROPE

Czechoslovakia Literature KOLLÁR, Jan. *Slávy Dcera* (The Daughter of Slava)
Russia Geography KRUSENSTERN, Adam Johann von. *Atlas de l'Océan Pacifique* bgn. (compl. 1827)

1825

GREAT BRITAIN

Biography PEPYS, Samuel. *Diary* (written 1659-69)
Chemistry FARADAY, Michael. Benzene first isolated
Literature HAZLITT, William. *The Spirit of the Age*
SCOTT, Walter. *The Talisman*
Technics First (Stockton-Darlington) railway opnd.

NORTHERN EUROPE

Sweden Literature TEGNÉR, Esaias. *Frithjofssaga*

CENTRAL EUROPE

Austria Music SCHUBERT, Franz. *Ave Maria*
Germany Literature PLATEN, August, Graf von. *Sonette aus Venedig*
Philology BOECKH, August. *Corpus Inscriptionum Graecarum* bgn. (compl. 1877)

LATIN EUROPE

France History THIERRY, Augustin. *Histoire de la Conquête d'Angleterre par les Normands*
Mathematics LEGENDRE, Adrien-Marie. *Traité des Fonctions elliptiques*
Music BOIELDIEU, François-Adrien. *La ' Dame Blanche*
Politics SAINT-SIMON, Claude-Henri, Comte de. *Le nouveau Christianisme*
Societies Société de Géographie, Paris, fnd.
Portugal Literature ALMEIDA GARRETT, João Baptista. *Camões*
Spain Literature OLMEDO, José Joaquín. *Canto de Junín*
Theatre Début of María Felicita Malibrán-García

SLAVONIC EUROPE

Poland Music CHOPIN, Frederik. *Rondo in C minor*, op. 1
Russia Literature PUSHKIN, Alexander. *Eugene Onyegin* bgn. (compl. 1832)
RYLÉYEV, Kondrati Fyedorovich. *Voynarovsky*

HUNGARY

Academies Hungarian Academy of Sciences, Budapest, fnd.

1826

GREAT BRITAIN

Literature	DISRAELI, Benjamin. *Vivian Grey* bgn. (compl. 1827)
	SCOTT, Walter. *Woodstock*
Painting	CONSTABLE, John. *The Cornfield* (Nat. Gal. Lond.)
Technics	First railway tunnel (Liverpool-Manchester railway) opnd.
Societies	Royal Astronomical Society fnd.

NORTHERN EUROPE

Norway   Mathematics   ABEL, Niels Henrik. *Beweis der Unmoeglichkeit algebraische Gleichungen von hoeheren Graden, als dem vierten, allgemein aufzuloesen*

CENTRAL EUROPE

Austria   Technics   RESSEL, Joseph. Ship's screw inv.

Germany   Architecture   KLENZE, Karl Leo. Alte Pinakothek, Munich, bgn. (compl. 1836)

Literature   EICHENDORFF, Joseph, Freiherr von. *Aus dem Leben eines Taugenichts*
HAUFF, Wilhelm. *Lichtenstein*
HOELDERLIN, Friedrich. *Gedichte*

Music   BEETHOVEN, Ludwig van. *String Quartet in B flat major* (first perf.; first pr. 1827)
MENDELSSOHN-BARTHOLDY, Felix. *Midsummer Night's Dream Overture in E major* (first public perf. 1827)
WEBER, Karl Maria von. *Oberon*

Universities   Munich fnd.

LATIN EUROPE

France   Literature   BRILLAT-SAVARIN, Anthèlme. *Physiologie du Goût*
HUGO, Victor. *Odes et Ballades*
VIGNY, Alfred de. *Cinq-Mars*

Mathematics   CAUCHY, Augustin-Louis. *Exercices de Mathématiques* bgn. (compl. 1830)

Philosophy   COUSIN, Victor. *Fragmens Philosophiques*

Physics   AMPÈRE, André-Marie. *Théorie mathématique des Phénomènes électro-dynamiques*
FRESNEL, Augustin-Jean. *Mémoire sur la Diffraction de la Lumière*

Italy   Literature   MANZONI, Alessandro. *I promessi Sposi*

1827

GREAT BRITAIN

Chemistry	FARADAY, Michael. *Chemical Manipulation; being Instructions to Students in Chemistry*
History	HALLAM, Henry. *The Constitutional History of England from the Accession of Henry VII to the Death of George II*
Literature	TENNYSON, Alfred. *Poems by Two Brothers* (i.e. Charles and Alfred Tennyson)
Painting	CONSTABLE, John. *The Glebe Farm* (Nat. Gal. Lond.)
	TURNER, William. *Ulysses deriding Polyphemus* (Nat. Gal. Lond.)

NORTHERN EUROPE

Finland

Universities	(Russian) University, Helsinki, fnd.

CENTRAL EUROPE

Austria
Germany

Music	SCHUBERT, Franz. *Die Winterreise* (songs)
Chemistry	WOEHLER, Friedrich. Aluminium first isolated
Geography	Gesellschaft fuer Erdkunde, Berlin, fnd.
Literature	HEINE, Heinrich. *Buch der Lieder*
Medicine	BAER, Karl Ernst von. Discovery of mammalian ovum
Physics	OHM, Georg Simon. *Die galvanische Kette*

LATIN EUROPE

France

History	GUIZOT, François-Pierre-Guillaume. *Histoire générale de la Civilisation en Europe* bgn.
Literature	BALZAC, Honoré de. *Les Chouans*, Pt. I
	HUGO, Victor. *Cromwell*
	STENDHAL; Henri Beyle. *Armance*
Painting	INGRES, Jean-Dominique. *Homère déifié* (Louvre)
Physics	NIEPCE, Joseph-Nicéphore. First photograph on metal plate prod.

Italy

Literature	LEOPARDI, Giacomo. *Operette morali*
Music	BELLINI, Vincenzo. *Il Pirata*

1828

GREAT BRITAIN

Literature	BULWER LYTTON, Edward George. *Pelham*
	SCOTT, Walter. *Tales of a Grandfather*
	SCOTT, Walter. *The Fair Maid of Perth*
Painting	CONSTABLE, John. *Dedham* (Nat. Gal. Edinburgh)
Periodicals	*The Athenaeum* iss.
Universities	University College, London, fnd.

[239]

CENTRAL EUROPE

Austria	Music	SCHUBERT, Franz. *Mass in E flat*
		SCHUBERT, Franz. *String Quintet in C major*
		SCHUBERT, Franz. *Symphony No. 7 in C major*
Germany	Chemistry	WOEHLER, Friedrich. First artificial preparation of urea
	Jurisprudence	GRIMM, Jakob. *Deutsche Rechtsaltertuemer*
	Philosophy	HERBART, Johann Friedrich. *Allgemeine Metaphysik* bgn. (compl. 1829)

LATIN EUROPE

France	Chemistry	DUMAS, Jean-Baptiste-André. *La Chimie, appliquée aux Arts*, Vol. I
	History	GUIZOT, François-Pierre-Guillaume. *Cours d'Histoire moderne* bgn. (compl. 1830)
	Music	AUBER, Daniel-François. *La Muette de Portici*
Italy	Theatre	Début of Giulia Grisi

SLAVONIC EUROPE

Russia	Literature	PUSHKIN, Alexander. *Poltava*

1829

GREAT BRITAIN

Periodicals	*London Review* iss.
Universities	King's College, London, fnd.

CENTRAL EUROPE

Germany	Chemistry	MITSCHERLICH, Eilhard. *Lehrbuch der Chemie* bgn. (compl. 1835)
	Literature	GRABBE, Christian Dietrich. *Don Juan und Faust*
	Mathematics	JACOBI, Carl Gustav Jacob. *Fundamenta Nova Theoriae Functionum Ellipticarum*
	Psychology	KERNER, Justinus. *Die Seherin von Prevorst*

LATIN EUROPE

France	History	GUIZOT, François-Pierre-Guillaume. *Histoire de la Civilisation en France*
		SAINT-SIMON, Louis de Rouvroy, Duc de. *Mémoires complets et authentiques* (posth.; compl. 1831)
	History of Art	STENDHAL; Henri Beyle. *Promenades dans Rome*
	Literature	HUGO, Victor. *Les Orientales*
	Periodicals	*Revue des deux Mondes* (new start in 1831) iss.

Italy   Academies   Archaeological Institute, Rome, fnd.
         Music   ROSSINI, Gioacchino. *Guillaume Tell*

SLAVONIC EUROPE

Czechoslovakia   Literature   ČELAKOVSKY, František Ladislav. *Ohlas písní ruských* (Echo of Russian Songs)
Russia   Literature   PUSHKIN, Alexander. *Poems* bgn. (compl. 1835)
         Mathematics   LOBACHEVSKY, Nicolai Ivanovich. *On the Principles of Geometry*

1830

GREAT BRITAIN

Geography   Royal Geographical Society fnd.
Geology   LYELL, Charles. *Principles of Geology* bgn. (compl. 1833)
             BULWER LYTTON, Edward George. *Paul Clifford*
Literature.   TENNYSON, Alfred. *Poems, chiefly lyrical*

NORTHERN EUROPE

Sweden   Literature   ALMQUIST, Carl Jonas Love. *Toernrosens Bok*

CENTRAL EUROPE

Germany   Architecture   KLENZE, Franz Karl Leo. Walhalla, nr. Regensburg (Ratisbon), bgn. (compl. 1847)
         Literature   IMMERMANN, Karl. *Tulifaentchen*
         Music   MENDELSSOHN-BARTHOLDY, Felix. *The Hebrides* bgn. (compl. 1832)
             MENDELSSOHN-BARTHOLDY, Felix. *Lieder ohne Worte*, Pt. I
             MENDELSSOHN-BARTHOLDY, Felix. *Symphony No. 5 in D (The Reformation)*

LATIN EUROPE

France   Literature   BALZAC, Honoré de. *Gobseck*
             BALZAC, Honoré de. *Physiologie du Mariage*
             HUGO, Victor. *Hernani*
             MÉRIMÉE, Prosper. *Colomba*
         Music   AUBER, Daniel-François. *Fra Diavolo*
             BERLIOZ, Hector. *Symphonie Phantastique* (compl. 1831)
         Philosophy   COMTE, Auguste. *Cours de Philosophie positive* bgn. (compl. 1842)

1831

GREAT BRITAIN

Discoveries	Ross, John. Magnetic North Pole discovered
Economics	Mill, John Stuart. *Essays on some unsettled questions of Political Economy*
Literature	Peacock, Thomas Love. *Crotchet Castle*
Physics	Faraday, Michael. Electric currents disc. and transformer inv.
Technics	London Bridge opnd.

CENTRAL EUROPE

Germany

Chemistry	Woehler, Friedrich. *Grundriss der anorganischen Chemie*
Literature	Grabbe, Christian Dietrich. *Napoleon*

LATIN EUROPE

France

Literature	Balzac, Honoré de. *La Femme de trente Ans*
	Balzac, Honoré de. *La Peau de Chagrin*
	Hugo, Victor. *Marion Delorme*
	Hugo, Victor. *Notre-Dame de Paris*
	Stendhal; Henri Beyle. *Le Rouge et le Noir*
	Vigny, Alfred de. *La Maréchale d'Ancre*
Music	Meyerbeer, Giacomo. *Robert le Diable*
Painting	Delacroix, Ferdinand. *The Barricade (Le 28 Juillet* 1830; Louvre)
Periodicals	*Revue des deux Mondes* re-iss.

Italy

Music	Bellini, Vincenzo. *Norma*

SLAVONIC EUROPE

Russia

Literature	Pushkin, Alexander. *Boris Godunov*

1832

GREAT BRITAIN

Jurisprudence	Austin, John. *The Province of Jurisprudence determined*
	Bulwer Lytton, Edward George. *Eugene Aram*
Literature	Disraeli, Benjamin. *Contarini Fleming*
	Tennyson, Alfred. *Poems*

NORTHERN EUROPE

Sweden

History	Geijer, Erik Gustaf. *Svenska folkets historia* bgn. (compl. 1836)
Literature	Runeberg, Johan Ludvig. *Elgskyttarne* (The Elk-Hunters)

CENTRAL EUROPE

Germany	Chemistry	LIEBIG, Justus, and WOEHLER, Friedrich. *Untersuchungen ueber das Radikal der Benzolsaeure* (in "Annalen der Chemie")
	Literature	GOETHE, Johann Wolfgang. *Faust. Der Tragoedie zweiter Teil* LENAU, Nikolaus. *Gedichte* MOERIKE, Eduard. *Maler Nolten*
	Politics	BÖRNE, Ludwig. *Briefe aus Paris* bgn. (compl. 1834)
Switzerland	Mathematics	STEINER, Jakob. *Systematische Entwicklung der Abhaengigkeit geometrischer Gestalten von einander*
	Universities	Zurich fnd.

LATIN EUROPE

France	Literature	BALZAC, Honoré de. *Contes Drôlatiques* BALZAC, Honoré de. *Le Colonel Chabert* DELAVIGNE, Casimir. *Louis XI* HUGO, Victor. *Le Roi s'amuse* SAND, George. *Indiana* SAND, George. *Valentine*
Italy	Press	*La Giovine Italia* iss. (ended 1836)
Spain	Literature	LARRA, Mariano José de. *El pobrecito hablador* bgn. (compl. 1833)

SLAVONIC EUROPE

Russia	Literature	PUSHKIN, Alexander. *Rusalka*

1833

GREAT BRITAIN

Literature	BULWER LYTTON, Edward George. *Godolphin* CARLISLE, Thomas. *Sartor Resartus* LAMB, Charles. *The Last Essays of Elia*
Physics	FARADAY, Michael. Laws of electrolysis discovered
Theology	*Tracts for the Times* bgn. (compl. 1841)

CENTRAL EUROPE

Austria	Literature	RAIMUND, Ferdinand. *Der Verschwender*
Germany	Literature	PLATEN, August, Graf von. *Gedichte*
	Mathematics	GAUSS, Karl Friedrich. *Intensitas Vis magneticae terrestris ad Mensuram absolutam revocata*

[243]

Germany	Medicine	MUELLER, Johannes. *Handbuch der Physiologie des Menschen*
	Music	MARSCHNER, Heinrich. *Hans Heiling*
		MENDELSSOHN - BARTHOLDY, Felix. *Symphony No. 4 in A (The Italian)*
	Philology	BOPP, Franz. *Vergleichende Grammatik* bgn. (compl. 1852)
Switzerland	Zoology	AGASSIZ, Louis-Jean-Rodolphe. *Recherches sur les Poissons fossiles* bgn. (compl. 1844)

LATIN EUROPE

France	History	MICHELET, Jules. *Histoire de France* bgn. (compl. 1867)
	Literature	BALZAC, Honoré de. *Eugénie Grandet*
		DESBORDES-VALMORE, Marceline. *Les Pleurs*
		HUGO, Victor. *Lucrèce Borgia*
		HUGO, Victor. *Marie Tudor*
		MUSSET, Alfred de. *Fantasio*
		SAND, George. *Lélia*
Italy	Biography	PELLICO, Silvio. *Le mie Prigioni*

SLAVONIC EUROPE

Poland	Literature	MICKIEVICZ, Adam. *Dziady* (Forefather's Eve)
	Music	CHOPIN, Frederik. *Douze Etudes*, op. 10
		CHOPIN, Frederik. *Concerto in E minor*, op. 11
Russia	Literature	PUSHKIN, Alexander. *The Bronze Horseman*

1834

GREAT BRITAIN

| | Literature | BULWER LYTTON, Edward George. *The Last Days of Pompeii* |
| | Philosophy | BENTHAM, Jeremy. *Deontology ; or, The Science of Morality* |

THE LOW COUNTRIES

| Belgium | Universities | Brussels fnd. |

CENTRAL EUROPE

Austria	Literature	GRILLPARZER, Franz. *Der Traum ein Leben*
Germany	Biology	MUELLER, Johannes. *Vergleichende Anatomie der Myxinoiden*
	History	RANKE, Leopold. *Die Roemischen Paepste* bgn. (compl. 1836)

LATIN EUROPE

France	Astronomy	ARAGO, Dominique-François-Jean. *Astronomie Populaire*
	Literature	BALZAC, Honoré de. *La Recherche de l'Absolu*
		LAMENNAIS, Hugues-Félicité-Robert de. *Paroles d'un Croyant*
		MUSSET, Alfred de. *Lorenzaccio*
Italy	Music	BELLINI, Vincenzo. *I Puritani*
Spain	Literature	MARTÍNEZ DE LA ROSA, Francisco. *La Conjuración de Venecia*

SLAVONIC EUROPE

Poland	Literature	MICKIEVICZ, Adam. *Pan Tadeusz*
	Music	CHOPIN, Frederik. *Quatre Mazurkas*, op. 17
		CHOPIN, Frederik. *Grande Valse brillante*, op. 18
Russia	Literature	GOGOL, Nicolai Vasilyevich. *Taras Bulba*
		PUSHKIN, Alexander. *The Queen of Spades*

1835

GREAT BRITAIN

	Literature	BROWNING, Robert. *Paracelsus*
		BULWER LYTTON, Edward George. *Rienzi*
		WORDSWORTH, William. *Yarrow Revisited*
	Painting	CONSTABLE, John. *The Valley Farm* (Nat. Gal. Lond.)

NORTHERN EUROPE

Denmark	Literature	ANDERSEN, Hans Christian. *Eventyr og Historier* (Fantasies and Sketches)
		ANDERSEN, Hans Christian. *Improvisatoren*
Finland	Literature	Ed. Prin. of *The Kalevala* (ed. Elias Lönnrot)
Sweden	Literature	GEIJER, Erik Gustaf. *Skaldestycken*

CENTRAL EUROPE

Austria	Literature	NESTROY, Johann Nepomuk. *Der boese Geist Lumpacivagabundus*
Germany	Folklore	GRIMM, Jakob. *Deutsche Mythologie*
	Literature	BUECHNER, Georg. *Dantons Tod*
		GRABBE, Christian Dietrich. *Hannibal*
		GUTZKOW, Karl. *Wally, die Zweiflerin*
	Painting	FRIEDRICH, Kaspar David. *Repose during the Harvest* (Dresden)
	Theology	STRAUSS, David Friedrich. *Das Leben Jesu*

LATIN EUROPE

France	Literature	BALZAC, Honoré de. *Le Père Goriot* GAUTIER, Théophile. *Mademoiselle de Maupin* HUGO, Victor. *Chants du Crépuscule* MUSSET, Alfred de. *Rolla* VIGNY, Alfred de. *Chatterton*
	Mathematics	POISSON, Siméon-Denis. *Théorie Mathématique de la Chaleur* (Supplement, 1837)
	Music	HALÉVY, Jacques-Fromentin-Elie. *La Juive*
	Philosophy	QUÉTELET, Lambert-Adolphe-Jacques. *Sur l'Homme*
	Politics	TOCQUEVILLE, Alexis de. *De la Démocratie en Amérique*
Italy	Music	DONIZETTI, Gaetano. *Lucia di Lammermoor*
	Politics	MAZZINI, Giuseppe. *Fede e Avvenire*
Spain	Literature	RIVAS, El Duque de. *Don Alvaro o la Fuerza del Sino*

SLAVONIC EUROPE

Poland	Literature	KRASINSKI, Zygmund. *Nieboska Komedya* (The Undivine Comedy)
Russia	Literature	GOGOL, Nicolai Vasilyevich. *Mirgorod*

1836

GREAT BRITAIN

	Painting	CONSTABLE, John. *The Cenotaph* (Nat. Gal. Lond.)
	Politics	OWEN, Robert. *The Book of the New Moral World*

CENTRAL EUROPE

Germany	Literature	BUECHNER, Georg. *Lenz* HEINE, Heinrich. *Die romantische Schule*
	Museums	Alte Pinakothek, Munich, fnd.
	Music	MENDELSSOHN-BARTHOLDY, Felix. *St. Paul*
	Philosophy	FECHNER, Gustav Theodor. *Das Buechlein vom Leben nach dem Tode*

LATIN EUROPE

France	Literature	DUMAS, Alexandre. *Kean* LAMARTINE, Alphonse de. *Jocelyn*
	Music	ADAM, Adolphe-Charles. *Le Postillon de Lonjumeau* MEYERBEER, Giacomo. *Les Huguenots*
Spain	Literature	GARCÍA GUTIÉRREZ, Antonio. *El Trovador* LARRA, Mariano José de. *El Día de Difuntos*

SLAVONIC EUROPE

Czechoslovakia	History	PALACKY, František. *Geschichte des Boehmischen Volkes* bgn. (compl. 1867)
Russia	Literature	GOGOL, Nicolai Vasilyevich. *Revizor* (The Inspector-General)
	Music	GLINKA, Michael. *A Life for the Tzar*

1837

GREAT BRITAIN

History	CARLYLE, Thomas. *The French Revolution*
Literature	DICKENS, Charles. *The Posthumous Papers of the Pickwick Club*
	LANDOR, Walter Savage. *The Pentameron*
Museums	Fitzwilliam Museum, Cambridge, fnd.

CENTRAL EUROPE

Germany	Education	Friedrich Wilhelm August Froebel's " Kindergarten," Blankenburg, fnd.
	Literature	EICHENDORFF, Joseph, Freiherr von. *Gedichte*
	Music	LORTZING, Albert. *Czaar und Zimmermann* SCHUMANN, Robert. *Carnaval*, op. 9 (comp. 1834-35)
	Painting	RICHTER, Ludwig. *Ueberfahrt am Schreckenstein* (Dresden)
Switzerland	Zoology	AGASSIZ, Louis-Jean-Rodolphe. *Monographies d'Echinodermes vivants et fossiles*

LATIN EUROPE

France	Geography	DUMONT D'URVILLE, Jules-Sébastien-César. *Voyage de l'Astrolabe* bgn. (compl. 1840)
	Literature	BALZAC, Honoré de. *César Birotteau* HUGO, Victor. *Les Voix Intérieures* SAND, George. *Mauprat*
	Mathematics	CHASLES, Michel. *Aperçu historique sur l'Origine et le Développement des Méthodes en Géométrie*
	Medicine	FLOURENS, Marie-Jean-Pierre. Discovery of respiratory centre in medulla
	Music	BERLIOZ, Hector. *Requiem*
	Theatre	Début of Elisa Rachel

SLAVONIC EUROPE

Russia	Literature	GOGOL, Nicolai Vasilyevich. *Dead Souls*

GREECE

Universities	Athens fnd.

1838

GREAT BRITAIN

Literature   DICKENS, Charles. *Oliver Twist*

THE LOW COUNTRIES

Belgium   Literature   CONSCIENCE, Hendrik. *De Leeuw van Vlaanderen*

CENTRAL EUROPE

Germany   Astronomy   BESSEL, Friedrich Wilhelm. Stellar parallax applied

Bacteriology   EHRENBERG, Christian Gottfried. *Die Infusionstierchen als vollkommene Organismen*

Literature   BRENTANO, Clemens. *Gockel, Hinkel und Gackeleia*
DROSTE-HUELSHOFF, Annette von. *Gedichte*
IMMERMANN, Karl, *Muenchhausen*
MOERIKE, Eduard. *Gedichte*

Mathematics   DIRICHLET, Peter Gustav Lejeune. *Sur l'Usage des Séries infinies dans la Théorie des Nombres*

Music   SCHUMANN, Robert. *Davidsbuendler Taenze*, op. 6 (comp. 1837)
SCHUMANN, Robert. *Kinderscenen*, op. 15

Physics   GAUSS, Karl Friedrich. *Allgemeine Theorie des Erdmagnetismus*

Physiology   SCHLEIDEN, Matthias, and SCHWANN, Theodor. *Mikroskopische Untersuchungen* bgn. (compl. 1839)

LATIN EUROPE

France   Literature   HUGO, Victor. *Ruy Blas*
LAMARTINE, Alphonse de. *La Chute d'un Ange*

Music   BERLIOZ, Hector. *Benvenuto Cellini*

SLAVONIC EUROPE

Russia   Architecture   Kremlin Palace, Moscow, bgn. (compl. 1849)

HUNGARY

Literature   EÖTVÖS, Joszef, Baron. *Karthausi* (The Carthusian)

1839

GREAT BRITAIN

Botany	Botanical Gardens, Kew, fnd.
Literature	DICKENS, Charles. *Nicholas Nickleby*
Natural History	DARWIN, Charles Robert. *Journal of Researches into Geology and Natural History of the various Countries visited by H.M.S. "Beagle"*
Painting	TURNER, William. *The Fighting Témeraire* (Nat. Gal. Lond.)
Technics	NASMYTH, James. First steam-hammer constr.

THE LOW COUNTRIES

Holland

Literature	BEETS, Nicolaas. *Camera Obscura*

CENTRAL EUROPE

Germany

Encyclo-paedia	*Meyers Neues Konversations-Lexikon* (compl. 1852)
History	RANKE, Leopold von. *Deutsche Geschichte im Zeitalter der Reformation* bgn. (compl. 1843)

Switzerland

Literature	TOEPFFER, Rodolphe. *Nouvelles Genevoises*

LATIN EUROPE

France

Literature	STENDHAL; Henri Beyle. *La Chartreuse de Parme*
Music	BERLIOZ, Hector. *Roméo et Juliette*
Physics	DAGUERRE, Louis-Jacques-Mandé. Daguerreotype process inv.

SLAVONIC EUROPE

Poland

Literature	SLOVACKI, Juliusz. *Lilla Weneda*
Music	CHOPIN, Frederik. *Préludes*, op. 28

1840

GREAT BRITAIN

Architecture	BARRY, Sir Charles. Houses of Parliament, London, bgn. (compl. 1852) Royal Exchange, London, bgn. (compl. 1844)
Libraries	London Library opnd.
Literature	DICKENS, Charles. *Barnaby Rudge* DICKENS, Charles. *Old Curiosity Shop* bgn. (compl. 1841)
Physics	JOULE, James Prescott. *On the production of Heat by Voltaic Electricity*

NORTHERN EUROPE

Denmark   Literature   ANDERSEN, Hans Christian. *Billedbog uden Billeder* (Picture-Book without Pictures)

CENTRAL EUROPE

Austria   Literature   GRILLPARZER, Franz. *Des Meeres und der Liebe Wellen*

Germany   Chemistry   LIEBIG, Justus. *Die Chemie in ihrer Anwendung auf Agrikultur und Physiologie*
WOEHLER, Friedrich. *Grundriss der organischen Chemie*

   Literature   ARNIM, Bettina von. *Die Guenderode*
GEIBEL, Emanuel. *Gedichte*
HEBBEL, Friedrich. *Genoveva*
TIECK, Ludwig. *Vittoria Accorombona*

   Music   SCHUMANN, Robert. *Dichterliebe* (songs)
SCHUMANN, Robert. *Frauenliebe und Leben* (eight songs)

   Physics   GAUSS, Karl Friedrich. *Dioptrische Untersuchungen*

Switzerland   Zoology   AGASSIZ, Louis-Jean-Rodolphe. *Etudes critiques sur les Mollusques fossiles* bgn. (compl. 1845)

LATIN EUROPE

France   Economics   PROUDHON, Pierre-Joseph. *Qu'est-ce que la Propriété?*

   History   SAINTE-BEUVE, Charles-Augustin. *Histoire de Port-Royal* bgn. (compl. 1860)
THIERRY, Augustin. *Récits des Temps Mérovingiens*

   Literature   MUSSET, Alfred de. *Comédies et Proverbes*

Italy   Music   DONIZETTI, Gaetano. *La Fille du Régiment*

SLAVONIC EUROPE

Czechoslovakia   History   PALACKY, František. *Archiv Cesky* bgn. (Czech Archives; compl. 1872)

Poland   Music   CHOPIN, Frederik. *Sonata in C flat minor, op. 35*
CHOPIN, Frederik. *Deux Nocturnes, op. 37*
CHOPIN, Frederik. *Deux Polonaises, op. 40*

Russia   Literature   LERMONTOV, Michael Yurievich. *A Hero of our Time*

1841

GREAT BRITAIN

   History   CARLYLE, Thomas. *On Heroes . . .*
   Literature   BROWNING, Robert. *Bells and Pomegranates* bgn. (compl. 1848)
   Periodicals   *Punch* iss.

NORTHERN EUROPE

Denmark   Philosophy   KIERKEGAARD, Søren. *Om begrebet Ironi*

Norway   Mathematics ABEL, Niels Henrik. *Mémoire sur une Propriété générale d'une Classe très étendue de Fonctions transcendantes* (posth.; written 1826)

CENTRAL EUROPE

Germany   Chemistry   BUNSEN, Robert Wilhelm. Carbon-zinc battery inv.

                 Economics   LIST, Friedrich. *Das nationale System der politischen Oekonomie*

                 Literature   HEBBEL, Friedrich. *Judith*

                              HERWEGH, Georg. *Gedichte eines Lebendigen* bgn. (compl. 1843)

                 Medicine   HENLE, Friedrich Gustav Jacob. *Allgemeine Anatomie*

                 Music   SCHUMANN, Robert. *Symphony No. 1 in B flat major*

                 Philosophy   FEUERBACH, Ludwig. *Das Wesen des Christentums*

                              LOTZE, Rudolf Hermann. *Metaphysik*

Switzerland Literature   GOTTHELF, Jeremias. *Uli der Knecht*

LATIN EUROPE

France   History   BLANC, Louis. *Histoire de dix Ans* bgn. (compl. 1845)

                 Literature   BALZAC, Honoré de. *Une ténébreuse Affaire*

                              DUMAS, Alexandre. *Le Comte de Monte-Christo* bgn. (compl. 1845)

                 Painting   DAUMIER, Honoré. *Physionomies tragico-classiques* (lithos)

                 Politics   BLANC, Louis. *Organisation du Travail*

Italy   Music   ROSSINI, Gioacchino. *Stabat Mater*

Spain   Literature   ESPRONCEDA, José de. *Canto a Teresa*

SLAVONIC EUROPE

Russia   Music   GLINKA, Michael Ivanovich. *Ruslan and Lyudmila*

1842

GREAT BRITAIN

                 History   MACAULAY, Thomas Babington. *Lays of Ancient Rome*

                 Painting   TURNER, William. *Burial at Sea* (Tate Gal. Lond.)

                 Periodicals *Illustrated London News* iss.

NORTHERN EUROPE

Denmark   Literature   ANDERSEN, Hans Christian. *En Digters Bazar*

Norway   Folklore   ASBJÖRNSON, Peter Christen, and MOE, Jörgen. *Norske Folke Eventyr* bgn. (compl. 1844 and 1871)

CENTRAL EUROPE

Austria   Medicine   ROKITANSKY, Carl von. *Lehrbuch der pathologischen Anatomie* bgn. (compl. 1846)

Germany   Botany   SCHLEIDEN, Matthias. *Grundzuege einer wissenschaftlichen Botanik* (-1843)

   Literature   HEBBEL, Friedrich. *Gedichte*
LENAU, Nikolaus. *Gedichte*

   Music   LORTZING, Albert. *Der Wildschuetz*
MENDELSSOHN-BARTHOLDY, Felix. *Symphony in A minor*, op. 56 (*The Scottish*)
WAGNER, Richard. *Rienzi* (first perf.; comp. 1840)

   Physics   MAYER, Julius Robert. *Bemerkungen ueber die Kraefte der unbelebten Natur*

LATIN EUROPE

France   Literature   BANVILLE, Théodore de. *Cariatides*
SAND, George. *Consuelo* bgn. (compl. 1843)
SUE, Eugène. *Les Mystères de Paris* bgn. (compl. 1843)

   Politics   CABET, Etienne. *Voyage en Icarie*

SLAVONIC EUROPE

Russia   Literature   BARATYNSKY, Evgeni Abramovich. *Twilight*
GOGOL, Nicolai Vasilyevich. *The Greatcoat*

1843

GREAT BRITAIN

Aesthetics   RUSKIN, John. *Modern Painters* bgn. (compl. 1860)

History   CARLYLE, Thomas. *Past and Present*
FINLAY, George. *History of Greece* bgn. (compl. 1861)
MACAULAY, Thomas Babington. *Essays*

Literature   BORROW, George. *The Bible in Spain*
BULWER LYTTON, Edward George. *The Last of the Barons*
DICKENS, Charles. *A Christmas Carol in Prose*

	Philosophy	MILL, John Stuart. *A System of Logic, ratiocinative and inductive*
	Physics	JOULE, James Prescott. *On the Heat evolved during Electrolysis of Water*
	Zoology	DARWIN, Charles Robert. *The Zoology of the Voyage of H.M.S. " Beagle "* (ed.)

NORTHERN EUROPE

| **Denmark** | Philosophy | KIERKEGAARD, Søren. *Enten—Eller* (Either—Or) |

CENTRAL EUROPE

Germany	Chemistry	LIEBIG, Justus. *Handbuch der organischen Chemie mit Ruecksicht auf Pharmazie*
	Music	SCHUMANN, Robert. *Das Paradies und die Peri* (choral work, op. 50)
		WAGNER, Richard. *Der fliegende Hollaender*
	Philosophy	LOTZE, Rudolf Hermann. *Logik*

LATIN EUROPE

France	History	THIERS, Adolphe. *Histoire du Consulat et de l'Empire* bgn. (compl. 1868)
	Literature	HUGO, Victor. *Les Burgraves*
Italy	Literature	NICCOLINI, Giovanni Battista. *Arnaldo da Brescia*
	Music	DONIZETTI, Gaetano. *Don Pasquale*
	Politics	GIOBERTI, Vincenzo. *Il Primato morale e civile degli Italiani*

SLAVONIC EUROPE

| **Russia** | Literature | TURGENIEV, Ivan Sergeievich. *Parasha* |

1844

GREAT BRITAIN

	Literature	BROWNING, Elizabeth Barrett. *Poems*
		DICKENS, Charles. *Martin Chuzzlewit*
		DISRAELI, Benjamin. *Coningsby*
	Painting	TURNER, William. *Rain, Steam and Speed* (Nat. Gal. Lond.)
		TURNER, William. *The Sun of Venice going to Sea* (Nat. Gal. Lond.)
	Physics	FARADAY, Michael. *Experimental Researches in Electricity* Vol. I (Vol. II, 1847)

NORTHERN EUROPE

| **Denmark** | Philosophy | KIERKEGAARD, Søren. *Begrebet Angst* |

[253]

CENTRAL EUROPE

Austria	Literature	STIFTER, Adalbert. *Studien*, Pt. I
Germany	Chemistry	LIEBIG, Justus. *Chemische Briefe*
	Literature	HEBBEL, Friedrich. *Maria Magdalena*
		HEINE, Heinrich. *Deutschland, ein Winter-maerchen*
		HEINE, Heinrich. *Neue Gedichte*

LATIN EUROPE

France	Literature	DUMAS, Alexandre. *Les Trois Mousquetaires*
		SUE, Eugène. *Le Juif errant* bgn. (compl. 1845)
Italy	Music	VERDI, Giuseppe. *Ernani*
	Politics	MAZZINI, Giuseppe. *Doveri dell'uomo*
Portugal	Literature	ALMEIDA GARRETT, João Baptista. *Frei Luiz de Sousa*
Spain	Literature	ZORRILLA, José. *Don Juan Tenorio*
	Theology	BALMES, Jaime. *El Protestantismo comparado con el Catolicismo*

SLAVONIC EUROPE

Russia	Literature	TURGENIEV, Ivan Sergeievich. *Andrei Kolosov*

HUNGARY

	Literature	PETÖFI, Sandor. *Versek* (verse)

1845

GREAT BRITAIN

Archaeology	Nimrud, British excavations bgn. by Sir A. H. Layard
Academies	College of Chemistry, London, fnd.
History	CARLYLE, Thomas. *Oliver Cromwell's Letters and Speeches*
	GROTE, George. *History of Greece* bgn. (compl. 1856)
Literature	DICKENS, Charles. *The Chimes*
	DISRAELI, Benjamin. *Sybil*
Mathematics	CAYLEY, Arthur. *On the Theory of linear Transformations*
Religion	NEWMAN, John Henry, received into the Roman Catholic Church

NORTHERN EUROPE

Denmark	Literature	HERTZ, Henrik. *Kong René's Datter*
	Philosophy	KIERKEGAARD, Søren. *Stadier paa Livetsvej*

CENTRAL EUROPE

Germany Astronomy   HUMBOLDT, Alexander von. *Kosmos* bgn.
and Natural   (compl. 1858)
History
Music   LORTZING, Albert. *Undine*
WAGNER, Richard. *Tannhaeuser*
Philosophy   STIRNER, Max. *Der Einzige und sein Eigentum*

LATIN EUROPE

France Architecture   VIGNON, Pierre (compl. by Jean-Jacques Huvé). The Madeleine, Paris, compl.
Literature   BALZAC, Honoré de. *Les Paysans*
Italy   Politics   GIOBERTI, Vincenzo. *Prolegomeni al Primato*
Spain   Philosophy   BALMES, Jaime. *El Criterio*

SLAVONIC EUROPE

Poland   Music   CHOPIN, Frederik. *Sonata in B minor*

1846

GREAT BRITAIN

Literature   THACKERAY, William Makepeace. *The Book of Snobs* bgn. (compl. 1847)
Medicine   MORTON, William Thomas Green. Ether anaesthesia first used
Press   *Daily News* iss. (founded by Charles Dickens)

CENTRAL EUROPE

Germany Aesthetics   VISCHER, Friedrich Theodor. *Aesthetik oder Wissenschaft des Schoenen* bgn. (compl. 1857)
Architecture   KLENZE, Franz Karl Leo. Propylaea, Munich, bgn. (compl. 1862)
Chemistry   SCHOENBEIN, Christian Friedrich. Improvement of the nitration of cellulose and first preparation of guncotton
Medicine   HENLE, Friedrich Gustav Jacob. *Lehrbuch der rationellen Pathologie* bgn. (compl. 1853)
Music   LORTZING, Albert. *Der Waffenschmied*
MENDELSSOHN-BARTHOLDY, Felix. *Elijah* (oratorio)
SCHUMANN, Robert. *Symphony No. 2 in C major*
Switzerland   Literature   KELLER, Gottfried. *Gedichte*

[255]

LATIN EUROPE

France   Astronomy   LEVERRIER, Urbain-Jean-Joseph. Mathematical detection of the planet Neptune

Economics   PROUDHON, Pierre-Joseph. *Philosophie de la Misère*

Literature   BALZAC, Honoré de. *Le Cousin Pons*
BANVILLE, Théodore de. *Les Stalactites*
SAND, George. *La Mare au Diable*

Mathematics   GALOIS, Evariste. *Œuvres*

Music   BERLIOZ, Hector. *La Damnation de Faust*

Italy   Chemistry   SOBRERO, Ascanio. Nitroglycerine first prepared

Politics   AZEGLIO, Massimo d'. *Degli ultimi Casi di Romagna*

Spain   Literature   CAMPOAMOR, Ramón de. *Doloras*

SLAVONIC EUROPE

Russia   Literature   DOSTOIEVSKY, Fyodor Michailovich. *Dvoynik* (Poor Folk)

HUNGARY

Literature   ARANY, Janos. *Toldi*

Music   LISZT, Franz. *Hungarian Rhapsody No.* 1

1847

GREAT BRITAIN

Discoveries   FRANKLIN, Sir John. Navigation of the North-West Passage

Literature   BRONTË, Charlotte. *Jane Eyre*
BROWNING, Elizabeth Barrett. *Sonnets from the Portuguese*
DISRAELI, Benjamin. *Tancred*
LANDOR, Walter Savage. *The Hellenics*
THACKERAY, William Makepeace. *Vanity Fair* bgn. (compl. 1848)

Medicine   SIMPSON, James Young. Chloroform anaesthesia first used

NORTHERN EUROPE

Denmark   Literature   ANDERSEN, Hans Christian. *Eventyr og Historier*, Pt. II

CENTRAL EUROPE

Germany   History   RANKE, Leopold von. *Neun Buecher Preussischer Geschichte* bgn. (compl. 1848)

Literature   HEINE, Heinrich. *Atta Troll*

Medicine   LUDWIG, Karl. Kymograph inv.

Music   FLOTOW, Friedrich von. *Marta*

Germany Philosophy MARX, Karl. *La Misère de la Philosophie* ...
   Physics HELMHOLTZ, Hermann. *Ueber die Erhaltung der Kraft*

LATIN EUROPE

France History LAMARTINE, Alphonse de. *Histoire des Girondins*
    MICHELET, Jules. *Histoire de la Révolution Française* bgn. (compl. 1853)
   Literature MÉRIMÉE, Prosper. *Carmen*
Italy Music VERDI, Giuseppe. *Macbeth*

SLAVONIC EUROPE

Poland Music CHOPIN, Frederik. *Trois Valses*, op. 64

1848

GREAT BRITAIN

Economics MILL, John Stuart. *Principles of Political Economy*
History MACAULAY, Thomas Babington. *The History of England* bgn. (compl. 1861)
Literature BRONTË, Emily. *Wuthering Heights*
   BULWER LYTTON, Edward George. *Harold, or the Last of the Saxon Kings*
   DICKENS, Charles. *Dombey and Son*
   GASKELL, Elizabeth Cleghorn. *Mary Barton*
   KINGSLEY, Charles. *Yeast*
   THACKERAY, William Makepeace. *Pendennis* bgn. (compl. 1850)
Painting Pre-Raphaelite Brotherhood fnd.
   HOLMAN HUNT, William. *The Hireling Shepherd* (Manchester)
   MILLAIS, John Everett. *Ophelia* (Tate Gal. Lond.)
Universities Queen's College, London, fnd.

NORTHERN EUROPE

Denmark Literature OEHLENSCHLÄGER, Adam Gottlob. *Ragnar Lqdbrok*
Finland Literature RUNEBERG, Johan Ludvig. *Fänrik Stals sägner* (Ensign Stal's Tales)

CENTRAL EUROPE

Germany Philology GRIMM, Jakob. *Geschichte der Deutschen Sprache*
   Politics MARX, Karl, and ENGELS, Friedrich. *Das Kommunistische Manifest*
   Press *Koelnische Zeitung* iss.
   Neue Preussische (Kreuz) *Zeitung* iss.

LATIN EUROPE

France   Chemistry   PASTEUR, Louis.   Optical resolution of racemic acid and recognition of molecular asymmetry

Literature   DUMAS, Alexandre, fils.   *La Dame aux Camélias*

Medicine   BERNARD, Claude.   Glycogenic function of the liver discovered

Italy   Politics   AZEGLIO, Massimo d'.   *Lutti della Lombardia*

1849

GREAT BRITAIN

Aesthetics   RUSKIN, John.   *The Seven Lamps of Architecture*

Universities   Bedford Square College, London, fnd. (from 1860, Bedford College for Women; chartered 1869)

CENTRAL EUROPE

Germany   Literature   LUDWIG, Otto.   *Der Erbfoerster*

Painting   RETHEL, Alfred.   *Auch ein Totentanz* (wood-engravings)

LATIN EUROPE

France   Literature   SCRIBE, Eugène.   *Adrienne Lecouvreur*

Music   MEYERBEER, Giacomo.   *Le Prophète*

Painting   COURBET, Gustave.   *L'Après-Dîner à Ornans* (Lille)

Physics   FIZEAU, Armand-Hippolyte-Louis.   First measurement of velocity of light

Spain   Literature   SARMIENTO, Domingo Fausto.   *Civilización y Barbarie: Vida de Facundo*

HUNGARY

Music   LISZT, Franz.   *Tasso*

1850

GREAT BRITAIN

Economics   SPENCER, Herbert.   *Social Statics*

Literature   BROWNING, Robert.   *Christmas Eve and Easter Day*

BULWER LYTTON, Edward George.   *The Caxtons*

DICKENS, Charles.   *David Copperfield*

KINGSLEY, Charles.   *Alton Locke*

Literature	ROSSETTI, Dante Gabriel. *The Blessed Damozel*
	TENNYSON, Alfred. *In Memoriam*
	WORDSWORTH, William. *The Prelude* (posth; written from 1798 to 1805)
Painting	HOLMAN HUNT, William. *The Two Gentlemen of Verona* (Birmingham)
	ROSSETTI, Dante Gabriel. *Ecce Ancilla Domini* (Tate Gall. Lond.)
Periodicals	*The Germ* iss.
Universities	Queen's University, Dublin, fnd. (Charter)

NORTHERN EUROPE

Norway   Literature   IBSEN, Henrik. *Catilina*

CENTRAL EUROPE

Germany

Chemistry	BUNSEN, Robert Wilhelm. Gas-burner inv.
Music	SCHUMANN, Robert. *Genoveva* (comp. 1848)
	WAGNER, Richard. *Lohengrin*
Painting	MENZEL, Adolf. *Round Table of Frederick the Great* (Nat. Gal. Berlin)
Philosophy	SCHOPENHAUER, Arthur. *Parerga und Paralipomena*
Physics	HELMHOLTZ, Hermann. Ophthalmoscope inv.

LATIN EUROPE

France

Medicine	DAVAINE, Casimir-Josèphe, and RAYER, Pierre-François-Olive. Anthrax bacillus disc. (first sighted by Pollender in 1849)
Painting	COROT, Camille. *Matinée* (Louvre)
	COURBET, Gustave. *L'Enterrement à Ornans* (Louvre)

Spain   Painting   GOYA Y LUCIENTES, Francisco de. *Proverbios* (engravings; first posth. pr.)

SLAVONIC EUROPE

Russia   Biography   HERZEN, Alexander Ivanovich. *My Past and Reflections* bgn. (compl. 1855)

1851

GREAT BRITAIN

Aesthetics	RUSKIN, John. *Pre-Raphaelitism*
History of Art	RUSKIN, John. *The Stones of Venice*
Literature	BORROW, George. *Lavengro*
	MEREDITH, George. *Poems*
Travels	LIVINGSTONE, David. Exploration of the Upper Zambesi bgn. (compl. 1853)

CENTRAL EUROPE

Germany   Literature   HEBBEL, Friedrich. *Herodes und Mariamne*
    HEINE, Heinrich. *Romanzero*
    Music   SCHUMANN, Robert. *Symphony No. 3 in E flat major* (" *Rhenish,*" comp. 1850)
    Sculpture   RAUCH, Christian Daniel, and SCHINKEL, Karl Friedrich. *Monument of Frederick the Great* (bgn. 1830; Berlin)

LATIN EUROPE

France   Literature   MURGER, Henri. *Scènes de la Vie de Bohème*
    Painting   COROT, Camille. *Danse des Nymphes* (Louvre)
    DAUMIER, Honoré. *Physionomies Tragiques* (lithos)
Italy   Music   VERDI, Giuseppe. *Rigoletto*
    Politics   GIOBERTI, Vincenzo. *Il Rinnovamento Civile d'Italia*
Spain   Politics   DONOSO CORTÉS, Juan. *Ensayo sobre el Catolicismo, el Liberalismo y el Socialismo*

1852

GREAT BRITAIN

Economics   SPENCER, Herbert. *Theory of Population*
Literature   BRONTË, Charlotte. *Villette*
    THACKERAY, William Makepeace. *Henry Esmond*
Mathematics   SYLVESTER, James Joseph. *On the Principles of the Calculus of Forms*
Painting   BROWN, Ford Madox. *The Last of England* (Fitzwilliam Mus., Cambridge)
Physics   THOMSON, William, and JOULE, James Prescott. *On the Thermal Effects of Fluids in Motion*

NORTHERN EUROPE

Norway   Literature   IBSEN, Henrik. *Gildet paa Solhaug*

CENTRAL EUROPE

Germany   History   RANKE, Leopold von. *Franzoesische Geschichte, vornehmlich im 16. und 17. Jahrhundert* bgn. (compl. 1861)
Jurisprudence   IHERING, Rudolf. *Geist des Roemischen Rechts*
Literature   BRENTANO, Clemens. *Romanzen vom Rosenkranz* (posth.)
    STORM, Theodor. *Gedichte*
    STORM, Theodor. *Immensee*

Germany   Music   SCHUMANN, Robert. *Manfred* (comp. 1848)
              Painting   MENZEL, Adolf. *Flute Concert at Sanssouci* (Nat. Gal. Berlin)
              Philosophy FISCHER, Kuno. *Geschichte der neueren Philosophie* bgn. (compl. 1893)

LATIN EUROPE

France   Literature GAUTIER, Théophile. *Emaux et Camées*
                             MUSSET, Alfred de. *Poésies*
              Painting   GAVARNI; Paul Chevalier. *Masques et Visages* bgn. (lithos; compl. 1848)
                             MÉRYON, Charles. *Eaux-Fortes sur Paris* bgn. (etchings; compl. 1854)
              Politics   COMTE, Auguste. *Système de Politique Positive*

SLAVONIC EUROPE

Russia   Literature TURGENIEV, Ivan Sergeievich. *A Sportsman's Sketches* (bgn. 1847)
              Music   RUBINSTEIN, Anton. *Dimitry Donskoy*

1853

GREAT BRITAIN

              Literature BULWER LYTTON, Edward George. *My Novel*
                             DICKENS, Charles. *Bleak House*
                             GASKELL, Elizabeth Cleghorn. *Cranford*
                             KINGSLEY, Charles. *Hypatia*
              Physics   THOMSON, William. *On transient Electric Currents*

CENTRAL EUROPE

Germany   Literature HEBBEL, Friedrich. *Gyges und sein Ring*
              Museums   Neue Pinakothek, Munich, compl. (bgn. 1846)
              Music   BRAHMS, Johannes. *First Sonata in C major*, op. 1
                             SCHUMANN, Robert. *Symphony No. 4 in in D minor* (comp. 1851)
                             WAGNER, Richard. *Der Ring des Nibelungen* (text)

LATIN EUROPE

France   Literature HUGO, Victor. *Les Châtiments*
              Politics   GOBINEAU, Joseph-Arthur, Comte de. *Essai sur l'Inégalité des Races humaines*
Italy   Music   VERDI, Giuseppe. *Il Trovatore*
                             VERDI, Giuseppe. *La Traviata*

HUNGARY

Literature   JOKAI, Maurus. *Egy Magyar Nábob* (A Hungarian Nabob)

1854

GREAT BRITAIN

Literature	DICKENS, Charles. *Hard Times*
	THACKERAY, William Makepeace. *The Newcomes*
	WISEMAN, Nicholas Patrick. *Fabiola*
Mathematics	BOOLE, George. *The Laws of Thought*
Painting	HOLMAN HUNT, William. *The Light of the World* (Manchester)
Universities	Working Men's College, London, fnd.

NORTHERN EUROPE

Norway   Literature   IBSEN, Henrik. *Fru Inger til Østraat*

CENTRAL EUROPE

Germany

Bacteriology	EHRENBERG, Christian Gottfried. *Mikrogeologie*
History	MOMMSEN, Theodor. *Roemische Geschichte*, Pt. I
Mathematics	RIEMANN, Georg Friedrich Bernhard. *Ueber die Hypothesen, welche der Geometrie zu Grunde liegen*
	WEIERSTRASS, Karl Wilhelm Theodor. *Zur Theorie der Abelschen Funktionen*
Medicine	VIRCHOW, Rudolf. *Handbuch der speziellen Pathologie und Therapie* bgn. (compl. 1862)
Painting	SCHWIND, Moritz von. *Life of St. Elisabeth* bgn. (compl. 1855; frescoes, Wartburg, nr. Eisenach)
Philology	GRIMM, Jakob. *Deutsches Woerterbuch*, Pt. I

Switzerland   Literature   KELLER, Gottfried. *Der gruene Heinrich*

LATIN EUROPE

France

Medicine	BERNARD, Claude. Function of vaso-dilator nerves discovered
Painting	DORÉ, Gustave. Illus. to Rabelais' *Gargantua*
Press	*Le Figaro* iss.
Societies	*Félibrige* fnd.

HUNGARY

Literature	ARANY, Janos. *Toldi Estéje* (The Downfall of Toldi)
Music	LISZT, Franz. *Les Préludes* (first perf.)
	LISZT, Franz. *Mazeppa*

1855

GREAT BRITAIN

History	FROUDE, James Anthony. *History of England from the Fall of Wolsey to the Defeat of the Spanish Armada*
Literature	GASKELL, Elizabeth Cleghorn. *North and South*
	KINGSLEY, Charles. *Westward Ho!*
	TROLLOPE, Anthony. *The Warden*
Press	*Daily Telegraph* iss.
Psychology	SPENCER, Herbert. *The Principles of Psychology*

NORTHERN EUROPE

Denmark   Literature   ANDERSEN, Hans Christian. *Mit Livs Eventyr* (The Story of my Life)

CENTRAL EUROPE

Germany

History	DROYSEN, Johann Gustav. *Geschichte der Preussischen Politik* bgn. (compl. 1886)
	GIESEBRECHT, Wilhelm. *Geschichte der Deutschen Kaiserzeit* bgn. (compl. 1895)
	HEFELE, Karl Josef. *Conciliengeschichte* bgn. (compl. 1874)
Literature	FREYTAG, Gustav. *Soll und Haben*
	HEBBEL, Friedrich. *Agnes Bernauer*
	SCHEFFEL, Joseph Viktor von. *Ekkehard*
Music	BRAHMS, Johannes. *First Trio in B major*, op. 8 (comp. 1853-54)
Philosophy	BUECHNER, Ludwig. *Kraft und Stoff*

Switzerland   History of Art   BURCKHARDT, Jakob. *Der Cicerone*

LATIN EUROPE

France

Astronomy	LEVERRIER, Urbain Jean Joseph. Publications in " Annales de l'Observatoire de Paris "
Literature	GÉRARD DE NERVAL; Gérard de Labrunie. *Aurélie*
Painting	COURBET, Gustave. *L'Atelier* (Louvre)

Italy   Music   VERDI, Giuseppe. *Les Vêpres Siciliennes*

Spain   Medicine   GARCIA, Manuel. Laryngoscope inv.

SLAVONIC EUROPE

Russia   Literature   TURGENIEV, Ivan Sergeievich. *Rudin*

1856

GREAT BRITAIN

Astronomy	MAXWELL, James Clerk. *Adams Prize Essay*	
Painting	HOLMAN HUNT, William. *The Scapegoat* (Manchester)	
	MILLAIS, John Everett. *The Blind Girl* (Birmingham)	
Theatre	Début of Henry Irving	

CENTRAL EUROPE

Germany	Literature	MOERIKE, Eduard. *Mozart auf der Reise nach Prag*
	Painting	MENZEL, Adolf. *Théâtre du Gymnase* (Nat. Gal. Berlin)
	Philosophy	LOTZE, Hermann. *Mikrokosmus* bgn. (compl 1864)
	Press	*Frankfurter Zeitung* iss.
Switzerland	Literature	KELLER, Gottfried. *Die Leute von Seldwyla,* Pt. I (Pt. II 1874)

LATIN EUROPE

France	History	TOCQUEVILLE, Alexis de. *L'Ancien Régime et la Révolution*
	Literature	HUGO, Victor. *Les Contemplations*
	Painting	INGRES, Jean-Dominique. *La Source* (Louvre)
	Philosophy	TAINE, Hippolyte. *Les Philosophes Français du Dix-neuvième Siècle*

SLAVONIC EUROPE

Russia   Literature   AKSAKOV, Sergei. *Family Chronicle*

1857

GREAT BRITAIN

History	BUCKLE, Henry Thomas. *History of Civilisation in England* bgn. (compl. 1861)
Literature	BORROW, George. *The Romany Rye*
	BROWNING, Elizabeth Barrett. *Aurora Leigh*

THE ANNALS 1857

Literature	DICKENS, Charles. *Little Dorrit* ELIOT, George; Mary Ann Evans. *Scenes from Clerical Life* KINGSLEY, Charles. *Two Years Ago* TROLLOPE, Anthony. *Barchester Towers*
Medicine	LISTER, Joseph. *The early Stages of Inflammation*
Museums	South Kensington Museum fnd.
Travels	LIVINGSTONE, David. *Missionary Travels in South Africa*

NORTHERN EUROPE

Norway Literature BJÖRNSON, Björnstjerne. *Synnöve Solbakken*

CENTRAL EUROPE

Austria Literature STIFTER, Adalbert. *Der Nachsommer*
Theatre Début of Charlotte Wolter
Germany Chemistry KEKULÉ, Friedrich August. *Ueber die s.g. gepaarten Verbindungen und die Theorie der mehratomigen Radicale*(Theory of molecular structure in organic chemistry; in "Annalen der Chemie ")
History CURTIUS, Ernst. *Griechische Geschichte* bgn. (compl. 1867)
Jurisprudence GNEIST, Heinrich Rudolf. *Das heutige englische Verfassungs- und Verwaltungsrecht*
Painting SCHWIND, Moritz von. *The Tale of the Seven Ravens* (Wartburg, nr. Eisenach)

LATIN EUROPE

France Literature BAUDELAIRE, Charles. *Les Fleurs du Mal*
FLAUBERT, Gustave. *Madame Bovary*
SAINTE-BEUVE, Charles-Augustin. *Causeries du Lundi*
Painting MILLET, Jean-François. *Les Glaneuses* (Louvre)
Italy Literature CARDUCCI, Giosuè. *Rime*
Music VERDI, Giuseppe. *Simone Boccanegra*

SLAVONIC EUROPE

Russia Literature GONCHAROV, Ivan Alexandrovich. *The Fregate Pallada*

HUNGARY

Music LISZT, Franz. *Eine Faust-Symphonie* (first perf.; first pr. 1861)

1858

GREAT BRITAIN

Discoveries	SPEKE, John. *Victoria Nyanza* disc.
History	CARLYLE, Thomas. *Frederick the Great* bgn. (compl. 1865)
Literature	MORRIS, William. *The Defence of Guenevere*
	THACKERAY, William Makepeace. *The Virginians* (compl. 1859)
	TROLLOPE, Anthony. *Doctor Thorne*
	TROLLOPE, Anthony. *The Three Clerks*

THE LOW COUNTRIES

Belgium

Literature	COSTER, Charles de. *Légendes Flamandes*
Music	FRANCK, César. *Messe Solennelle*

NORTHERN EUROPE

Norway

Folklore	BUGGE, Elseus Sophus. *Gamle Norske Folkeviser*
Literature	BJÖRNSON, Björnstjerne. *Mellem Slagene*
	IBSEN, Henrik. *Haermaendene paa Helgeland*

CENTRAL EUROPE

Germany

Medicine	VIRCHOW, Rudolf. *Cellularpathologie*
Music	CORNELIUS, Peter. *Der Barbier von Bagdad*

LATIN EUROPE

France

History	*Correspondance de Napoléon*
	GUIZOT, François-Pierre-Guillaume. *Mémoires pour servir à l'Histoire de mon Temps* bgn. (compl. 1868)
Medicine	BERNARD, Claude. Function of vaso-constrictor nerves discovered
Music	OFFENBACH, Jacques. *Orphée aux Enfers*
Painting	MANET, Edouard. *Le Concert aux Tuileries* (Dublin)

1859

GREAT BRITAIN

Biology	DARWIN, Charles Robert. *Origin of Species by Means of Natural Selection*
Chemistry	FARADAY, Michael. *Experimental Researches in Chemistry and Physics*
	MAXWELL, James Clerk. *Illustrations of the dynamical theory of gases*
Discoveries	LIVINGSTONE, David. Lake Nyassa discovered
Literature	DICKENS, Charles. *A Tale of Two Cities*
	ELIOT, George; Mary Ann Evans. *Adam Bede*

Literature	FITZGERALD, Edward. *Rubáiyát of Omar Khayyam* MEREDITH, George. *The Ordeal of Richard Feverel* TENNYSON, Alfred. *Idylls of the King*
Museums	Scottish National Gallery, Edinburgh, opnd.
Philosophy	MILL, John Stuart. *On Liberty*

CENTRAL EUROPE

Germany

Chemistry	BUNSEN, Robert W., and KIRCHHOFF. Spectrum analysis discovered
Economics	MARX, Karl. *Zur Kritik der politischen Oekonomie*
History	FREYTAG, Gustav. *Bilder aus der Deutschen Vergangenheit* bgn. (compl. 1867) GREGOROVIUS, Ferdinand. *Geschichte der Stadt Rom in Mittelalter* bgn. (compl. 1873) RANKE, Leopold von. *Englische Geschichte im 16. und 17. Jahrhundert* bgn. (compl. 1868)
Mathematics	RIEMANN, Georg Friedrich Bernhard. *Ueber die Anzahl der Primzahlen unter einer gegebenen Groesse*
Physics	HELMHOLTZ, Hermann. *Handbuch der physiologischen Optik* bgn. (compl. 1866)

LATIN EUROPE

France

Literature	HUGO, Victor. *La Légende des Siècles* MISTRAL, Frédéric. *Mirèio*
Music	GOUNOD, Charles. *Faust* (Marguerite)
Painting	MILLET, Jean-François. *L'Angélus* (Louvre)
Physics	PLANTÉ, Gaston. Accumulator inv.

Italy

Music	VERDI, Giuseppe. *Un Ballo in Maschera*
Theatre	Début of Adelina Patti

SLAVONIC EUROPE

Russia

Literature	DOSTOIEVSKY, Fyodor Michailovich. *The Mayor of Stepanchikovo* GONCHAROV, Ivan Alexandrovich. *Oblomov*

1860

GREAT BRITAIN

Chemistry	BESSEMER, Henry. Bessemer converter introd.
Literature	ELIOT, George ; Mary Ann Evans. *The Mill on the Floss* SWINBURNE, Algernon Charles. *The Queen Mother*
Physics	MAXWELL, James Clerk. *On the Theory of Compound Colours*

THE LOW COUNTRIES

Holland   Literature   MULTATULI; Eduard Douwes Dekker. *Max Havelaar*

CENTRAL EUROPE

Germany   Physics   FECHNER, Gustav Theodor. *Elemente der Psychophysik*

Switzerland   History   BURCKHARDT, Jakob. *Die Kultur der Renaissance in Italien*

LATIN EUROPE

France   Chemistry   BERTHELOT, Marcellin. *Chimie Organique*

    Literature   BAUDELAIRE, Charles. *Les Paradis Artificiels*

Italy   Politics   MAZZINI, Giuseppe. *Ai Giovani d'Italia*

Rumania   Universities   Jassy fnd.

Spain   Philosophy   SANZ DEL RIO, Julián. *Analítica, Metafísica* bgn. (compl. 1874)

SLAVONIC EUROPE

Czechoslovakia   Medicine   CZERMAK, Johann Nepomuk. Rhinoscopy introd.

Russia   Colonization   Vladivostok fnd.

    Literature   OSTROVSKY, Alexander Nicolaievich. *The Thunderstorm*

1861

GREAT BRITAIN

Literature   DICKENS, Charles. *Great Expectations*

ELIOT, George; Mary Ann Evans. *Silas Marner*

MEREDITH, George. *Evan Harrington*

ROSSETTI, Dante Gabriel. *Dante and his Circle*

THACKERAY, William Makepeace. *Lovel, the Widower*

TROLLOPE, Anthony. *Framley Parsonage*

Pedagogy   SPENCER, Herbert. *Education: intellectual, moral, and physical*

Philology   MUELLER, Friedrich Max. *The Science of Language*

Physics   MAXWELL, James Clerk. *Physical Lines of Force*

Politics   MILL, John Stuart. *Considerations on Representative Government*

THE LOW COUNTRIES

Belgium   Literature   COSTER, Charles de. *Contes Brabançons*

Holland   Literature   MULTATULI; Eduard Douwes Dekker.
        Minnebrieven

CENTRAL EUROPE

Austria   Medicine   SEMMELWEISS, Ignaz. *Die Aetiologie, der
        Begriff und die Prophylaxe des Kind-
        bettfiebers*
Germany   Chemistry   KEKULÉ, Friedrich August. *Lehrbuch der
        organischen Chemie* bgn. (compl. 1887)
      Literature   FONTANE, Theodor. *Balladen*
      Medicine   PETTENKOFER, Max, and VOIT, Karl. *Ueber
        einen neuen Respirationsapparat* (construc-
        tion of calorimeter; basal metabolism)
      Music   BRAHMS, Johannes. *First Quartet in G
        minor*, op. 25
Switzerland   Philosophy   BACHOFEN, Johann Jakob. *Das Mutterrecht*

LATIN EUROPE

France   Medicine   BROCA, Paul. *Remarques sur le Siège de la
        Faculté du Langage articulé* . . .
      Painting   MANET, Edouard. *Guitariste* (Fauré Coll.)
Spain   Politics   ARENAL, Concepción. *La Beneficencia, la
        Filantropía, y la Caridad*

SLAVONIC EUROPE

Russia   Literature   DOSTOIEVSKY, Fyodor Michailovich. *The
        Insulted*
        DOSTOIEVSKY, Fyodor Michailovich. *The
        House of the Dead*

HUNGARY

      Literature   MADACH, Imre. *Az ember tragédiája* (The
        Tragedy of Man)

1862

GREAT BRITAIN

      Literature   BORROW, George. *Wild Wales, its People,
        Language and Scenery*
        ROSSETTI, Christina Georgina. *Goblin
        Market*
        THACKERAY, William Makepeace. *The
        Adventures of Philip*
        TROLLOPE, Anthony. *Orley Farm*
      Music   SULLIVAN, Arthur Seymour. *Five Songs
        from Shakespeare*
      Sociology   RUSKIN, John. *Unto this Last*
        SPENCER, Herbert. *First Principles*

THE LOW COUNTRIES

Holland	Literature	MULTATULI; Eduard Douwes Dekker. *Ideen* bgn. (compl. 1877)

CENTRAL EUROPE

Germany	Chemistry	WOEHLER, Friedrich. Acetylene first prep. from calcium carbide
	Literature	HEBBEL, Friedrich. *Die Nibelungen*
	Politics	LASSALLE, Ferdinand. *Arbeiter-Programm*

LATIN EUROPE

France	Literature	FLAUBERT, Gustave. *Salammbô*
		HUGO, Victor. *Les Misérables*
		LECONTE DE LISLE, Charles-Marie. *Poèmes Barbares*
	Theatre	Début of Sarah Bernhardt
Italy	Music	VERDI, Giuseppe. *La Forza del Destino*

SLAVONIC EUROPE

Russia	Literature	TURGENIEV, Ivan Sergeievich. *Fathers and Sons*
	Music	BALAKIREV, Mily Alexeivich. *Islamey*
		BALAKIREV, Mily Alexeivich. *Tamara*

1863

GREAT BRITAIN

	Biology	HUXLEY, Thomas Henry. *Evidence as to Man's Place in Nature*
	History	GARDINER, Samuel Rawson. *The History of England from the Accession of James I to the Restoration* bgn. (compl. 1901)
	Literature	ELIOT, George; Mary Ann Evans. *Romola*
	Painting	ROSSETTI, Dante Gabriel. *Beata Beatrix* (Tate Gal. Lond.)
	Philosophy	MILL, John Stuart. *Utilitarianism*
	Travels	SPEKE, John. *Journal of the Discovery of the Source of the Nile*

THE LOW COUNTRIES

Belgium	Literature	GEZELLE, Guido. *Gedichten*

CENTRAL EUROPE

Germany	Philology	MOMMSEN, Theodor *Corpus Inscriptionum Latinarum*, Vol. I (ed.)
	Physics	HELMHOLTZ, Hermann. *Die Lehre von den Tonempfindungen*
	Politics	LASSALLE, Ferdinand. *Arbeiter-Lesebuch*

LATIN EUROPE

France   History   RENAN, Ernest. *Histoire des Origines du Christianisme.* Vol. I

Literature   SAINTE-BEUVE, Charles-Augustin. *Nouveaux Lundis* bgn. (compl. 1872)

Music   BIZET, Georges. *Les Pêcheurs de Perles*

Painting   DORÉ, Gustave. Illus. to Cervantes' *Don Quixote*

MANET, Edouard. *Le Déjeuner sur l'Herbe* (Luxembourg, Paris)

Italy   Literature   CARDUCCI, Giosuè. *Inno a Satana*

Spain   History   COLMEIRO, Manuel. *Historia de la Economía política en España*

Literature   CASTRO, Rosalía de. *Cantares gallegos*

1864

GREAT BRITAIN

Biography   NEWMAN, John Henry. *Apologia pro Vita sua*

Biology   SPENCER, Herbert. *The Principles of Biology*

Literature   BROWNING, Robert. *Dramatis Personae*

DICKENS, Charles. *Our Mutual Friend*

TENNYSON, Alfred. *Enoch Arden*

TROLLOPE, Anthony. *The Small House at Allington*

Physics   MAXWELL, James Clerk. *On a Dynamical Theory of the Electromagnetic Field*

NORTHERN EUROPE

Norway   Literature   IBSEN, Henrik. *Kongs-emnerne* (The Pretenders)

Sweden   Chemistry   NOBEL, Alfred. Detonator inv.

CENTRAL EUROPE

Austria   Literature   STIFTER, Adalbert. *Witiko*

Music   BRUCKNER, Anton. *Mass No. 1 in D minor,* (revised 1881-82)

Press   *Neue Freie Presse* iss.

Germany   Literature   RAABE, Wilhelm. *Der Hungerpastor*

REUTER, Fritz. *Ut mine Stromtid*

Medicine   TRAUBE, Ludwig. *Erwaegungen ueber die Ursache der Fieberwaerme*

Zoology   BREHM, Alfred. *Tierleben,* Pt. I

Switzerland Painting   BOECKLIN, Arnold. *Villa at the Sea* (Munich)

LATIN EUROPE

France   Archaeology   FUSTEL DE COULANGES, Numa Denis. *La Cité Antique*

[271]

France	Literature	VIGNY, Alfred de. *Les Destinées* (posth.)
		ZOLA, Emile. *Contes à Ninon*
	Music	OFFENBACH, Jacques. *La Belle Hélène*
	Painting	FANTIN-LATOUR, Henri. *L'Hommage à Delacroix* (Mus. des Arts décoratifs, Paris)
	Sculpture	RODIN, Georges. *L'Homme au Nez cassé*
Italy	Psychology	LOMBROSO, Cesare. *Genio e Follia*
Rumania	Universities	Bucharest, fnd.

SLAVONIC EUROPE

Russia	Literature	TOLSTOI, Leo Nicolaievich. *War and Peace* bgn. (compl. 1869)
Yugoslavia	Universities	Belgrade fnd.

ROMAN CATHOLIC CHURCH

Syllabus Errorum

1865

GREAT BRITAIN

	Aesthetics	RUSKIN, John. *Sesame and Lilies*
	Literature	CARROLL, Lewis; Charles Lutwidge Dodgson. *Alice in Wonderland*
		GASKELL, Elizabeth Cleghorn. *Wives and Daughters*
		SWINBURNE, Algernon Charles. *Atalanta in Calydon*
		SWINBURNE, Algernon Charles. *Chastelard*
	Medicine	LISTER, Joseph. First use of carbolic acid on a compound wound
	Societies	Salvation Army fnd.
	Travels	LIVINGSTONE, David. *Expedition to the Zambesi and its Tributaries*

CENTRAL EUROPE

Austria	Biology	MENDEL, Gregor. *Versuche ueber Pflanzenhybriden*
Germany	Literature	BUSCH, Wilhelm. *Max und Moritz*
	Music	WAGNER, Richard. *Tristan und Isolde* (first perf.; comp. 1859)

LATIN EUROPE

France	Aesthetics	TAINE, Hippolyte. *Philosophie de l'Art* bgn. (compl. 1869)
	Literature	GONCOURT, Edmond and Jules de. *Germinie Lacerteux*
	Music	MEYERBEER, Giacomo. *L'Africaine*
	Painting	MANET, Edouard. *Olympia* (Louvre)
		MOREAU, Gustave. *Head of Orpheus* (Luxembourg, Paris)

SLAVONIC 'EUROPE

Russia   Music   RIMSKY-KORSAKOV, Nicolai Andreievich. *First Symphony in E minor*
Universities   Odessa fnd.

1866

GREAT BRITAIN

Literature   ELIOT, George ; Mary Ann Evans. *Felix Holt, the Radical*
KINGSLEY, Charles. *Hereward the Wake*
NEWMAN, John Henry. *The Dream of Gerontius*
SWINBURNE, Algernon Charles. *Poems and Ballads*

THE LOW COUNTRIES

Belgium   Architecture   Palais de Justice, Brussels, bgn. (compl. 1883; Polaert)

NORTHERN EUROPE

Norway   Literature   IBSEN, Henrik. *Brand*
Sweden   Chemistry   NOBEL, Alfred. Dynamite inv.

CENTRAL EUROPE

Germany   Biology   HAECKEL, Ernst. *Generelle Morphologie der Organismen*
Chemistry   KEKULÉ, Friedrich August. *Untersuchungen ueber aromatische Verbindungen* (theory of the benzene ring ; in "Annalen der Chemie ")

LATIN EUROPE

France   Encyclo-   LAROUSSE, Pierre. *Grand Dictionnaire Universel du XIX⁶ Siècle*
paedia
History of Art   TAINE, Hippolyte. *Voyage en Italie*
Literature   BAUDELAIRE, Charles. *Les Epaves*
DAUDET, Alphonse. *Lettres de mon Moulin*
HUGO, Victor. *Les Travailleurs de la Mer*
VERLAINE, Paul. *Poèmes Saturniens*
Music   THOMAS, Ambroise. *Mignon*
Painting   DORÉ, Gustave. Illus. to the Bible
MONET, Claude. *Camille* (Bremen)
Italy   Press   *Il Secolo* iss.

SLAVONIC EUROPE

Czechoslovakia   Music   SMETANA, Frederik. *Prodand nevěsta* (The Bartered Bride)
Poland   Periodicals   *Przeglad Polski* (Polish Review) iss.
Russia   Literature   DOSTOIEVSKY, Fyodor Michailovich. *Crime and Punishment*

1867

GREAT BRITAIN

Education   MILL, John Stuart. *Essays on a Liberal Education*
Literature   MORRIS, William. *The Life and Death of Jason*
   TROLLOPE, Anthony. *The Last Chronicle of Barset*
Physics   THOMSON, William (Lord Kelvin), and TAIT, Peter Guthrie. *Treatise on Natural Philosophy*, Pt. I (Pt. II, 1874)
Politics   BAGEHOT, Walter. *The English Constitution*

THE LOW COUNTRIES

Belgium   Literature   COSTER, Charles de. *Légende de Thyl Uylenspiegel et de Lamme Goedzak*

NORTHERN EUROPE

Norway   Literature   IBSEN, Henrik. *Peer Gynt*

CENTRAL EUROPE

Austria   Music   STRAUSS, Johann. *An der schoenen blauen Donau*
Germany   Economics   MARX, Karl. *Das Kapital. Kritik der politischen Oekonomie*
   Medicine   COHNHEIM, Julius. *Ueber Entzuendung und Eiterung*

LATIN EUROPE

France   Literature   ZOLA, Emile. *Thérèse Raquin*
Italy   Biography   AZEGLIO, Massimo d'. *I miei Ricordi*
   Music   VERDI, Giuseppe. *Don Carlos*

SLAVONIC EUROPE

Russia   Music   TCHAIKOVSKY, Pyotr Ilyich. *Symphony No. 1 in G minor*, op. 13 (*Winter Day-Dreams*)
Yugoslavia   Academies   South Slavonic Academy, Zagreb, fnd.

1868

GREAT BRITAIN

Biology | DARWIN, Charles Robert. *The Variation of Animals and Plants under Domestication*
Literature | BROWNING, Robert. *The Ring and the Book* bgn. (compl. 1869)
| MORRIS, William. *The Earthly Paradise* bgn. (compl. 1870)
Physics | TAIT, Peter Guthrie. *Thermodynamics*
Societies | Royal Historical Society fnd.

CENTRAL EUROPE

Germany Biology | HAECKEL, Ernst. *Natuerliche Schoepfungsgeschichte*
Music | BRAHMS, Johannes. *Ein Deutsches Requiem*, op. 45 (comp. 1857-66)
| WAGNER, Richard. *Die Meistersinger zu Nuernberg* (first perf.)
Painting | LEIBL, Wilhelm. *Portrait of Frau Gedon* bgn. (compl. 1869; Munich)
| SCHWIND, Moritz von. *Melusine Cyclus* bgn. (compl. 1869; Schubert Mus., Vienna)

LATIN EUROPE

France Painting | DEGAS, Edgar. *L'Orchestre* (Louvre)
| MANET, Edouard. *Execution of Emperor Maximilian* (Mannheim)
| MANET, Edouard. *Portrait of Emile Zola* (Louvre)
Italy Music | BOITO, Arrigo. *Mefistofele*

SLAVONIC EUROPE

Russia Literature | DOSTOIEVSKY, Fyodor Michailovich. *The Idiot*
Politics | BAKUNIN, Michael. *People's Business*

1869

GREAT BRITAIN

Literature | TROLLOPE, Anthony. *Phineas Finn, the Irish Member*
Painting | HOLMAN HUNT, William. *The Shadow of the Cross* (Manchester)

NORTHERN EUROPE

Norway Literature | IBSEN, Henrik. *De Unges Forbund*

[275]

CENTRAL EUROPE

Austria	Music	BRUCKNER, Anton. *Mass No. 2 in E minor* (first perf.; comp. 1866)
Germany	Music	BRAHMS, Johannes. *Hungarian Dances, Nos. I and II*
		WAGNER, Richard. *Rheingold* (first perf.)
	Philosophy	HARTMANN, Eduard von. *Die Philosophie des Unbewussten*

LATIN EUROPE

France	Literature	FLAUBERT, Gustave. *L'Education sentimentale*
		VERLAINE, Paul. *Fêtes galantes*
	Painting	MANET, Edouard. *The Balcony* (Louvre)
	Sculpture	CARPEAUX, Jean-Baptiste. *La Danse* (Paris)
Portugal	Literature	DEUS, João de. *Flores de Campo*

SLAVONIC EUROPE

Russia	Chemistry	MENDELÉEV, Dmitry Ivanovich. *Elements of Chemistry*
	Literature	GONCHAROV, Ivan Alexandrovich. *The Precipice*
	Music	TCHAIKOVSKY, Pyotr Ilyich. *The Voievoda* (comp. 1868)

1870

GREAT BRITAIN

Literature	DICKENS, Charles. *The Mystery of Edwin Drood* (uncompleted)
	DISRAELI, Benjamin. *Lothair*
	ROSSETTI, Dante Gabriel. *Poems*
Painting	ROSSETTI, Dante Gabriel. *The House of Life* (Tate Gal. Lond.)
Universities	Keble College, Oxford, fnd.

THE LOW COUNTRIES

Belgium	Literature	COSTER, Charles de. *Voyage de Noce*

CENTRAL EUROPE

Germany	Archaeology	SCHLIEMANN, Heinrich. *Excavations at Hissarlik* (Troy) bgn.
	Music	WAGNER, Richard. *Die Walkuere* (first perf.)
	Politics	DOELLINGER, Ignaz von. *Der Papst und das Konzil*

LATIN EUROPE

France Literature VERLAINE, Paul. *La bonne Chanson*
Music DELIBES, Léo. *Coppélia*
Philosophy TAINE, Hippolyte. *De l'Intelligence*
Zoology PASTEUR, Louis. *Etudes sur la Maladie des Vers-à-Soie*
Portugal History of Literature BRAGA, Joaquim Theophilo Fernandes. *Historia da Litteratura Portugueza* bgn. (compl. 1892)
Spain Education GINER DE LOS RÍOS, Francisco. *La Universidad Española* bgn. (compl. 1916)

SLAVONIC EUROPE

Russia Music TCHAIKOVSKY, Pyotr Ilyich. *Overture to Romeo and Juliet*

ROMAN CATHOLIC CHURCH

Vatican Council

1871

GREAT BRITAIN

Biology DARWIN, Charles Robert. *The Descent of Man, and Selection in relation to Sex*
Economics RUSKIN, John. *Fors Clavigera* bgn. (compl. 1887)
Literature BULWER LYTTON, Edward George. *The Coming Race*
CARROLL, Lewis; Charles Lutwidge Dodgson. *Through the Looking Glass and what Alice found there*
ELIOT, George; Mary Ann Evans. *Middlemarch* bgn. (compl. 1872)
SWINBURNE, Algernon Charles. *Songs before Sunrise*

NORTHERN EUROPE

Norway Literature IBSEN, Henrik. *Digte* (poems)
Medicine HANSEN, Armauer. Bacillus leprae discovered

CENTRAL EUROPE

Germany History MOMMSEN, Theodor. *Roemisches Staatsrecht* bgn. (compl. 1888)
Medicine WEIGERT, Karl. First staining of bacteria with carmine
Music BRAHMS, Johannes. *Schicksalslied*, op. 54 (comp. 1868)

Germany	Painting	FEUERBACH, Anselm. *Iphigenie* (Stuttgart)
	Philosophy	NIETZSCHE, Friedrich. *Die Geburt der Tragoedie*

LATIN EUROPE

France	Academies	Ecole Libre des Sciences Politiques, Paris, fnd.
	Literature	ZOLA, Emile. *Les Rougon-Macquart.* Pt. I, *La Fortune des Rougon*
	Music	SAINT-SAËNS, Camille. *Le Rouet d'Omphale*
	Painting	COURBET, Gustave. *La Vague* (Louvre)
Italy	Music	VERDI, Giuseppe. *Aïda* (first European perf.)
Spain	Literature	BÉCQUER, Gustavo Adolfo. *Leyendas*
		BÉCQUER, Gustavo Adolfo. *Rimas*

SLAVONIC EUROPE

Russia	Chemistry	MENDELÉEV, Dmitry Ivanovich. *Die periodische Gesetzmaessigkeit der chemischen Elemente*
	Literature	DOSTOIEVSKY, Fyodor Michailovich. *The Demons*
		OSTROVSKY, Alexander Nicolaievich. *The Forest*

1872

GREAT BRITAIN

	Economics	RUSKIN, John. *Munera Pulveris*
	Literature	BUTLER, Samuel. *Erewhon*
		HARDY, Thomas. *Under the Greenwood Tree*
		HARDY, Thomas. *A Pair of Blue Eyes*
	Travels	STANLEY, Henry Morton. *How I found Livingstone*

NORTHERN EUROPE

Denmark	History of Literature	BRANDES, Georg. *Hovedströmninger i det 19. Aarhundrededs Litteratur* bgn. (compl. 1890)
	Literature	JACOBSEN, Jens Peter. *Mogens*
Norway	Literature	BJÖRNSON, Björnstjerne. *Sigurd Jorsalfar*

CENTRAL EUROPE

Austria	Medicine	BILLROTH, Albert Christian Theodor. First resection of the oesophagus
	Music	BRUCKNER, Anton. *Mass No. 3 in F minor* (first perf.; comp. 1867-68)

Germany	Jurisprudence	GNEIST, Heinrich Rudolf. *Der Rechtsstaat*
		IHERING, Rudolf. *Der Kampf um's Recht*
		Edition of the *Corpus Juris Civilis* by Theodor Mommsen
		Deutsches Reichsstrafgesetzbuch (German Criminal Code)
	Literature	FREYTAG, Gustav. *Die Ahnen*, Pt. I
Switzerland	Literature	KELLER, Gottfried. *Sieben Legenden*

LATIN EUROPE

France	Literature	DAUDET, Alphonse. *Tartarin de Tarascon*
	Painting	DEGAS, Edgar. *La Femme à la Potiche* (Louvre)
		DEGAS, Edgar. *Le Foyer de la Danse* (Louvre)
		MANET, Edouard. *Le bon Bock* (Tyson Coll. Philadelphia)
Italy	Theatre	Début of Eleonora Duse
Spain	Literature	HERNÁNDEZ, José. *El Gaucho Martín Fierro*

SLAVONIC EUROPE

Russia	Music	DARGOMIJSKY, Alexander Sergeievich. *The Stone Guest* (Don Juan)
		TCHAIKOVSKY, Pyotr Ilyich. *Symphony No. 2 in C minor*, op. 17

HUNGARY

	Universities	Koloszvar (Klausenburg, Cluj; Transsylvania) fnd.

1873

GREAT BRITAIN

	History	PATER, Walter Horatio. *The Renaissance*
	Literature	BULWER LYTTON, Edward George. *Kenelm Chillingly*
	Physics	MAXWELL, James Clerk. *Treatise on Electricity and Magnetism*
	Sociology	SPENCER, Herbert. *Study of Sociology*
	Universities	Girton College, Cambridge, fnd.

THE LOW COUNTRIES

Belgium	Music	FRANCK, César. *Prélude, Fugue et Variations*

NORTHERN EUROPE

Norway	Literature	BJÖRNSON, Björnstjerne. *Brude-Slaatten* (The Bridal March)
		IBSEN, Henrik. *Kejser og Galilaeer*

[279]

CENTRAL EUROPE

Austria Medicine BILLROTH, Albert Christian Theodor. First excision of the larynx made

Germany Painting FEUERBACH, Anselm. *Plato's Symposium* (? Berlin)
LIEBERMANN, Max. *Women plucking Geese* (Nat. Gal. Berlin)
MARÉES, Hans von. Frescoes in the Zoological Institute, Naples
Philosophy SIGWART, Christoph von. *Logik*

LATIN EUROPE

France Literature DAUDET, Alphonse. *Contes du Lundi*
RIMBAUD, Arthur. *Une Saison en Enfer*
Mathematics HERMITE, Charles. *Sur la Fonction exponentielle*
Medicine CHARCOT, Jean-Martin. *Leçons sur les Maladies du Système nerveux*, Series I
Music BIZET, Georges. *L'Arlésienne*
Painting CÉZANNE, Paul. *La Maison du Pendu* (Luxembourg, Paris)
CÉZANNE, Paul. *Straw Hat* (Metropolitan Mus., New York)
FROMENTIN, Eugène. *Fauconnier Arabe* (Luxembourg, Paris)

Italy Astronomy SCHIAPARELLI, Giovanni Virginio. *Le Stelle cadenti*

Portugal Literature HERCULANO, Alexandre. *Opusculos* bgn. (compl. 1908)

Spain History CARDENAS, Francisco de. *Historia de la Propriedad territorial en España*
Literature PÉREZ GALDÓS, Benito. *Episodios Nacionales* bgn. (compl. 1912)

SLAVONIC EUROPE

Czechoslovakia Music DVOŘÁK, Antonin. *Symphony in E flat* (originally op. 10)

Russia Literature TOLSTOI, Leo Nicolaievich. *Anna Karenina*
Politics BAKUNIN, Michael. *Statecraft and Anarchy*

1874

GREAT BRITAIN

History STUBBS, William. *Constitutional History of England in its Origin and Development*
Literature ELIOT, George ; Mary Ann Evans. *Daniel Deronda*
HARDY, Thomas. *Far from the Madding Crowd*
Philosophy SIDGWICK, Henry. *The Methods of Ethics*
Physics THOMSON, William. *Electrostatics and Magnetism*

THE LOW COUNTRIES

Holland   Chemistry   VAN'T HOFF, Jacobus Hendricus. *La Chimie dans l'Espace*

CENTRAL EUROPE

Austria   Music   STRAUSS, Johann. *Die Fledermaus*
Germany   Biology   HAECKEL, Ernst. *Anthropogenie*

LATIN EUROPE

France   Literature   BARBEY D'AUREVILLY, Jules-Amédée. *Les Diaboliques*
         FLAUBERT, Gustave. *La Tentation de Saint-Antoine*
    Music   SAINT-SAËNS, Camille. *La Danse Macabre*
    Painting   RENOIR, Auguste. *La Loge* (Norwich)
Spain   Literature   ALARCÓN, Pedro Antonio de. *El Sombrero de tres Picos*
         VALERA, Juan. *Pepita Jiménez*

SLAVONIC EUROPE

Czechoslovakia   Music   DVOŘÁK, Antonin. *Symphony in D minor* (originally op. 13)
         DVOŘÁK, Antonin. *First String Quartet in A minor*, op. 16
         SMETANA, Frederik. *Ma Vlast* bgn. (My Country ; compl. 1879)
Russia   Music   MOUSSORGSKY, Modest Petrovich. *Boris Godunov*
         MOUSSORGSKY, Modest Petrovich. *Pictures from an Exhibition*
         MOUSSORGSKY, Modest Petrovich. *Fantasia, Night on the Bare Mountain*

1875

GREAT BRITAIN

    Literature   TENNYSON, Alfred. *Queen Mary*
    Universities   Newnham College, Cambridge, fnd.

NORTHERN EUROPE

Norway   Literature   BJÖRNSON, Björnstjerne. *En Fallit*

CENTRAL EUROPE

Austria   Universities   Austrian University, Czernowitz, fnd.
Germany   Biology   WEISMANN, August. *Studien zur Descendenztheorie*
    Painting   MENZEL, Adolf. *Eisenwalzwerk* (The Forge; Nat. Gal. Berlin)
Switzerland   Painting   BOECKLIN, Arnold. *Triton and Nereid* (Berlin)

LATIN EUROPE

France History TAINE, Hippolyte. *Les Origines de la Frame contemporaine* bgn. (compl. 1890)

 Music BIZET, Georges. *Carmen*

 Painting CÉZANNE, Paul. *Madame Cézanne in a striped blouse* (Coll. Reber, Lausanne)
MONET, Claude. *Le Bassin d'Argenteuil* (Louvre)

 Theatre " Grand Opéra," Paris, opnd. (blt. betw. 1862 and 1874 by Charles Garnier)
Début of Gabrielle Réjane

SLAVONIC EUROPE

Czechoslovakia Music DVOŘÁK, Antonin. *Symphony No. 3 in F,* op. 76 (originally Symphony No. 1)

Russia Music TCHAIKOVSKY, Pyotr Ilyich. *Symphony No. 3 in D major* (*The "Polish"*), op. 29
TCHAIKOVSKY, Pyotr Ilyich. *First Piano Concerto in B flat minor,* op. 23

1876

GREAT BRITAIN

 Literature HARDY, Thomas. *The Hand of Ethelberta*
MORRIS, William. *Sigurd the Volsung*
STEVENSON, Robert Louis. *The New Arabian Nights*

 Philosophy BRADLEY, Francis Herbert. *Ethical Studies*

 Sociology SPENCER, Herbert. *The Principles of Sociology*

 Zoology WALLACE, Alfred Russel. *The Geographical Distribution of Animals*

THE LOW COUNTRIES

Belgium Music FRANCK, César. *Les Eolides*

NORTHERN EUROPE

Denmark Literature DRACHMANN, Holger. *I Storm og Stille*
JACOBSEN, Jens Peter. *Fru Marie Grubbe*

CENTRAL EUROPE

Germany Aesthetics FECHNER, Gustav Theodor. *Vorschule der Aesthetik*

 Music BRAHMS, Johannes. *Symphony No. 1 in C minor,* op. 68 (comp. 1875)
WAGNER, Richard. *Siegfried* (first perf.)
WAGNER, Richard. *Goetterdaemmerung* (first perf.)

[282]

Germany	Palaeontology	ZITTEL, Karl Alfred von. *Handbuch der Palaeontologie* bgn. (compl. 1893)
Switzerland	Literature	MEYER, Conrad Ferdinand. *Georg Jenatsch*
	Universities	Geneva fnd.

LATIN EUROPE

France	History of Art	FROMENTIN, Eugène. *Maîtres d'autrefois*
	Literature	MALLARMÉ, Stéphane. *L'Après-midi d'un Faune*
	Music	DELIBES, Léo. *Sylvia*
	Painting	DEGAS, Edgar. *L'Absinthe* (Louvre) MOREAU, Gustave. *Apparition* (Luxembourg, Paris) RENOIR, Auguste. *Le Moulin de la Galette* (Louvre, Paris)
Italy	Music	PONCHIELLI, Amilcare. *La Gioconda*
Portugal	Literature	EÇA DE QUEIROS, José Maria. *O Crime do Padre Amaro*
Spain	Literature	PÉREZ GALDÓS, Benito. *Doña Perfecta* VERDAGUER, Jacinto. *L'Atlántida*
	Politics	GINER DE LOS RÍOS, Francisco. *Principios de Derecho natural*

SLAVONIC EUROPE

Czechoslovakia	Music	DVOŘÁK, Antonin. *The Heirs of the White Mountain,* op. 30

1877

GREAT BRITAIN

Music	SULLIVAN, Arthur Seymour. *The Lost Chord*

THE LOW COUNTRIES

Holland	Universities	Amsterdam, re-fnd.

NORTHERN EUROPE

Norway	Literature	BJÖRNSON, Björnstjerne. *Kongen* IBSEN, Henrik. *Samfundets Stötter*

CENTRAL EUROPE

Germany	Literature	STORM, Theodor. *Aquis submersus*
	Music	BRAHMS, Johannes. *Symphony No. 2 in D major,* op. 73

LATIN EUROPE

France	Literature	FLAUBERT, Gustave. *Trois Contes* GOBINEAU, Joseph-Arthur, Comte de. *La Renaissance* ZOLA, Emile. *L'Assommoir*

[283]

France	Music	SAINT-SAËNS, Camille. *La jeunesse d'Hercule*
		SAINT-SAËNS, Camille. *Samson et Dalila*
	Painting	MANET, Edouard. *Nana* (Luxembourg, Paris)
	Sculpture	RODIN, Auguste. *The Bronze Age*
Italy	Literature	CARDUCCI, Giosuè. *Odi Barbare*
Spain	Encyclopaedia	*Diccionario enciclopédico Hispano-Americano* bgn. (compl. 1899)

SLAVONIC EUROPE

| Russia | Music | TCHAIKOVSKY, Pyotr Ilyich. *Symphony No. 4 in F minor*, op. 36 |

1878

GREAT BRITAIN

	History	LECKY, William Edward Hartpole. *The History of England in the Eighteenth Century* bgn. (compl. 1890)
	Literature	HARDY, Thomas. *The Return of the Native*
		STEVENSON, Robert Louis. *An Inland Voyage*
	Music	SULLIVAN, Arthur Seymour. *H.M.S. Pinafore*

NORTHERN EUROPE

Denmark	Literature	BANG, Hermann. *Hverdagskamp*
Sweden	Discoveries	NORDENSKJÖLD, Niels Adolf Erik. North-East Passage disc.
	Literature	STRINDBERG, August. *Mäster Olof*
	Universities	Stockholm fnd.

CENTRAL EUROPE

Germany	Literature	FONTANE, Theodor. *Vor dem Sturm*
	Medicine	KOCH, Robert. *Untersuchungen ueber die Aetiologie der Wundinfektionskrankheiten* (discovery of causes of traumatic infections)
	Painting	LEIBL, Wilhelm. *Women in Church* bgn. (compl. 1882; Hamburg)
	Philosophy	NIETZSCHE, Friedrich. *Menschliches Allzumenschliches*

LATIN EUROPE

| France | Literature | GONCOURT, Edmond de. *La Fille Elisa* |
| | Painting | PUVIS DE CHAVANNES, Pierre. *Childhood of St. Geneviève* (Panthéon, Paris) |

SLAVONIC EUROPE

Czechoslovakia Music DvoŘÁK, Antonin. *Three Slavonic Rhapsodies, op. 56*

1879

GREAT BRITAIN

Literature HARDY, Thomas. *The Trumpet Major*
      MEREDITH, George. *The Egoist*
      STEVENSON, Robert Louis. *Travels with a Donkey in the Cevennes*
Music SULLIVAN, Arthur Seymour. *The Pirates of Penzance*
Philosophy SPENCER, Herbert. *The Principles of Ethics* bgn. (compl. 1893)
Physics CAVENDISH, Henry. *Electrical Researches of the Hon. Henry Cavendish*, ed. by James Clerk Maxwell (posth.)
Universities Somerville College, Oxford, fnd.

THE LOW COUNTRIES

Belgium Music FRANCK, César. *Les Béatitudes*
        FRANCK, César. *Quintet in F minor*
Holland Chemistry VAN'T HOFF, Jacobus Hendricus. *Ansichten ueber die organische Chemie* bgn. (compl. 1881)

NORTHERN EUROPE

Norway Literature IBSEN, Henrik. *Et Dukkehjem*
Sweden Literature STRINDBERG, August. *Röde Rummet*

CENTRAL EUROPE

Germany History TREITSCHKE, Heinrich von. *Deutsche Geschichte im 19. Jahrhundert* bgn. (compl. 1895)
Medicine KRAFFT-EBING, Richard, Freiherr von. *Lehrbuch der Psychiatrie*
     NEISSER, Albert. *Ueber eine der Gonorrhöe eigentuemliche Mikrokokkenform* (discovery of gonococcus)
Switzerland Painting BOECKLIN, Arnold. *Ruggiero and Angelica* (Duesseldorf)

LATIN EUROPE

France Chemistry BERTHELOT, Marcellin. *Essai de Mécanique Chimique*
Painting MANET, Edouard. *Dans la Serre* (Berlin)
Sculpture RODIN, Auguste. *St. John the Baptist*
Zoology FABRE, Jean-Henri. *Souvenirs entomologiques* bgn. (compl. 1907)

SLAVONIC EUROPE

Russia Literature DOSTOIEVSKY, Fyodor Michailovich. *The Brothers Karamazov* bgn. (compl. 1880)

Music TCHAIKOVSKY, Pyotr Ilyich. *Eugene Onyegin*

HUNGARY

Literature ARANY, Janos. *Toldi Szerelme* (Toldi's Love)

1880

GREAT BRITAIN

Universities Manchester fnd.

NORTHERN EUROPE

Denmark Literature BANG, Hermann. *Haablöse Slögter*
JACOBSEN, Jens Peter. *Niels Lynhe*

CENTRAL EUROPE

Germany Chemistry BAEYER, Adolf von. Synthesis of indigotin from o-nitrocinnamic acid

History RANKE, Leopold von. *Weltgeschichte*, Vols. I and II

Medicine EBERTH, Karl. *Die Organismen in den Organen bei Typhus abdominalis* (first isolation of typhoid bacillus)

Music BRAHMS, Johannes. *Hungarian Dances*, Nos. 3 and 4

Philosophy WUNDT, Wilhelm. *Logik* bgn. (compl. 1883)

LATIN EUROPE

France Literature MAUPASSANT, Guy de. *Boule de Suif*
MAUPASSANT, Guy de. *Des Vers*
ZOLA, Emile. *Nana*

Medicine PASTEUR, Louis. Streptococcus, staphylococcus and pneumococcus discovered

Music DEBUSSY, Claude. *La Belle au Bois dormant*

Spain Philosophy MENÉNDEZ Y PELAYO, Marcelino. *Historia de los Heterodoxos Españoles* bgn. (compl. 1881)

SLAVONIC EUROPE

Czechoslovakia Music DVOŘÁK, Antonin. *Symphony No. 1 in D*, op. 60

Russia Music BORODIN, Alexander Porphyrievich. *In the Steppes*
TCHAIKOVSKY, Pyotr Ilyich. *String Quartet No. 3 in F flat minor*, op. 30

1881

GREAT BRITAIN

Literature	ROSSETTI, Dante Gabriel. *Ballads and Sonnets* STEVENSON, Robert Louis. *Virginibus Puerisque* SWINBURNE, Algernon Charles. *Mary Stuart*
Museums	Natural History Museum, Kensington, opnd.
Music	SULLIVAN, Arthur Seymour. *Patience*
Painting	ROSSETTI, Dante Gabriel. *Dante's Dream* compl. (bgn. 1869; Liverpool)
Theology	Revised Version of the New Testament

THE LOW COUNTRIES

Belgium   Literature   LEMONNIER, Camille. *Un Mâle*

NORTHERN EUROPE

Norway   Literature   IBSEN, Henrik. *Gengangere* (Ghosts)

CENTRAL EUROPE

Germany

Music	BRAHMS, Johannes. *Naenie*, op. 82 (comp. 1880)
Painting	LIEBERMANN, Max. *Asylum for old Men* (Berlin) LIEBERMANN, Max. *Courtyard of the Amsterdam Orphanage* (Berlin)
Philosophy	NIETZSCHE, Friedrich. *Morgenroete*
Technics	SIEMENS, Werner von. First electric railway constr.

LATIN EUROPE

France

Literature	FLAUBERT, Gustave. *Bouvard et Pécuchet* FRANCE, Anatole. *Le Crime de Sylvestre Bonnard* VERLAINE, Paul. *Sagesse*
Medicine	LAVERAN, Charles-Louis Alphonse. Parasite of malaria discovered PASTEUR, Louis. Anthrax vaccine disc.
Music	OFFENBACH, Jacques. *Contes d'Hoffmann*
Painting	RENOIR, Auguste. *Le Déjeuner des Canotiers* (Washington)

Spain   Literature   ECHEGARAY, José. *El Gran Galeotto*

1882

GREAT BRITAIN

Literature	HARDY, Thomas. *Two on a Tower* SWINBURNE, Algernon Charles. *Tristram of Lyonesse* WILDE, Oscar. *Poems*
Music	SULLIVAN, Arthur Seymour. *Iolanthe*
Physics	THOMSON, William. *Mathematical and Physical Papers* bgn. (compl. 1911)
Universities	Selwyn College, Cambridge, fnd.

NORTHERN EUROPE

Denmark	Literature	JACOBSEN, Jens Peter. *Noveller*
Norway	Literature	IBSEN, Henrik. *En Folkefiende*

CENTRAL EUROPE

Germany	Medicine	KOCH, Robert. Tuberculosis bacillus disc. EHRLICH, Paul. Tuberculosis bacillus stained
	Music	WAGNER, Richard. *Parsifal*
	Press	*Berliner Tageblatt* iss.
Switzerland	Literature	KELLER, Gottfried. *Das Sinngedicht* MEYER, Conrad Ferdinand. *Gedichte*

LATIN EUROPE

France	Literature	MAUPASSANT, Guy de. *Une Vie*
	Painting	MANET, Edouard. *Le Bar aux Folies-Bergères* (Tate Gal. Lond.)

SLAVONIC EUROPE

Russia	Literature	TURGENIEV, Ivan Sergeievich. *Poems in Prose*
	Music	GLAZOUNOV, Nicolai Konstantinovich. *Symphony No. 1 in E major*

1883

GREAT BRITAIN

Economics	SIDGWICK, Henry. *The Principles of Political Economy*
Literature	BRIDGES, Robert. *Prometheus the Firegiver* STEVENSON, Robert Louis. *Treasure Island*

NORTHERN EUROPE

Norway	Literature	BJÖRNSON, Björnstjerne. *Over Aevne*, Pt. I
Sweden	Physics	ARRHENIUS, Svante August. *Recherche sur la Conductibilité des Electrolytes*

CENTRAL EUROPE

Germany	Medicine	KLEBS, Edwin. Diphtheria bacillus discovered
		KOCH, Robert. Cholera bacillus discovered
	Music	BRAHMS, Johannes. *First Quintet in F major*, op. 88 (comp. 1881)
		BRAHMS, Johannes. *Symphony No. 3 in F major*, op. 90
	Philosophy	NIETZSCHE, Friedrich. *Also sprach Zarathustra*

LATIN EUROPE

France	Painting	CÉZANNE, Paul. *Rocky Landscape* (Paris)
		RENOIR, Auguste. *Umbrellas* (Tate Gal., Lond.)
Italy	Press	*La Tribuna* iss.
Spain	Literature	PALMA, Ricardo. *Tradiciones Peruanas*
	Philosophy	MENÉNDEZ Y PELAYO, Marcelino. *Historia de las Ideas estéticas en España* bgn. (compl. 1891)

SLAVONIC EUROPE

Czechoslovakia	Music	DVOŘÁK, Antonin. *Stabat Mater*, op. 58 (originally op. 28, as comp. 1876-77)

1884

GREAT BRITAIN

Music	SULLIVAN, Arthur Seymour. *Princess Ida*
Painting	BURNE-JONES, Edward. *King Cophetua and the Beggar Maid* (Tate Gal. Lond.)
Philology	*The Oxford English Dictionary*, Pt. I
Physics	THOMSON, William. *On Molecular Dynamics and the Wave Theory of Light* (Baltimore Lectures)
Theology	Revised Version of the Old Testament

THE LOW COUNTRIES

Belgium	Literature	EEKHOUD, Georges. *Kermesses*
	Music	FRANCK, César. *Les Djinns*
Holland	Chemistry	VAN'T HOFF, Jacobus Hendricus. *Etudes de Dynamique Chimique*

NORTHERN EUROPE

Denmark	Literature	DRACHMANN, Holger. *Smaa Fortöllinger*
Norway	Literature	IBSEN, Henrik. *Vildanden* (The Wild Duck)

CENTRAL EUROPE

Germany   Mathematics   MINKOWSKI, Hermann. *Mémoire sur la Théorie des Formes quadratiques à Coefficients entiers*

Medicine   NIKOLAIER, Arthur. Tetanus bacillus disc.

LATIN EUROPE

France   Literature   LECONTE DE LISLE, Charles-Marie. *Poèmes tragiques*

VERLAINE, Paul. *Jadis et naguère*

Medicine   BERNHEIM, Hippolyte. *De la suggestion*

Music   MASSENET, Jules. *Manon*

Painting   SEURAT, Georges. *Baignade* (Tate Gal., Lond.)

Press   *Le Matin* iss.

Sculpture   RODIN, Auguste. *The Burghers of Calais* bgn. (compl. 1895)

Spain   Literature   CASTRO, Rosalía de. *En las orillas del Sar*

PEREDA, José Maria de. *Sotileza*

SLAVONIC EUROPE

Russia   Bacteriology   METCHNIKOV, Ilya. *Daphnia*

1885

GREAT BRITAIN

Biography   *The Dictionary of National Biography*, Pt. I

Literature   MEREDITH, George. *Diana of the Crossways*

PATER, Walter Horatio. *Marius the Epicurean*

STEVENSON, Robert Louis. *A Child's Garden of Verses*

SWINBURNE, Algernon Charles. *Marino Faliero*

Music   SULLIVAN, Arthur Seymour. *The Gondoliers*

SULLIVAN, Arthur Seymour. *The Mikado*

Painting   WATTS, George Frederick. *Hope* (Tate Gal. Lond.)

NORTHERN EUROPE

Denmark   Literature   BANG, Hermann. *Excentriske Noveller*

CENTRAL EUROPE

Austria   Music   BRUCKNER, Anton. *Te Deum in C major* (comp. 1881-84)

STRAUSS, Johann. *Der Zigeunerbaron*

Germany Chemistry OSTWALD, Wilhelm. *Lehrbuch der allgemeinen Chemie* bgn. (compl. 1887)

       Medicine FRAENKEL, Albert. Diplococcus pneumoniae discovered

       Music BRAHMS, Johannes. *Symphony No. 4 in E minor*, op. 98 (compl. 1884-85)

       Technics DAIMLER, Gottlieb. First motor-bicycle const.

LATIN EUROPE

France History SOREL, Albert. *L'Europe et la Révolution Française* bgn. (compl. 1892)

     Literature MAUPASSANT, Guy de. *Bel Ami*
         ZOLA, Emile. *Germinal*

     Medicine PASTEUR, Louis. First anti-rabies inoculation

     Painting RENOIR, Auguste. *Baigneuses* (Philadelphia)

SLAVONIC EUROPE

Czechoslovakia Music DVOŘÁK, Antonin. *Symphony No. 2 in D minor*, op. 70

Russia Literature TOLSTOI, Leo Nicolaievich. *The Dominion of Darkness*

    Music GLAZOUNOV, Nicolai Konstantinovich. *Stenka Razin* (symphonic poem)

1886

GREAT BRITAIN

   Literature HARDY, Thomas. *The Mayor of Casterbridge*
         KIPLING, Rudyard. *Departmental Ditties*
         STEVENSON, Robert Louis. *Dr. Jekyll and Mr. Hyde*
         STEVENSON, Robert Louis. *Kidnapped*

THE LOW COUNTRIES

Belgium Literature VERHAEREN, Emile. *Les Soirs*

     Music FRANCK, César. *Symphony in D minor*

NORTHERN EUROPE

Denmark Literature BANG, Hermann. *Stille Eksistenzer*
Norway Literature IBSEN, Henrik. *Rosmersholm*
Sweden Literature STRINDBERG, August. *Tjensteqvinnans Son* (The Son of a Servant)

CENTRAL EUROPE

Germany History HARNACK, Adolf. *Lehrbuch der Dogmengeschichte* bgn. (compl. 1890)

Germany   Medicine   KRAFFT-EBING, Richard, Freiherr von. *Psychopathia Sexualis*

    Philosophy   NIETZSCHE, Friedrich. *Jenseits von Gut und Boese*

        WUNDT, Wilhelm. *Ethik*

    Technics   BENZ, Karl. First motor car prod.

LATIN EUROPE

France   Literature   LOTI, Pierre. *Pêcheurs d'Islande*

    RIMBAUD, Arthur. *Les Illuminations*

    ZOLA, Emile. *L'Œuvre*

    Painting   SEURAT, George. *La grande Jatte* (Chicago)

    Sculpture   RODIN, Auguste. Monument to Victor Hugo (first design)

Spain   Literature   PARDO BAZÁN, Emilia, Condesa de. *Los Pazos de Ulloa*

    PÉREZ GALDÓS, Benito. *Fortunata y Jacinta* bgn. (compl. 1887)

SLAVONIC EUROPE

Czechoslovakia Music   DVOŘÁK, Antonin. *New Slavonic Dances*, op. 72

Russia   Literature   TCHEKHOV, Anton Pavlovich. *Ivanov*

1887

GREAT BRITAIN

    Literature   HARDY, Thomas. *The Woodlanders*

    KIPLING, Rudyard. *Plain Tales from the Hills*

    PATER, Walter Horatio. *Imaginary Portraits*

    Music   SULLIVAN, Arthur Seymour. *Ruddigore*

    Technics   DUNLOP, John Boyd. Pneumatic tyre inv.

THE LOW COUNTRIES

Belgium   Literature   EEKHOUD, Georges. *Nouvelles Kermesses*

Holland   Literature   VAN EEDEN, Frederik. *De kleine Johannes*

NORTHERN EUROPE

Sweden   Literature   STRINDBERG, August. *Fadren*

    Universities   Gothenburg, fnd.

CENTRAL EUROPE

Austria   Medicine   WEICHSELBAUM, Anton. Meningococcus disc.

Germany   Philosophy   NIETZSCHE, Friedrich. *Zur Genealogie der Moral*

    Physics   HERTZ, Heinrich. *Ueber sehr schnelle elektrische Schwingungen* . . . (discovery of electric waves)

LATIN EUROPE

France   Literature   MALLARMÉ, Stéphane. *Poèmes complets*
MAUPASSANT, Guy de. *Le Horla*
SARDOU, Victorien. *La Tosca*
ZOLA, Emile. *La Terre*
Italy   Music   VERDI, Giuseppe. *Otello*
Spain   Literature   GENER, Pompeyo. *Herejías*

1888

GREAT BRITAIN

Literature   WILDE, Oscar. *The Happy Prince*
Music   SULLIVAN, Arthur Seymour. *Yeomen of the Guard*

NORTHERN EUROPE

Norway   Literature   HAMSUN, Knut. *Sult* (Hunger)
IBSEN, Henrik. *Fruen fra Havet*
   Mathematics   LIE, Sophus. *Theorie der Transformationsgruppen* (compl. 1893)
   Music   GRIEG, Edvard. *Peer Gynt Suite No.* 1
Sweden   Literature   STRINDBERG, August. *Fröken Julie*

CENTRAL EUROPE

Austria   Music   WOLF, Hugo. Setting of Moerike Poems
Germany   Literature   STORM, Theodor. *Der Schimmelreiter*
   Mathematics   DEDEKIND, Julius Wilhelm Richard. *Was sind und was sollen die Zahlen?*
   Painting   LIEBERMANN, Max. *Net-menders* (Hamburg)

LATIN EUROPE

France   Academies   Institut Pasteur, Paris, fnd.
   History   RENAN, Ernest. *Histoire du Peuple d'Israël* bgn. (compl. 1894)
   Literature   MAUPASSANT, Guy de. *Pierre et Jean*
MAUPASSANT, Guy de. *Sur l'Eau*
VERLAINE, Paul. *Amour*
   Painting   VAN GOGH, Vincent. *L'Arlésienne* (Paris)
VAN GOGH, Vincent. *Sunflowers* (Tate Gal. Lond.)
GOGH, Vincent van. *Yellow Chair* (Tate Gal. Lond.)
Italy   Physics   FERRARIS, Galileo. *Rotationi Elettrodinamiche*
Spain   Literature   DARÍO, Rubén. *Azul*

SLAVONIC EUROPE

Bulgaria   Universities   Sofia fnd.

[293]

Russia   Music   RIMSKY-KORSAKOV, Nicolai Andreyevich.
                          Scheherezade Symphony Suite, op. 39
                          TCHAIKOVSKY, Pyotr Ilyich. *Symphony
                          No. 5 in E minor*, op. 64

1889

GREAT BRITAIN
            Literature   JEROME, Jerome Klapka. *Three Men in a Boat*
                          STEVENSON, Robert Louis. *The Master of
                          Ballantrae*
                          YEATS, William Butler. *The Wanderings of
                          Oisin*

THE LOW COUNTRIES
Belgium   Literature   MAETERLINCK, Maurice. *La Princesse
                          Maleine*
                          MAETERLINCK, Maurice. *Serres Chaudes*

CENTRAL EUROPE
Austria   Music   MAHLER, Gustav. *Symphony No. 1* (first
                          perf.; publ. 1898)
Germany   Literature   HAUPTMANN, Gerhart. *Vor Sonnenaufgang*
                Medicine   BEHRING, Emil. Discovery of antitoxins
                          BERGMANN, Ernst. *Die chirurgische Behand-
                          lung von Hirnkrankheiten*
                Music   STRAUSS, Richard. *Don Juan*
                          STRAUSS, Richard. *Tod und Verklaerung*
Switzerland Universities Fribourg fnd.

LATIN EUROPE
France   Architecture Eiffel Tower, Paris, compl.
                Painting   VAN GOGH, Vincent. *Portrait of Dr. Gachet*
                          (Frankfurt)
                          VAN GOGH, Vincent. *Landscape with Cypress
                          Tree* (Tate Gal. Lond.)
                Philosophy   BERGSON, Henri. *Essai sur les Données im-
                          médiates de la Conscience*
Italy   Jurisprudence LOMBROSO, Cesare. *L'uomo delinquente*
                Literature   D'ANNUNZIO, Gabriele. *Il Piacere*
Spain   Literature   PALACIO VALDÉS, Armando. *La hermana
                          San Sulpicio*

SLAVONIC EUROPE
Czechoslovakia Music   DVOŘÁK, Antonin. *Symphony No. 4 in G*,
                          op. 88
Russia   Medicine   METCHNIKOV, Ilya. *Etudes sur l'Immunité*
                          (phagocytic theory of immunity)
                Music   BORODIN, Alexander Porphyrievich. *Prince
                          Igor* (compl. by Rimsky-Korsakov and
                          Glazounov)
                          TCHAIKOVSKY, Pyotr Ilyich. *The Sleeping
                          Beauty*

1890

GREAT BRITAIN

Economics	MARSHALL, Alfred. *Principles of Economics*
Folklore	FRAZER, James George. *The Golden Bough* bgn. (compl. 1915)
Literature	BRIDGES, Robert. *Shorter Poems*
Music	ELGAR, Edward. *Froissart Overture*, op. 19 (first perf.)
Travels	STANLEY, Henry Morton. *In Darkest Africa*

THE LOW COUNTRIES

Belgium Literature MAETERLINCK, Maurice. *Les Aveugles*
MAETERLINCK, Maurice. *L'Intruse*

NORTHERN EUROPE

Norway Literature IBSEN, Henrik. *Hedda Gabler*

CENTRAL EUROPE

Germany Chemistry FISCHER, Emil. First synthesis of glucose
Literature GEORGE, Stefan. *Die Fibel*

LATIN EUROPE

Italy Jurisprudence *Codice Penale d'Italia*
Music MASCAGNI, Pietro. *Cavalleria Rusticana*

SLAVONIC EUROPE

Russia Literature TOLSTOI, Leo Nicolaievich. *The Kreutzer Sonata*
Music TCHAIKOVSKY, Pyotr Ilyich. *Pique-Dame*

1891

GREAT BRITAIN

Aesthetics	SHAW, George Bernard. *The Quintessence of Ibsenism*
Chemistry	RAMSAY, William. *A System of Chemistry*
Literature	HARDY, Thomas. *Tess of the D'Urbervilles* KIPLING, Rudyard. *The Light that Failed* WILDE, Oscar. *The Picture of Dorian Gray*
Printing	The Kelmscott Press estab.

THE LOW COUNTRIES

Belgium Literature HUYSMANS, Joris-Karl. *Là-bas*

NORTHERN EUROPE

Sweden Literature LAGERLÖF, Selma. *Gösta Berlings Saga*

[295]

CENTRAL EUROPE

Germany	Literature	DEHMEL, Richard. *Erloesungen*
		WEDEKIND, Frank. *Fruehlings Erwachen*
Switzerland	Universities	Lausanne fnd.

LATIN EUROPE

France	Medicine	BERNHEIM, Hippolyte. *Hypnotisme, Suggestion, Psychothérapie*
	Painting	CÉZANNE, Paul. *Les Joueurs de Cartes* (Courtauld Coll., Lond.)
		CÉZANNE, Paul. *Man with a Pipe* (Courtauld Coll., Lond.)
Italy	Literature	PASCOLI, Giovanni. *Myricae*
Spain	Literature	PÉREZ GALDÓS, Benito. *Angel Guerra*

SLAVONIC EUROPE

Russia	Music	TCHAIKOVSKY, Pyotr Ilyich. *Casse-Noisette Suite*, op. 71a

1892

GREAT BRITAIN

Literature	KIPLING, Rudyard. *Barrack-Room Ballads*
	SHAW, George Bernard. *Widowers' Houses*
	WILDE, Oscar. *Lady Windermere's Fan*

THE LOW COUNTRIES

Belgium	Literature	MAETERLINCK, Maurice. *Pelléas et Mélisande*
		RODENBACH, Georges. *Bruges la Morte*

NORTHERN EUROPE

Denmark	Literature	PONTOPPIDAN, Henrik. *Det forjöttede Land* bgn. (compl. 1895)
Norway	Literature	IBSEN, Henrik. *Bygmester Solness*

CENTRAL EUROPE

Austria	Literature	HOFMANNSTHAL, Hugo von. *Gestern*
	Music	BRUCKNER, Anton. *150th Psalm*
Germany	Literature	HAUPTMANN, Gerhart. *Die Weber*
		HAUPTMANN, Gerhart. *College Crampton*

LATIN EUROPE

France	Astronomy	POINCARÉ, Henri. *Les Méthodes nouvelles de la Mécanique céleste* bgn. (compl. 1899)
	Literature	HEREDIA, José-Maria de. *Les Trophées*
		ZOLA, Emile. *La Débâcle*
	Music	DEBUSSY, Claude. *L'Après-midi d'un Faune*

France	Painting	TOULOUSE-LAUTREC, Henri. *Jane Avril leaving the Moulin Rouge* (Courtauld Coll., Lond.)
Italy	Music	LEONCAVALLO, Ruggiero. *Pagliacci*
Spain	Museums	National Library and Museum, Madrid, opnd.

1893

GREAT BRITAIN

	Academies	Imperial Institute, Kensington, opnd.
	Biology	HUXLEY, Thomas Henry. *Collected Essays*
	Literature	KIPLING, Rudyard. *Many Inventions*
		ROSSETTI, Christina Georgina. *Verses*
		SHAW, George Bernard. *Mrs. Warren's Profession*
		STEVENSON, Robert Louis. *Island Nights' Entertainments*
		WILDE, Oscar. *A Woman of No Importance*
		WILDE, Oscar. *Salome*
	Painting	BEARDSLEY, Aubrey. Illus. to Sir Thomas Malory's *Morte d'Arthur*
	Philosophy	BRADLEY, Francis Herbert. *Appearance and Reality*
	Universities	Wales (Aberystwyth, Bangor, Cardiff) fnd.

NORTHERN EUROPE

Denmark	Medicine	FINSEN, Niels Ryberg. Light therapy introd.
Norway	Literature	HAMSUN, Knut. *Redaktör Lynge*
Finland	Music	SIBELIUS, Jan. *Karelia*, op. 10 and 11
		SIBELIUS, Jan. *Malinconia*, op. 20

CENTRAL EUROPE

Austria	Literature	SCHNITZLER, Arthur. *Anatol*
	Chemistry	NERNST, Walter Hermann. *Theoretische Chemie vom Standpunkt der Avogadro'schen Regel und der Thermodynamik*
Germany	Literature	HAUPTMANN, Gerhart. *Der Biberpelz*
		HAUPTMANN, Gerhart. *Hanneles Himmelfahrt*
	Medicine	BEHRING, Emil. *Die Geschichte der Diphtherie*
	Music	HUMPERDINCK, Engelbert. *Haensel und Gretel*
	Physics	DIESEL, Rudolf. *Theorie und Konstruktion eines rationellen Waermemotors*

LATIN EUROPE

France	History	AULARD, François-Victor-Alphonse. *Etudes et Leçons sur la Révolution Française* bgn. (compl. 1908)

France	Literature	FRANCE, Anatole. *La Rôtisserie de la Reine Pédauque*
Italy	Music	PUCCINI, Giacomo. *Manon Lescaut*
		VERDI, Giuseppe. *Falstaff*
	Physics	TESLA, Nicola. Tesla transformer disc.

SLAVONIC EUROPE

Czechoslovakia	Music	DVOŘÁK, Antonin. *Symphony No. 5* ("*From the New World*")
		DVOŘÁK, Antonin. *Violin Concerto*, op. 53
Russia	Music	TCHAIKOVSKY, Pyotr Ilyich. *Symphony No. 6 in B minor*, op. 74 (*Pathétique*)

1894

GREAT BRITAIN

	History	WEBB, Sidney and Beatrice. *The History of Trade Unionism*
	Literature	KIPLING, Rudyard. *The Jungle Book*
		SHAW, George Bernard. *Arms and the Man*
		SWINBURNE, Algernon Charles. *Astrophel*
		WILDE, Oscar. *The Sphinx*
	Painting	BEARDSLEY, Aubrey. Illus. to Oscar Wilde's *Salome*
	Printing	The Ashendene Press estab.

THE LOW COUNTRIES

| Belgium | Literature | COSTER, Charles de. *Lettres à Elisa* (posth.) |
| | | VERHAEREN, Emile. *Les Villages Illusoires* |

NORTHERN EUROPE

| Norway | Literature | HAMSUN, Knut. *Pan* |
| | | IBSEN, Henrik. *Lylle Eyolf* |

CENTRAL EUROPE

Austria	Music	BRUCKNER, Anton. *Symphony No. 5* (comp. 1875; rev. 1876-78)
		WOLF, Hugo. *Italian Serenade*
Germany	Music	STRAUSS, Richard. *Guntram* (first perf.; first pr. 1895)
	Painting	KLINGER, Max. *Brahms-Phantasie* (etchings)
Switzerland	Medicine	YERSIN, Alexander-Jean-Emile (simultaneously with Shibasaburo Kitasato). Plague bacillus discovered

LATIN EUROPE

France	Literature	FRANCE, Anatole. *Le Lys Rouge*
		ZOLA, Emile. *Lourdes*
Spain	Literature	BLASCO IBÁÑEZ, Vicente. *Arroz y Tartana*

1895

GREAT BRITAIN

Chemistry RAMSAY, William, and STRUTT, John William, Lord Rayleigh. Discovery of argon and helium in the atmosphere

Jurisprudence MAITLAND, Frederick William, and POLLOCK, Frederick. *History of English Law before the Time of Edward I*

Literature CONRAD, Joseph. *Almayer's Folly*
HARDY, Thomas. *Jude the Obscure*
SHAW, George Bernard. *Candida*
WILDE, Oscar. *The Importance of being Earnest*
YEATS, William Butler. *Poems*

THE LOW COUNTRIES

Belgium Literature VERHAEREN, Emile. *Les Villes Tentaculaires*

NORTHERN EUROPE

Sweden Travels HEDIN, Sven. *En Färd genom Asien* bgn. (compl. 1902)

CENTRAL EUROPE

Austria Medicine FREUD, Sigmund. *Studien ueber Hysterie* (with Joseph Breuer)
Music MAHLER, Gustav. *Symphony No. 2* (first perf.; publ. 1896)

Germany Literature FONTANE, Theodor. *Effi Briest*
GEORGE, Stefan. *Die Buecher der Hirten- und Preisgedichte*
Mathematics CANTOR, Georg. *Beitraege zur Begruendung der transfiniten Mengenlehre* bgn. (compl. 1897)
Music STRAUSS, Richard. *Till Eulenspiegels lustige Streiche*
Physics ROENTGEN, Wilhelm. X-rays discovered

LATIN EUROPE

France Literature BARRÈS, Maurice. *Du Sang, de la Volupté et de la Mort*
Italy Physics MARCONI, Guglielmo. Wireless telegraphy inv.
Spain Literature VALLE-INCLÁN, Ramón María del. *Femeninas*
SANTOS CHOCANO, José. *En la Aldea*

[299]

SLAVONIC EUROPE

Czechoslovakia Politics   MASARYK, Tómas Garrigue. *Českav ázka* (The Czech Question)
MASARYK, Tómas Garrigue. *Naše nynejši krise* (Our present Crisis)

1896

GREAT BRITAIN

Chemistry   RAMSAY, William. *The Gases of the Atmosphere*
Literature   CONRAD, Joseph. *An Outcast of the Islands*
HOUSMAN, Alfred Edward. *A Shropshire Lad*
ROSSETTI, Christina Georgina. *New Poems* (posth.)
STEVENSON, Robert Louis. *Weir of Hermiston*
Painting   BEARDSLEY, Aubrey. Illus. to Pope's *Rape of the Lock*
Periodicals   *The Savoy* iss.
Physics   RUTHERFORD, Ernest. Magnetic detector of electrical waves inv.
Press   *Daily Mail* iss.

THE LOW COUNTRIES

Belgium   Literature   MAETERLINCK, Maurice. *Aglavaine et Sélysette*
VERHAEREN, Emile. *Les Heures Claires*
Philosophy   MAETERLINCK, Maurice. *Le Trésor des Humbles*

NORTHERN EUROPE

Norway   Literature   IBSEN, Henrik. *John Gabriel Borkman*

CENTRAL EUROPE

Austria   Music   MAHLER, Gustav. *Symphony No. 3* (date of composition; publ. 1898; first complete perf. 1902)
WOLF, Hugo. *Der Corregidor*
Germany   Jurisprudence *Buergerliches Gesetzbuch fuer das Deutsche Reich* (date of publ.)
Literature   HAUPTMANN, Gerhart. *Florian Geyer*
Music   BRAHMS, Johannes. *Vier ernste Gesaenge*, op. 121
STRAUSS, Richard. *Also sprach Zarathustra*
Periodicals   *Jugend* iss.

LATIN EUROPE

France	Chemistry	BECQUEREL, Henri. Uranium radiation disc.
	Literature	ZOLA, Emile. *Rome*
	Painting	GAUGUIN, Paul. *Birth of Christ* (Munich)
	Philosophy	BERGSON, Henri. *Matière et Mémoire*
	Universities	Clermont-Ferrand, Nancy and Marseilles fnd.
Italy	Music	PUCCINI, Giacomo. *La Bohème*
Spain	Literature	BENAVENTE, Jacinto. *Gente conocida*
		GUTIÉRREZ NAJERA, Manuel. *Poesías*
		MENÉNDEZ PIDAL, Ramón. *La Leyenda de los Infantes de Lara*

SLAVONIC EUROPE

Poland	Literature	SIENKIEWICZ, Henryk. *Quo vadis?*
Russia	Literature	TCHEKHOV, Anton Pavlovich. *The Sea-Gull*

1897

GREAT BRITAIN

	Literature	CONRAD, Joseph. *The Nigger of the Narcissus*
		GALSWORTHY, John. *From the Four Winds*
		HARDY, Thomas. *The Well-Beloved*
		KIPLING, Rudyard. *Captains Courageous*
	Medicine	ROSS, Ronald. Discovery of malaria bacillus in the stomach of Anopheles mosquito
	Museums	Tate Gallery, London, opnd.
	Politics	WEBB, Sidney and Beatrice. *Industrial Democracy*

NORTHERN EUROPE

Norway	Travels	NANSEN, Fridtjof. *Fram over Polhaved* (Eng. ed. *Farthest North*)
Sweden	Literature	STRINDBERG, August. *Inferno*

CENTRAL EUROPE

Austria	Music	MAHLER, Gustav. *Lieder eines fahrenden Gesellen* (comp. 1884)
	Technics	SCHWARZ, David. Dirigible airship inv.
Germany	Literature	GEORGE, Stefan. *Das Jahr der Seele*
		HAUPTMANN, Gerhart. *Die versunkene Glocke*
	Medicine	EHRLICH, Paul. *Zur Kenntnis der Antitoxinwirkung* (side-chain theory of immunity)
	Painting	KLINGER, Max. *Christus in Olymp* (Mod. Gal. Vienna)
Switzerland	Painting	HODLER, Ferdinand. *Retreat from Marignano* (Zurich)

LATIN EUROPE

France	Chemistry	BERTHELOT, Marcellin. *Thermochimie*
	Literature	ROSTAND, Edmond. *Cyrano de Bergerac*
		ZOLA, Emile. *Paris*
	Painting	CÉZANNE, Paul. *Lake of Annecy* (Courtauld Coll. Lond.)
		GAUGUIN, Paul. *La Orana Maria* (Lewisohn Coll., New York)
		PISSARRO, Camille. *Boulevard des Italiens* (Tate Gall. Lond.)
Italy	Literature	PASCOLI, Giovanni. *Poemetti e Poemi*
Spain	Literature	GANIVET, Angel. *Idearium Español*
		GUIMERÁ, Angel. *Terra baixa*
		LUGONES, Leopoldo. *Las Montañas de Oro*

SLAVONIC EUROPE

Russia	Music	SCRIABIN, Alexander. *Symphony No. 1 in E major*, op. 26 (comp. 1895)

1898

GREAT BRITAIN

Literature	HARDY, Thomas. *Wessex Poems*
	WILDE, Oscar. *The Ballad of Reading Gaol*
Music	ELGAR, Edward. *Caractacus Cantata* (first perf.)
Painting	CRANE, Walter. Illus. to Spenser's *Shepheardes Calender*
Theology	Evangelical Free Church Catechism

THE LOW COUNTRIES

Belgium	Philosophy	MAETERLINCK, Maurice. *La Sagesse et la Destinée*

NORTHERN EUROPE

Denmark	Literature	PONTOPPIDAN, Henrik. *Lykke Per* bgn. (compl. 1904)
Norway	Literature	HAMSUN, Knut. *Victoria*
Sweden	Literature	STRINDBERG, August. *Legender*
		STRINDBERG, August. *Till Damaskus* bgn. (compl. 1904)

CENTRAL EUROPE

Germany	History	BISMARCK, Otto von. *Gedanken und Erinnerungen*
	Literature	HAUPTMANN, Gerhart. *Fuhrmann Henschel*

Switzerland   Painting   HODLER, Ferdinand. *Day* bgn. (compl.
                           1900; Berne)

LATIN EUROPE

France   Chemistry   CURIE, Marie (*née* Sklodowska) and Pierre.
                       Radium disc.
          Painting   GAUGUIN, Paul. *The Idol* (Moscow)
                       GAUGUIN, Paul. *Whence come we? What
                       are we? Whither go we?* (Oslo)ᵛ
          Sculpture   RODIN, Auguste. *Balzac*
                       RODIN, Auguste. *The Kiss*
Italy   Literature   D'ANNUNZIO, Gabriele. *La Città Morte*
Spain   Economics   COSTA, Joaquín. *Colectivismo agrario*
          Literature   BLASCO IBÁÑEZ, Vicente. *La Barraca*
                       NERVO, Amado. *Perlas negras*
                       RUSIÑOL, Santiago. *L'Alegría que pasa*
                       VALENCIA, Guillermo. *Ritos*
          Philosophy   GINER DE LOS RÍOS, Francisco. *Filosofía del
                       Derecho*

SLAVONIC EUROPE

Russia   Music   RIMSKY-KORSAKOV, Nicolai Andreyevich.
                   Sadko (opera)

1899

GREAT BRITAIN

          Libraries   John Rylands Library, Manchester, opnd.
          Literature   KIPLING, Rudyard. *Stalky and Co.*
                       SHAW, George Bernard. *Caesar and Cleo-
                       patra*
          Music   ELGAR, Edward. *Enigma Variations*
                       ELGAR, Edward. *Sea Pictures*

NORTHERN EUROPE

Denmark   Literature   DRACHMANN, Holger. *Gurre*
Finland   Music   SIBELIUS, Jan. *Finlandia*, op. 26
                       SIBELIUS, Jan. *Symphony No. 1 in E minor*
Sweden   Literature   STRINDBERG, August. *Advent*
                       STRINDBERG, August. *Erik XIV*

CENTRAL EUROPE

Austria   Literature   HOFMANNSTHAL, Hugo von. *Theater in
                       Versen*
Germany   Literature   GEORGE, Stefan. *Der Teppich des Lebens*
          Music   STRAUSS, Richard. *Ein Heldenleben*
          Natural   HAECKEL, Ernst. *Die Weltraetsel*
          History

[303]

LATIN EUROPE

France   Literature   GIDE, André. *Le Prométhée mal enchaîné*

SLAVONIC EUROPE

Russia   Literature   GORKI, Maxim. *Foma Godeyev*
TOLSTOI, Leo Nikolaievich. *Resurrection*

1900

GREAT BRITAIN

Chemistry   RUTHERFORD, Ernest. Radium emanation discovered
Literature   DOWSON, Ernest Christopher. *Collected Verse*
Museums   Wallace Collection, London, opnd.
Music   ELGAR, Edward. *The Dream of Gerontius*
Press   *Daily Express* iss.
Universities   Birmingham fnd.

NORTHERN EUROPE

Norway   Literature   IBSEN, Henrik. *Naar vi döde vaagner*
Sweden   Literature   STRINDBERG, August. *Gustaf Adolf*
   Physics   ARRHENIUS, Svante August. *Lärebok i teoretik elektrokemi*

CENTRAL EUROPE

Austria   Literature   HOFMANNSTHAL, Hugo von. *Der Tor und der Tod*
   Music   MAHLER, Gustav. *Symphony No. 4*
   Psychology   FREUD, Sigmund. *Ueber Traumdeutung*
Germany   Chemistry   OSTWALD, Wilhelm. *Grundlinien der anorganischen Chemie*
   Psychology   WUNDT, Wilhelm. *Voelkerpsychologie*, Pt. I. " Die Sprache "
   Technics   ZEPPELIN, Ferdinand von. First " Zeppelin " constr.

LATIN EUROPE

France   Literature   GAUGUIN, Paul. *Noa Noa*
ROLLAND, Romain. *Danton*
ROSTAND, Edmond. *L'Aiglon*
   Painting   TOULOUSE-LAUTREC, Henri. *Messalina* (Lewisohn Coll., N. York)
Italy   Literature   D'ANNUNZIO, Gabriele. *Il Fuoco*
   Music   PUCCINI, Giacomo. *Tosca*

[304]

Spain   History   ALTAMIRA, Rafael. *Historia de España y de la Civilización española* bgn. (compl. 1929)

    Literature   BAROJA, Pío. *La Casa de Aizgorri*

    BLASCO IBÁÑEZ, VICENTE. *Entre Naranjos*

    MARAGALL, Joan. *Visions y Cants*

    RODÓ, José Enrique. *Ariel*

    UNAMUNO, Miguel. *Tres Ensayos*

SLAVONIC EUROPE

Russia   Literature   TCHEKHOV, Anton Pavlovich. *Uncle Vanya*

    TOLSTOI, Leo Nicolaievich. *The Living Corpse*